Best Coast Hikes
of Northern California

Best Coast Hikes

of Northern California

Marc J. Soares

Sierra Club Books
San Francisco

The Sierra Club, founded in 1892 by John Muir, has devoted itself to the study and protection of the Earth's scenic and ecological resources—mountains, wetlands, woodlands, wild shores and rivers, deserts and plains. The publishing program of the Sierra Club offers books to the public as a nonprofit educational service in the hope that they may enlarge the public's understanding of the Club's basic concerns. The point of view expressed in each book, however, does not necessarily represent that of the Club. The Sierra Club has some sixty chapters coast to coast, in Canada, Hawaii, and Alaska. For information about how you may participate in its programs to preserve wilderness and the quality of life, please address inquiries to Sierra Club, 85 Second Street, San Francisco, CA 94105.
www.sierraclub.org/books

Copyright © 1998 by Marc J. Soares

LIBRARY OF CONGRESS CATALOGING-IN-PUBLICATION DATA
Soares, Marc J.
    Best coast hikes of Northern California / Marc Soares.
      p.   cm.
    Includes index.
    ISBN 0-87156-904-3 (soft)
      1. Hiking—California, Northern—Guidebooks. 2. Hiking—California—Pacific Coast—Guidebooks. 3. California, Northern—Guidebooks. 4. Pacific Coast (California)—Guidebooks. I. Title.
GV199.42.C2S636   1998
917.94—DC21   97–43531
                                                    CIP

Cover design by Mark Ong
Book design and composition by BookMatters
Maps by Nick Gregoric
Photos by Marc J. Soares

CONTENTS

Lost Coast—Mendocino and Sonoma Counties

Marin County and San Francisco Bay Area

San Mateo County/Santa Cruz Mountains Area

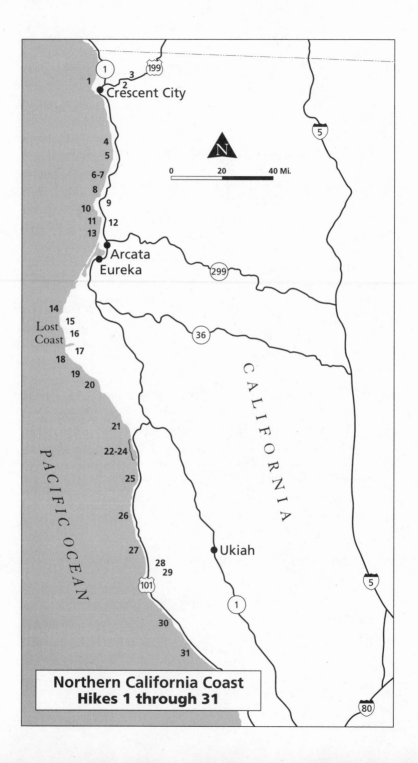

1

(1)

3 (199)

2

Crescent City

(5)

4

5

6-7

8

9

10

11 12

13

Arcata

Eureka

(299)

14

Lost 15

Coast 16

17

18

19

20

21

22-24

25

26

27

28

29

(101)

30

31

PACIFIC OCEAN

C A L I F O R N I A

36

Ukiah

(1)

(5)

80

Northern California Coast
Hikes 1 through 31

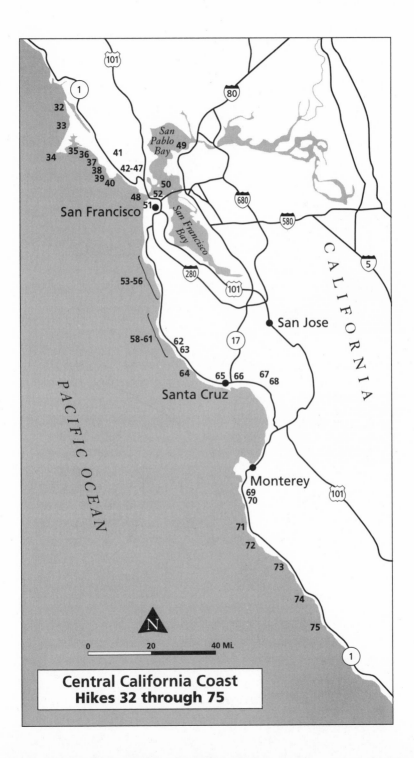

**Central California Coast
Hikes 32 through 75**

FOREWORD

It has always seemed plain to me that in order to work and struggle to save beaches in California, or natural habitat anywhere, you must be willing to go there, and that the creepy crawlers, the four-legged ones, the winged ones can't be fully appreciated without going into the wild. Yet in a busy, demanding, complicated world just getting there can be difficult. At a minimum it requires time, careful planning, transportation, and money. Overcrowding, access and camping fees, pollution, strip malls, fast food outlets, and miles-long caravans of RVs can entangle matters even worse.

The significance of this book by Marc Soares is that it puts you in position to make the most of your time in the wild. It gets you there. It describes in detail how to easily access California's finest old growth redwood groves, secret beaches, vistas, ridgelines, valleys, and wetlands. From the giant trees and wild coast of Del Norte south to the San Francisco Bay Area and through Big Sur, whether you have only a couple of hours or weeks to explore.

The trails and hikes presented in this book are public trails on public lands. Most of the places revealed here are already saved and permanently protected for future generations. In nearly every case they were saved through the dedication and perseverance of one or more individuals, a nonprofit organization or governmental agency. In every case it took work—fund-raising, donations, persistence, determination, dedication, vision, popular votes, political organizing, lobbying, bond acts, tax dollars, etc., in order to save these special places.

Yet for every place saved others have been lost. Trees clear-cut, rivers dammed, wetlands drained and beaches built on and eroded. Commercial strip malls with giant "big box" retail outlets, miles of beaches privatized by luxury housing, pollution of groundwater supplies, and construction of golf resorts. Existing special places are being lost every single month in counties throughout California's coastal region at a pace both confusing and relentless. The very same public participation and single-minded determination that saved the special places in this book must be brought to bear on California's remaining coastal habitat if these remnant wildlands are to be permanently protected. Use this book, then, in two ways. Go into the wild. Then come home and fight for the special places remaining in your community. Good luck. And good hiking.

Mark Massara

ACKNOWLEDGMENTS

For Patricia: Whenever I'm alone in another paradise, my first and main thought is to share it with you.

I'm so blessed that my wife, Patricia, is my number one hiking mate. My daughter Dionne also shares my deep love of nature, and keeps going and going. My son Jake shares my thirst for adventure, often sprinting ahead of me, up the mountain. Thanks for coming, family. Thank you, brother John, for showing me the way (hike writing); sister Camille, for so many quality outings together, both past and present; brother Eric for your kindness, go-for-it attitude, and sense of humor; mother Mozelle, for your spiritual guidance and warm and approving smile; and stepfather Les, for loving my mom.

I received lots of spiritual, outdoor, plant, and musical awareness from my friends—hiking partner and naturalist Rick Ramos, Greg Haling, Derek Moss, and plant guru Gary Matson. Much praise goes to the photographic experts at Crown Camera in Redding—Ed Beier, Gary Engell, and Lisa Fuller.

So many rangers and naturalists at various parks along the Northern California coast helped out big time, especially Neill Fogarty at Marin Municipal Water District. Many thanks to manuscript readers at Henry Cowell Redwoods State Park, the Point Reyes National Seashore Ranger Staff, Peter Keller at Redwood National Park, Mary Hazel at Armstrong Redwoods State Park, and Shawn

Gillette at Muir Woods National Monument. Other assisting rangers and naturalists include Tony Stagnaro at Año Nuevo State Reserve, Mike Rydjord at Sinkyone Wilderness State Park, Suzanne Westover at Salt Point State Park, and Diane Pierce and James Wheeler at Redwood National Park.

INTRODUCTION

From the Oregon border down to Big Sur country, the Northern California coast is typically wild and arguably the most beautiful stretch of shoreline in the world. This hiking book describes and shares 75 carefully chosen hikes from this remarkable region. The intent of the book is for you to take some of these hikes, and in doing so, have more fun, be more comfortable, more informed, more interested, and above all, more touched.

Experience just a few hikes from this book, and it's obvious the rugged and pristine Northern California coast is wonderfully varied. People tend to be in awe of its numerous scenic blessings—the world's tallest trees, the pretty ponds and clear creeks, precipitous bluffs and cliffs, enchanting and solitary beaches and coves, intriguing islands and bays, precious marshes, wildflower-dotted meadows and slopes, the wide mouths of untamed rivers, jagged rock outcrops, the California coast's tallest mountain, lush green canyons, abundant wildlife, and historical lighthouses.

This guidebook features hikes to suit all hikers' abilities and moods. There's a balanced blend of "cakewalks" and "butt-kickers," backpacking trips, family outings, hikes with views, hikes with color, hikes with deep shade and deep peace, beach strolls, and mountain climbs.

How to Use This Book

The beginning of each hike description has an information block, which helps you size up the hike. Here's what each brief topic means:

LENGTH: This provides the hike's total mileage, up and back. If there are other ideal destinations within the total hike, those up and back hiking lengths are also listed. Keep in mind that many of the long hikes feature great scenes within a couple of miles, and therefore most people lacking time and/or energy often turn back early (which makes total sense).

DIFFICULTY: The terms "easy," "moderate," and "strenuous" are subjective, factoring in distance, elevation gain and loss, and to a lesser extent, trail conditions. A triathlete may deem a strenuous hike as moderate, and a nonhiker may call an easy hike a "toughie." Some hikes combine two adjectives (example "easy to moderate") to better describe the difficulty. Other factors can make hikes more difficult, such as being hungry or thirsty, sore, recovering from illness, or high winds. Some hikes rated as strenuous are easy for the first couple of miles, and sometimes make ideal short hikes.

TOTAL ELEVATION GAIN: This is an approximate measure of actual feet you'll climb, taking into account the various little ups and downs trails tend to go over. Keep in mind that most hikers consider a thousand feet of gradual climbing much easier than a thousand feet of steep ascent.

WATER: This is a listing of freshwater streams and lakes where water can be filtered or purified for drinking purposes. Be sure the filter does not need to be replaced, and that it eliminates giardia bacteria. Keep in mind that some of these water sources may dry up by late summer/early autumn, particularly during low-rainfall years. It's best to bring your own water, but always take along iodine-purifying tablets for emergency situations.

SEASON: Most of the hikes described in this book can be done any time of year. This section will inform you of that and suggest certain seasons for enjoying certain features (flowers, views, waterfalls, and so forth). Keep in mind that some trails either are closed for certain seasons, get temporarily overgrown, or require a swollen stream crossing. It makes sense to call the agency that has jurisdiction (see next sections).

MAP: Each hike description in this book is accompanied by a computer-generated map that includes all the place-names contained in the hike description, and that generally will more than suffice. (There are sometimes several hikes on one map in this book.) Park brochures and USGS (U.S. Geological Survey) topo maps are listed in this section because they usually include more details and information. This may come in handy if you're temporarily lost or simply enjoy spending time studying maps. Some topo maps are outdated, however. For getting to your destination, consult a state highway map, state atlas, and/or Forest Service map.

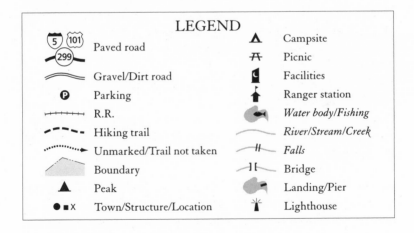

LEGEND

5 101 299 Paved road	▲ Campsite
Gravel/Dirt road	⛩ Picnic
℗ Parking	Facilities
R.R.	Ranger station
Hiking trail	*Water body/Fishing*
Unmarked/Trail not taken	*River/Stream/Creek*
Boundary	*Falls*
▲ Peak	*Bridge*
● ■ X Town/Structure/Location	Landing/Pier
	Lighthouse

INFORMATION: This section lists the governing agency and its phone number. Call to determine weather, fees (if any), trail conditions, and camping. To write to them, see the appendix sections at the end of this book. Most parks covered in this book have an entrance station, visitor center, and/or ranger station for acquiring information, permits (if any, usually not necessary), maps, and brochures.

DIRECTIONS TO TRAILHEAD: This leads you from the nearest town or highway to where you park to begin hiking at the trailhead, with mileages included. If a road is rough, steep, and/or winding, this section will generally mention it. Those with travel trailers or motor homes should call ahead to make sure they can make it. Factor in extra driving time for these roads, and drive alertly and cautiously. Most of the hikes are close to Highway 1 (often slow, narrow, and winding) and Highway 101 (straight, but subject to traffic jams in the San Francisco Bay area).

The first two or three paragraphs below the Information block are meant to whet the appetite and provide a feel for the hike. Hikers in a subjective mood may choose or pass on the hike by sampling its flavor from the lead paragraphs. This text section usually lists the place-names, benefits, and bonuses of the hike.

The rest of the hike description details a blow-by-blow account of the actual hike. The idea is to take this book with you and read excerpts along the way (sort of a semi-interpretive guide).

Climate

The Northern California coastal climate is typically mild, with distinctively less and less rainfall the farther south you go. The Eureka/Crescent City area (far north) tends to receive between 40 and 50 inches of annual rainfall in a normal year. The Mendocino/Sonoma Counties region often gets half that, and Big Sur country (this book's far south section) generally gets about a quarter the annual precipitation that Crescent City acquires.

It's not uncommon for the entire North Coast to be frost free for an entire winter, but there's sometimes a small handful of days in a given winter when the mercury dips slightly below freezing, particularly a few miles inland. Every few years, a light dusting of snow occurs in some areas at sea level. Temperatures seldom exceed 80ºF on the immediate coast during summer, but just inland can reach the 90s.

The flora of the Northern California coast typically benefit from supplementary moisture from summer fog. The hillsides stay greener longer the farther north one goes.

The rainy season generally ranges from November through March, with plenty of clear spells. April and May tend to be the windiest but lushest, and the summer months are the foggiest. The clearest and calmest days are usually in September and October, a time of golden hills and splendid sunsets.

Things to Do for Added Enjoyment

1 Walk in deep fog, deep into the redwoods.
2 Hike to a destination with a view, stay for the entire sunset, then return with flashlight (for open areas and wide trails only).
3 Have dinner at a favorite hiking spot with your favorite person, then return together under a full moon.
4 Hike a popular trail in pouring rain.
5 Do at least part of a beach hike barefoot.
6 Stroll the beach, play a favorite song in your mind, then get lost in a major daydream.
7 Reach a beautiful spot, then take a nap under a coast live oak tree.
8 Assemble yourself at the edge of an estuary, wait quietly, then watch the bird show.
9 Take some young kids to a rocky surf zone in winter, then anticipate whale sightings and big waves pounding sea stacks.
10 Spend hang time near a coastal waterfall in late winter or in a coastal wildflower meadow in late spring.

Hiking Tips and Things to Consider

1 Parks and gates often close at dusk (call ahead).
2 Most parks charge fees, usually from $3 to $6 for day use (some hikes are feeless, because the trailhead is alongside the road).
3 Hikes with far-reaching views should be done on clear days, but deep forest and heavy woods hikes often are embellished by fog or thick cloud cover.
4 Arranging car shuttles eliminates the return trip, allowing more time to enjoy the hike or affording the opportunity to hike farther and see more.
5 Plan one of these hikes on an off-season weekday, and enjoy substantially fewer people, if any.
6 Mosey along, check things out, and stop often, which adds to your enjoyment (key tip for hiking success with kids).
7 Use your senses a lot.
8 Consider a hike as therapy for your soul, a spiritual treatment, a cleansing and healing tool.
9 Keep in mind there are roughly two high tides and two low tides daily. Some beaches are safer and best explored at low tide. For dramatic views, it's often best to schedule a visit during high tide.
10 If traveling the coast extensively, consider acquiring a tide table every 100 miles or so.

Wilderness Ethics

Most hikers who've explored the Northern California coast deeply appreciate its beauty and wildness, and therefore want it to be kept clean and protected. Here are several useful, thoughtful, productive and practical tips, ideas, and suggestions to feel good about helping preserve and improve the Northern California coast environment. Its trees are the big picture. Conservationist John Muir wrote,

> Any fool can destroy trees. They cannot run away, and if they could, they would still be destroyed, chased and hunted down as long as fun

or a dollar could be got out of their bark hides or branching horns . . . it took more than 3,000 years to make some of the trees of the western woods—trees that are still standing in perfect strength and beauty, waving and singing in the mighty forests. . . . Through all the wonderful, eventful centuries . . . God has cared for these trees, saved them from drought, disease, avalanches . . . and floods; but He cannot save them from a fool—only Uncle Sam can do that.

Here are some important things we should continue to do:

1 Get involved in an environmental activist group(s). Their addresses are listed in Appendix 2 at the end of the book. It's fun, rewarding, and you get to meet nice people.

2 If you come across an overgrown or hazardous trail, or a trail being ruined by off-road vehicles, please report it to the park ranger or office.

3 Stay on the trail over switchback sections. In cross-country areas, try to step on firm ground or rocks. When in meadows, keep in mind that grasses tend to be more forgiving than wildflowers.

4 Camp at least 100 feet away from all bodies of water so that you don't pollute water or bother riparian habitat. Use existing sites whenever possible. Instead of digging trenches to keep rainwater out of the tent, use a plastic tarp.

5 Spending the night without a fire can heighten the senses, and it certainly doesn't pollute the air, remove some of the local ecosystem's important organic supply, or scare off animals, as fires do. Consider instead bringing extra clothes for warmth, a flashlight for light, and a gas stove for cooking.

6 When washing, protect bodies of water and their aquatic life by not using soaps. A person can be fresh and clean by using fresh mud for soap (it works), deodorant, and a toothbrush (dry brushing is best in the boonies).

7 Besides packing out your own garbage, it's a good idea to toss other people's glass and plastic in your garbage bag as well. People tend to litter less often in litter-free areas.

8 Bury feces at least 6 inches deep, preferably in forest duff, where it will decompose faster. Go at least 200 feet away

from bodies of water, and far away from camps and trails to defecate. When urinating, spread it around to enrich the soil with nitrogen from urea.

9 Allow nature's sound to prevail. It's best to speak in quiet to normal tones.

10 Uphold a philosophy of minimum impact and an environmental vision, do more than your share, and remember that actions always speak louder than words.

Things to Bring

The absolute essentials, which keep hikers much safer (some also heighten enjoyment and overall hike success), have come in handy for me (rescuing me!) many a time. They include water (plenty of it, in a water bottle[s]), extra food, extra clothing (in layers, plus a thin poncho or light raincoat), a first-aid kit with Swiss Army knife, matches in a waterproof container, trail maps, compass, and a flashlight (with extra batteries and bulbs).

I leave most of those items in my daypack at all times, updating the first-aid kit and matches annually. It's also best to include a whistle, fire starter (for wet wood), iodine, water filter, toilet paper, and this book.

For hikes involving any distance or heavy climbing, a pair of broken-in (important), lightweight hiking boots (an ankle-high tennis shoe with Vibram-like soles) are suggested. The sun is meant to be worshiped, but—easier than most people think—it can drain one's energy and cause sunburn. When the sun is out, wear a shirt, a wide-brimmed hat, and sunglasses. Apply sunblock (level 15 or higher) every 4 hours or so.

Staying Safe

Mention risks and getting hurt in the boonies and most folks think of bears, mountain lions, and rattlesnakes. Ironically, more people by far are harmed or killed from bee stings than bears, lions, and snakes combined. In the Northern California coast, getting lost or dehydrated or falling are probably the main factors hikers should take into account.

In the long run, hiking can easily be among the safest activities if a hiker does three things:

1 Be prepared. Do things such as study maps beforehand. Keep the daypack on your back full of the essentials (see Things to Bring section). Take walks in your shoes beforehand to make sure they don't cause blisters. Make sure you can handle the mileage and elevation of a given hike. Make sure you don't have to struggle to keep up.

2 AA stands for "always alert." Twisted ankles, a common hiking injury, are most often caused when someone lets his or her guard down, usually on the way back during a long hike. Assume in the back of your mind that each and every step could result in a fall. This way, your foot placement tends to be consistently good. "Watch your eyes." This means make sure branch tips don't poke a person in the eye. Burns and cuts, two typical hiking injuries, can often be avoided through alertness (always take a first-aid kit, though).

3 Make good decisions. If the watch says it'll be dark sooner than later, allow enough return time. If the creek is too swollen to cross, then it's too swollen to cross. When you come to a trail junction, stop, study the map and wait for the others to catch up.

HIKING ALONE: It's important to leave a definite hiking itinerary with a family member or close friend, then stick to it. The three measures just detailed are especially imperative for those hiking alone. Also, a solo hiker must keep the mind-set that there is no room for error.

WEATHER: Make a habit of always getting an accurate, updated report before venturing out. If it's stormy weather, properly use raingear, waterproof tents, and so on. It's imperative to keep clothes dry, or have dry clothes to change into. Cold air, cold winds, and wetness can cause hypothermia, a life-threatening condition characterized by a big drop in body temperature, shivering, disorientation, and inarticulate speech. Anyone suffering those symptoms needs to change into dry clothes, and get near a warm fire or curl up in a sleeping bag.

POISONOUS PLANTS: Poison oak and stinging nettles cause skin discomfort. Learn to recognize and avoid these plants. In the case of the more common poison oak, anyone can get it anytime, even those who swear they never get it, even in winter when the plant is out of leaf. People can get the itchy rash poison oak causes simply by handling clothes that rubbed against it, or petting a dog that came in contact with it, or by standing by a fire that is burning it. If you suspect you came into contact with it, wash your clothes and take a cold or warm shower, soaping the potentially affected areas twice.

TICKS: Living in brushy and grassy areas that people tend to come into contact with, ticks are more of a problem than rattlesnakes, bears, and mountain lions combined. The likelihood of a tick latching on to drink your blood is substantially lessened by wearing long-sleeve shirts and sweatpants tucked into socks. If hiking along an overgrown trail in late spring, check for ticks often. If they just came aboard, they can be flicked off. If a tick does attach, it can be dislodged by a tick removal kit or a doctor. Get it off right away, for some ticks (very small ones) can cause Lyme disease, which usually makes people very sick.

RATTLESNAKES: Two key things about these slant-eyed vipers with rattlers for tails: They usually strike only when cornered or touched, and most people get bit because they're handling them. For a rattlesnake bite, stay calm and promptly get to a hospital.

BEARS: The Northern California coast has black bears, and they typically hightail it in high gear when they see a human. If you ever come between a mother bear and her cubs, walk away while saying nice things. If you ever discover a bear ransacking your food, walk away, swear if it helps you feel better, then return when the bear is done. Remember, the bear found this food and thinks it's his. He believes it so much, he may swat you around if you come to claim it.

Also, keep your sleeping quarters and the clothes you're wearing free of such things as fish stains and jelly smears. Bears are rarely a threat.

MOUNTAIN LIONS: Most hikers will never see this predator. That's because lions are smart enough to fear humans, and each lion requires a lot of private roaming territory. If, by freak accident, you come into contact with a mountain lion, don't run, as sheep do. Stand your ground, look it in the eye, look big, and talk loud. Chances are, that cat is already gone.

WATER: Assume that all water from streams, ponds, and lakes carry the microorganism called giardia, which gives humans symptoms like stomach flu. Use a filter that is claimed to eliminate giardia, or use iodine tablets, or boil the water briskly for a couple of minutes. Better yet, bring your own, and always refill your water bottles at safe faucets.

The Amazing Redwoods

Nature's noblest legacy doubles as the tallest living thing on earth. The stately coast redwood has rewarded humans for countless generations with faithful grace and beauty.

To take a walk in a peaceful, primeval redwood forest is to feel a close, spiritual connection with nature. Imagine the ancient history the winds told these enduring trees (redwoods can live for more than 2,000 years). Perhaps this anonymous haiku best describes the sentiment of being in a redwood forest: "It is not easy to leave this cool green garden for the dusty road."

It would be so easy for some bearded elves to hide behind a coast redwood's massive trunk, buttressed at the base (some thicken to 20 feet in diameter). Follow the trunk as it tapers to the sky—you can sometimes barely discern the foliage reaching for the sun at heights above 300 feet.

When dinosaurs roamed the earth, they were dwarfed by these redwood kings. Fossil records prove redwoods blanketed the northern hemisphere when the climate was wetter and warmer over a 100 million years ago. The gradual advancement and retraction of ice sheets eventually limited the coast redwood into isolated coastal patches of Southern Oregon and Northern California, extending to Monterey and Big Sur.

In nature, the hugest redwoods grow in pure stands along protected, sheltered flats in well-drained soil and a climate of extra winter and spring rainfall with fog-moistened summers. The largest redwood in the world, rising 387 feet from the forest floor, thrives in this ideal growing situation. Growing for 600 years on an alluvial flat (which consists of loam soil deposited by periodic floods), this superlative monarch joins thousands of other redwoods in Redwood National Park north of Eureka, California, as a World Heritage Site and International Biosphere Reserve.

California's state tree, the coast redwood, is attractive in youth, with branches growing laterally from near the ground. It can even grow 4 feet a year during its first few years of life. The needles of this conifer are bright, deep green, with new foliage yellowish green. In seven or eight years, the tree will produce olive-sized, reddish-brown cones in clusters.

Each year the fire-resistant bark becomes more dark cinnamon-brown to reddish, tinged with gray. The bark keeps getting more deeply furrowed and ridged, sometimes becoming up to a foot thick. Often the main attraction in a redwood forest is the overwhelmingly thick trunks with shredded bark.

Most coast redwoods in the forest feature interesting scorch marks, fire scars, and burnt hollows, all resulting from periodic fires covering several centuries. The term "goosepen" refers to the large, burnt cavities, and early settlers may have used them to confine geese and chickens. Although redwood's thick and fibrous bark lacks resin and therefore supplies little fuel, repeated fires (perhaps two per century) gradually weaken the affected trees.

But unlike other conifers, the redwood is capable of sprouting additional trunks, as evidenced by the typically multiple-trunked specimens that abound in a redwood forest. The swollen and bumpy bases of many large redwoods contain burls—dormant buds capable of sprouting if the tree is injured. With a root system already firmly established, these sprout trees can grow much faster than seedlings.

In 1769, world traveler Fray Juan Crespi named the coast redwood *palo colorado* (colored tree). Botanical credit goes to Archibald Menzies, who documented it in 1794. In 1874, it was given its scientific name, *Sequoia sempervirens,* honoring Cherokee leader Sequoyah (*sempervirens* means evergreen, or ever living).

The Tolowa, Chilula, and Yurok Indians effectively used the abundant and diverse resources within the California redwood forests to achieve the most evolved cultures and highest population density known among any food-gathering peoples. Canoes, houses, and sweathouses were crafted from redwood by these Native American Indians.

Coast redwood, a close relative of the giant sequoia native to the Sierra, features several landscape uses. A shady grove of coast redwoods can be established in quick order with regular watering. An uneven but natural-looking line of redwoods planted as close as 10 feet apart can be grown as a windbreak in a north–south direction.

One can mimic nature by scattering redwoods as they sometimes appear in a riparian community. This can be done by mixing in bigleaf maples, Pacific dogwood, and white alder (red alder grows on the coast, but white alder fares better inland).

Three native shrubs that often accompany redwoods in the California coastal redwood forests that would look great and grow well in most zones include California huckleberry, Oregon grape, and salal. These trees and shrubs can be mail-ordered by calling Forest Farms at (541) 846-7269. These shrubs can be placed a few feet from the trunk, and a couple of limbs per year can be entirely removed from the very bottom until there's head room clearance to show off the redwood trunk and the shrubs for a delightful coastal motif landscape.

A mixed native conifer forest can be easily created in a large garden setting by giving enough room for ponderosa pine, gray pine, incense cedar, and coast redwood (if too crowded, a redwood becomes lanky and thin). As stand-alones, redwoods make handsome specimens. They continue to be used frequently along California's freeways, in parks, and even on golf courses. Redwoods are suitable as backgrounds for redbud, toyon, and shrubs with bold flowers, such as wild mock orange, forsythia, and ocean spray. They also make good dividers and screens.

Always fresh looking, with a pleasing woodsy scent, this evergreen is a standout on a wet and gray winter's day. Plant some on the lawn's edge, since the comparatively shallow-rooted redwoods thrive with water. Although it won't look its best, a redwood should also manage in boggy conditions, like its cousin, the bald cypress native to the south.

Redwood needles tend to cling to the branches for a year or two after they are dead, when they are a pale and dull brown. This irregular occurrence is to be expected at times.

Although generally considered to be pest free, sometimes yellowing of the foliage may indicate iron deficiency or overwatering. Cut back on the frequency of waterings, and apply chelated iron according to the package directions.

The only pruning that needs to be done to the pyramid-shaped redwood is to remove the suckers at the base. It's best to cut into the bark to assure getting rid of these suckers.

The more water the redwood gets, the faster it grows. Protect from drying winds and summer heat by mimicking nature and keeping a supply of rotting needles and leaves under the tree.

Although the coast redwood doesn't tolerate extreme freezes, the blue-green foliaged Aptos Blue and the fine-textured Soquel redwood varieties are more freeze tolerant.

To fully admire the trees that existed since humankind began, check out grand groves in Northern California, which include Tall Trees Grove in Redwood National Park, Jedediah Smith Redwoods near Crescent City, Prairie Creek Redwoods State Park north of Trinidad, Armstrong Redwoods State Park west of Santa Rosa, and Muir Redwoods National Monument in Marin County.

There's a feeling of magic in a redwood grove. Many who've wandered deep within a peaceful grove claim major inspiration and a touched soul. To depart a redwood forest is to leave with renewed spirit and the promise of many much-awaited returns.

Far Northern California Coast

Del Norte and Humboldt Counties

Hike 1

Point St. George, Pelican Bay, and Lake Earl

LENGTH: 9 miles round-trip as described; 1.5 miles round-trip to Point St. George and its tidepools; the total beach hike can be shortened if Lake Earl is skipped.
DIFFICULTY: easy.
TOTAL ELEVATION GAIN: 100 feet.
WATER: none; bring your own.
SEASON: all—most likely to get a clear day in the autumn; portions of the dunes are extra wet in winter and spring.
MAP: Del Norte County Park map or USGS topos for Crescent City and Smith River.
INFORMATION: Del Norte County Park, (707) 464-7230.
DIRECTIONS TO TRAILHEAD: Just north of Crescent City on Highway 101, take the Washington Boulevard exit. Follow this road west 4 miles until it dead-ends in a large, paved parking lot next to a former Coast Guard Station.

Tidepools to frolic in, a point for scintillating views, a beach for barefoot strolling, seemingly endless sand dunes, and large marshes for birdwatching—this hike's got it. The fact that all this takes place on little known and seldom visited Pelican Bay makes the journey more charming.

Most who do know Pelican Bay consider it among the most abundant fisheries in California, with bountiful sole, salmon, and rockfish catches offshore. The Tolowa Indians camped on this beach long ago and harvested these fish and also gathered mussels and clams.

The main mission of this odyssey is to reach two coastal lagoons separated from Pelican Bay by a sandbar. Two hundred and fifty species of birds feed and drink from the mostly freshwater Lake Earl and more saline Lake Talawa. Ornithologists estimate that 100,000 birds can be sighted here at the same time.

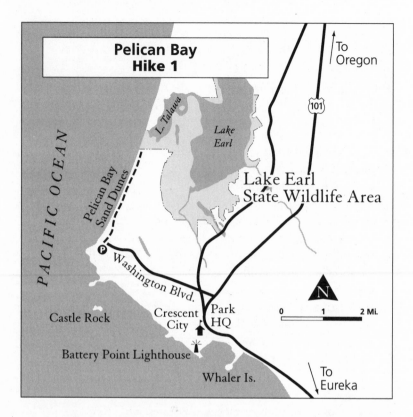

To begin, head for the roar of the surf by crossing next to the metal gate and traipsing along an unused gravel road. Grassy hillocks dotted with low-growing, spring-flowering wildflowers escort you to the driftwood-lined beach. During high tide you may have to walk on the foot-sized boulders and twig-sized driftwood to reach the Point St. George tidepools on the left.

The short side trip south to Point St. George has enough enticing stopover scenes to make you feel like a kid again. Clusters of sea stacks rise from the surf, and frequently seabirds are perched atop them. The low banks here are roughly an even mix of smooth, low-growing grasses higher up, and stark, wave-worn sandstone and shale rock faces toward the bottom. Your goal is to spot at least two of the sea caves located on the rocky shore near the rich tidepools.

During exceptionally high tides, it's safer and drier to zip over the grassy hills more inland to reach the top of Point St. George. From atop this hefty knob (choose the easiest way to scramble up this blufftop), the ocean photographic possibilities are varied. The smooth, brown beach sprawls below. Telephoto shots of the waves smashing against the sea stacks look dramatic. The seemingly infinite sand dunes and Pelican Bay encompass the view north.

Back on the beach, stroll north with the dual destination of Lakes Talawa and Earl in mind. The rolling grassy hillocks soon graduate into more flat sand dunes. The driftwood becomes more scant and the beach gets wider the further one ventures northward. The occasional car-sized chunks augment the seascape. How the heck they got there in the first place is a good conversation starter.

To keep the beach walk refreshing, consider scurrying up sand dunes and sink your feet into them for a half mile or so. To avoid wet feet, skirt around the numerous water seepage spots in the low areas of the dunes. It's a cinch to feel like a speck of sand when surrounded by undulating dunes in all directions.

Marshy terrain engulfs the lakes, curtailing access to them. A hiker can get into sections of the marsh and a little closer to the wide variety of waterfowl for the small price of getting their shoes wet and muddy. Binoculars and a picnic lunch are the two top-priority items here. It's an absorbing scene—extensive sand dunes encasing freshwater wetlands and saltwater marshlands. Birds in several sizes, shapes, and colors swoop, zoom, and even run about.

Hike 2

Stout Redwood Grove and Hiouchi Trail
in Jedediah Smith Redwoods State Park

LENGTH: 5.4 miles round-trip as described; 1.5 miles round-trip to and through Stout Grove.

DIFFICULTY: easy.

TOTAL ELEVATION GAIN: 300 feet.

WATER: available from Smith River (purify) and Mill Creek (purify); bring your own.

SEASON: all—call ahead in winter and early spring to make sure Mill Creek is crossable to get on the Hiouchi Trail.

MAP: Jedediah Smith Redwoods State Park map or USGS topo Hiouchi.

INFORMATION: Jedediah Smith Redwoods State Park, (707) 458-3310 or (707) 464-9533.

DIRECTIONS TO TRAILHEAD: Just north of Crescent City on Highway 101, turn east onto Highway 199. Drive 8.6 miles, then turn right onto South Fork Road. After 0.4 mile, turn right onto Douglas Park Road for another 1.6 miles to the trailhead. There's more parking space in the large clearing 70 feet up a side road on the left.

A soul wandering through giant redwoods along the banks of the Smith River is as close to heaven on earth as one can get. This journey is loaded with large redwoods, traversing the south shore of wide and clear Smith River, showing off its wild passages and its gracefully flowing segments.

Pure and smooth Smith River, the largest undammed river in California, features a few prime swimming spots along the trek. Mill Creek, the park's largest and most popular creek, climaxes into the river where a gravel beach and Stout Redwood Grove meet. This is an ideal place for a picnic/meditation/nap, and kids just dig it. They can play hide and seek behind some of the world's largest trees grouped in Stout Grove, then skip rocks over the Smith River.

Shaded and mostly flat Stout Grove and Hiouchi Trails are well designed and constructed. At times, they rise gently, always to reveal rewarding vistas down on gently curving Smith River. The trails are dust free, instead softly carpeted with needles and other leaves in various stages of decay. You can wear your most comfortable and well-worn tennis shoes over these cushioned trails.

In a quarter mile, the Stout Grove Trail leads to a rustic wooden bridge crossing vine-maple-decorated Cedar Creek where it finishes into Smith River. Shortly thereafter the trail loops, taking you through an alluvial flat that provides sheltered conditions and deep loam for the old-growth redwoods here in Stout Grove. This bountiful assembly of ancient gargantuan redwoods gives a good idea of what large redwood groves looked like back in the dinosaur age.

To connect with the Hiouchi Trail, take the spur trail that leaves the Stout Grove loop and promptly winds up at the intersection of

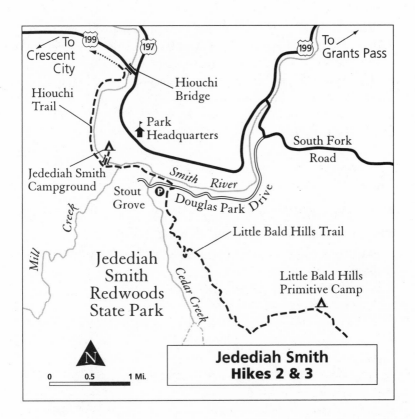

To Crescent City
199
197
To Grants Pass
199
Hiouchi Bridge
Hiouchi Trail
Park Headquarters
South Fork Road
Jedediah Smith Campground
Smith River
Stout Grove
Douglas Park Drive
Little Bald Hills Trail
Mill Creek
Cedar Creek
Jedediah Smith Redwoods State Park
Little Bald Hills Primitive Camp
N
0   0.5   1 Mi.

Jedediah Smith
Hikes 2 & 3

Mill Creek and the Smith River. This is a scenic spot for spending hang time, since this meeting point of creek and river is photogenic, with a gravel beach and places to swim. You may have to wade Mill Creek barefoot here to access the Hiouchi Trail that climbs its banks on the other side.

Secluded Hiouchi Trail has a few brief ups and downs, but steady flowing Smith River is rarely out of earshot or eyeshot. Gravel beaches and gravel bar islands are recurring scenes along the Smith River, which parallels the trails, and they are ideal places for spawning salmon to lay eggs.

Redwoods continue to dominate the dreamlike forest, accompanied by this region's understory associates—rhododendron, California and red huckleberry shrubs, sword fern, and redwood sorrel.

At 2.2 miles the trail comes to a steep cliffside, where redwood railings and a bench overlook river ripples at a major bending point in the river's course. Just before reaching Highway 199, a spur trail leads down to a large gravel beach and a deep section of Smith River, ideal for taking a dip. This is also a good turnaround point once you've checked out Hiouchi Bridge to the left and a series of river ripples to the right.

Hike 3

Little Bald Hills Trail
in Jedediah Smith Redwoods State Park

LENGTH: 7 miles round-trip to Little Bald Hills Primitive Camp.

DIFFICULTY: moderate to strenuous.

TOTAL ELEVATION GAIN: 1,600 feet.

WATER: available from Smith River (purify); bring lots of your own.

SEASON: all—most of the flowers here bloom in mid spring.

MAP: USGS topo Hiouchi or Jedediah Smith Redwoods State Park brochure. See p. 7.

INFORMATION: Jedediah Smith Redwoods State Park, (707) 458-3310 or (707) 464-9533.

DIRECTIONS TO TRAILHEAD: Just north of Crescent City on Highway 101, turn east onto Highway 199. Drive 8.6 miles, then turn right onto South Fork Road. After 0.4 mile, turn right onto Douglas Park Road for another 1.6 miles to the trailhead. There's more parking space in a large clearing 70 feet up a side road on the left.

One thing about nature—it's predictably mysterious. Little Bald Hills Trail used to climb to sloping prairies, now it rises to meet a mix of chaparral and open woodlands. Nobody can predict which native plants will occupy what spots when once common fires are suppressed. It's been decades since controlled fires swept this area.

Your mission is to find out the latest scenario as the shrubs multiply and the trees grow up in the Little Bald Hills.

Native American Indians here were experts at using timely fires to restore nutrients and increase beneficial bacteria and fungi in the soil, increase useful plants, and allow more sunshine to strike them. A hiker gets to see a mosaic of tiny prairie patches and thickening plant cover advancing as fast as patient time and mysterious nature dictates.

As part of the natural cycle, a lot of hunting goes on here. Bears feed on lots of fish that are bountiful in the Smith River, while the spotted owl patrols the redwood section of the hike. The Little Bald Hills Trail winds up in the open chaparral, which is prime stomping grounds for the coyote, bobcat, and mountain lion. Quiet hikers may get lucky and spy one of these animals off in the distance.

After checking out adjacent Smith River, proceed into the tall redwoods on the Little Bald Hills Trail. Many of the oldest redwoods with the largest trunks have amazingly survived despite being zapped by lightning.

The wide trail climbs moderately at first, past shiny green sword fern and huckleberry, rhododendron, and salal shrubs amply shaded in the redwood forest. Listen for the "squeaky brake" sound of the varied thrush here. Marbled murrelets fly low in these redwoods, especially at dawn and dusk.

The trail then flattens along a dinky annual streambed flanked by an alder thicket. It then switches into and climbs earnestly in a hardwood forest of tan oak and California bay laurel trees, with Douglas fir mixed in. Then the grayish-needled Port Orford cedar, which grows in just a few isolated areas of northwest California, soon joins the forest canopy.

Eventually you reach some clearings above 1,000 feet where Jeffrey pines decorate an open woodland that the trail goes through. A close relative of the ponderosa pine, this three-needled conifer usually grows much more inland and at elevations above 6,000 feet. The fact that nature allows their presence here is a bit of a mystery, but Jeffrey pines tend to thrive in lean soil, and there's some of that up here. Other trees and shrubs occupying what was once prairie in-

clude young madrones, manzanita, and coffeeberry shrubs. They all
add to the food variety for the drier-dwelling wildlife.

At 3.3 miles, a spur trail darts to the left, leading to Little Bald
Hills Primitive Campground (an overnight stopover for backpackers who plan to continue another few miles on this trip). Continuing
on the Little Bald Hills Trail, fleeting glimpses of the ocean in the far
distance soon appear. Conifer-coated canyons and mountainsides
sprawl in front of the ocean.

Hike 4

Damnation Creek Trail to Damnation Beach
in Del Norte Redwoods State Park

LENGTH: 4.5 miles round-trip.

DIFFICULTY: moderate.

TOTAL ELEVATION GAIN: 1,000 feet.

WATER: available from Damnation Creek (purify); bring your
own.

SEASON: all—most likely to get clear weather for views in
autumn.

MAP: Del Norte Coast Redwoods State Park brochure or
USGS topo map for Sister Rocks.

INFORMATION: Del Norte Coast Redwoods State Park, (707)
464-6101.

DIRECTIONS TO TRAILHEAD: On Highway 101 south of
Crescent City, look for mileage marker 16 on the west side,
about 4 miles past Del Norte Coast Redwoods State Park
campground entrance.

The perfect remedy for sweeping away cobwebs in the mind and
cleansing the spirit is to take this fine ramble. It plunges through
virgin redwoods so huge you might gasp with inspiration, then climaxes at a rocky beach so remote, some people pretend they discovered it.

Along the way, Damnation Creek gets into the act. Trailblazer

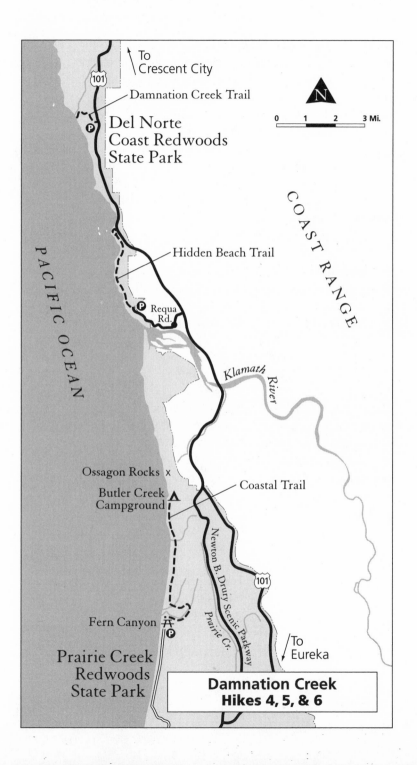

To
Crescent City

101

Damnation Creek Trail

Del Norte
Coast Redwoods
State Park

P

PACIFIC OCEAN

Hidden Beach Trail

P Requa
Rd.

Klamath River

COAST RANGE

N

0   1   2   3 Mi.

Ossagon Rocks ✕

Butler Creek
Campground

Coastal Trail

Newton B. Drury Scenic Parkway

101

Fern Canyon

P

Prairie Cr.

Prairie Creek
Redwoods
State Park

To
Eureka

**Damnation Creek
Hikes 4, 5, & 6**

Jedediah Smith, who founded nearby Jedediah Smith Redwoods State Park (Hikes 2 and 3), indicated while camping here back in 1828 that crashing along the creek was tough going. Other settlers agreed, and that's probably how the rough-and-tumble creek got its name. Yurok Indians used the Damnation Creek Trail to get to the beach to gather shellfish and seaweed.

Needle-carpeted Damnation Creek Trail is a wide path as it climbs gently for the first quarter mile under giant redwoods. Tropical-looking rhododendrons grow here like small, sparse patio trees, often canopying evergreen and red huckleberry, salal shrubs, and sword ferns.

As the trail commences gently downhill, the largest redwoods on the hike show up, some up to 4 yards thick at the base. Shortly after the junction with the Coastal Trail (the old Highway 101) at 0.7 mile (keep left), Damnation Creek Trail becomes more narrow, and begins its rapid plummet to the ocean.

Fleeting and teasing glimpses of the sea accompany the muffled purr of the surf. Although this well-made trail dips steeply at times, the impact of footsteps are cushioned by the accumulated duff from the redwoods, which by now aren't quite as big.

By the time you notice the heavily forested canyon that drains Damnation Creek on the right, salty-air-tolerant Sitka spruce takes over as the forest's dominant conifer. Salmonberry, gooseberry, and thimbleberry join the aforementioned shrubs in the understory. Soon after the trail parallels above the creek, look for a massive, moss-covered bigleaf maple tree hovering over the trail—it has ferns growing from many of its branches.

You soon cross two rustic wooden footbridges—the latter features a pair of handsome and windswept Sitka spruce trees—then the awaited union with the ocean promptly follows at the mouth of the creek.

The surf here is so populated with sea stacks that the only virtual access to this secluded and rough shoreline strip is the way you came. The whole scene is so surreal, secretive, and secluded it's easy to pretend to be an eighteenth-century explorer here. Imagine that there are several undiscovered shipwrecks hidden beneath the wild surf.

It's a treat to watch big waves crash against and then rinse over the two largest rock pillars, called Sister Rocks.

Low-growing lizard's-tail plants control erosion along the steep banks overlooking the beach. Aerial views of the polished boulders that nestle along the beach below are captured from atop these 50-foot-high bluffs. Boulder hopping the beach can be done anytime except high tide. A tremendous pile of driftwood logs partially dams Damnation Creek. A thicket of salal (edible berries and small, bell-shaped flowers) hugs the trail 50 feet prior to reaching the creek's mouth.

Hike 5

Klamath River to Hidden Beach and False Klamath Rock in Redwood National Park

LENGTH: 8.2 miles round-trip as described; 5.6 miles round-trip to Hidden Beach.

DIFFICULTY: moderate.

TOTAL ELEVATION GAIN: 600 feet.

WATER: bring your own.

SEASON: all—ideal for California gray whale watching in winter; wildflowers in spring; most likely to get best views in the autumn.

MAP: Redwood National Park brochure or USGS topo Requa. See p. 11.

INFORMATION: Redwood National Park, (707) 464-6101.

DIRECTIONS TO TRAILHEAD: About 60 miles north of Eureka on Highway 101 (2 miles north of the town of Klamath), turn west on Requa Road. Drive 2.3 miles to the trailhead next to a stop sign.

To truly capture the essence of this view-filled trek, one must go on a fog-free day. When the line of vision is long, the vistas of notable place-names allow splendid photos. It's an impressive list of popular and pretty sites—the wide mouth of the Klamath River, spectacular

Hidden Beach and sea stacks galore, featuring massive False Klamath Rock.

This journey follows a fabulous section of the Coastal Trail, which ultimately spans 40 miles. You wander in and out of lush grasslands and forests of alder and Sitka spruce, and along rocky cliffs and coastal bluffs. As an added bonus, there's the self-guided Yurok Indian Loop Trail halfway into the excursion, which details the Yurok way of life when they once roamed the territory you've been hiking in.

In the beginning, Coastal Trail descends to jaw-dropping views of the Klamath River union with the Pacific Ocean at a huge sandbar. For 0.7 mile the hawk's-eye views keep coming, through open grasslands sporting horsetail, bracken fern, lupine, and berry bushes.

Perhaps the prime vista occurs from a trailside bench, where you can admire the Klamath River, loaded with sediment washed down from the coastal mountains. Northern California's second longest river, the Klamath, drains a lot of the Klamath and Trinity mountains.

The steep cliffs overlooking the ocean and river here are gradually sinking into the sea, unlike most of the coastline southward, which continues to rise. The largest of the three nearby sea stacks was named Oregos, for the Yurok Indian spirit who lives there.

From here, you begin a series of short climbs in a red alder and Sitka spruce forest, where the main understory plants are salmonberry and California huckleberry. At 1.2 miles into the journey, another wondrous view is granted, this one revealing the rugged coastline to the south, climaxed by Patrick's Point (Hike 13) some 30 miles away. Listen for sea lions barking from the ocean rocks some 400 steep feet below.

The forest walking continues, graced by the distant roar of the surf. The hike's highlight, driftwood-laden Hidden Beach, is reached via a spur trail at 2.7 miles. From the dark gray sands of this isolated beach, you can admire False Klamath Rock dominating the surf to the north. Wildflowers decorate a grassy strip behind you while big waves crash against jagged sea stacks that attempt to block the waves that rinse Hidden Beach.

Horsetails flourish just above Hidden Beach.

Back on Coastal Trail, you pass near the north tail of Hidden Beach, then reenter grasslands, where a steady surf chant complements unblocked ocean views. Take the side path at 3.3 miles to appreciate a breathtaking view of Hidden Beach. Signed Yurok Loop Trail (go right onto it) appears 0.1 mile farther on Coastal Trail. Farther on, pick up the interpretive brochure from a dispenser west of the bridge.

Lagoon Creek spills into a freshwater pond here, bordered by a thicket of oaks, alders, and willows. Yellow pond lilies are perched on the still water along with several species of native and migrating waterbirds. Spot False Klamath Rock dominating to the north at 3.8 miles. The Yurok Tribe named this 209 foot-high rock "*olrgr*," meaning "digging place." Here they harvested Indian potatoes from Brodiaea plants. The Yurok Indians named the neighboring, smaller, jagged rock "*prgris-o-tsiguk,*" meaning "where bald eagle rests."

The trail winds westward at 4.0 miles, returning you in the direction you came. To cut the hike in half, take the path that briefly goes to the Lagoon Creek Parking Area (which has restrooms and a drinking fountain), and your prearranged car shuttle.

Hike 6

Fern Canyon to Ossagon Rocks in Prairie Creek Redwoods State Park

LENGTH: 8.6 miles round-trip.
DIFFICULTY: easy.
TOTAL ELEVATION GAIN: 200 feet.
WATER: available from Home and Butler Creeks (purify); or bring your own.
SEASON: all—wildflowers in late spring; slick spots on Coastal Trail after heavy winter rains; Home Creek may be difficult to cross when swollen after heavy winter rains.
MAP: Prairie Creek Redwoods State Park brochure or USGS topo Fern Canyon. See p. 11.
INFORMATION: Prairie Creek Redwoods State Park, (707) 464-6101 or (707) 488-2171.
DIRECTIONS TO TRAILHEAD: Get to the tiny town of Orick on Highway 101 first, which is north of Eureka and south of Crescent City. Turn west on bumpy Davison Road (2.5 miles north of Orick), then drive the 6.8 curving and dusty miles to the Fern Canyon trailhead parking lot.

This wild and wonderful trip features three dramatic settings that are virtually unduplicated anywhere in California. Part 1 goes along the bottom of moist and lush Fern Canyon, where several varieties of ferns literally cling to and coat the steep and narrow walls. A masterpiece of a small waterfall gushes into crystal-clear Home Creek, combining for an intimate experience.

Coastal Trail traipses through forests of Sitka spruce and alder, alternating with grasslands where you're bound to meet several massive Roosevelt elk. Oh, sure, there are other hikes near here (see Hikes 7, 8, and 10) where the elk graze, but the lush grassy flat on

This California gray whale perished on Gold Bluffs Beach near Ossagon Rocks.

this hike provides ideal habitat and lots of roaming room to attract more elk.

This walk's third unique setting, and the ultimate destination, is a cluster of sea stacks called Ossagon Rocks that are uncommonly close to the headlands. At low tide, many of these massive rock outcrops can be easily scaled, giving a hiker the refreshing illusion of being a temporary sea king.

To start, get on Fern Canyon Loop Trail, which crosses Home Creek via planks several times along this level and completely shaded 0.8-mile stroll. The 50- to 60-foot-tall vertical walls are covered mainly with sword and five-finger ferns, and with some lady and bracken ferns. Thimbleberry and salmonberry drape the banks of Home Creek, which swirls through 30-foot-wide Fern Canyon.

A towering red alder tree stands in front of a spiral-staircase trail section that takes you to a smaller canyon coated with five-finger ferns and featuring a slender 12-foot waterfall. A bit farther, a walkway departs the canyon into a redwood grove (Hike 8). Our hike retraces your steps, then travels through a red alder forest on the Coastal Trail, also called Beach Trail.

Level Coastal Trail soon hugs the cliff bottoms, displaying grassy dunes and numerous Sitka spruce groves. The next couple of miles provide lots of chances to encounter herds of Roosevelt elk, California's largest land animals (stags can weigh a half ton). Named after former President Theodore Roosevelt, these gregarious grazers are native to this area. The stags tend to be docile, but the females are alert and protective during calving season in May.

Coastal Trail skirts a marsh 2.4 miles into the journey, then passes Butler Creek Primitive Camp (for bicyclists) a bit farther. Native grasses reach 6 feet tall near the banks of Butler Creek.

Large banana slugs are often massed along a dark and moist jungle the trail goes into just past a 50-yard cobblestone section at 2.9 miles. Look for California salamanders, pigeons, and frogs here, before the trail switches back into grassy sand dunes.

At 3.9 miles, the trail heads inland near a small brook. You stay left here, near Gold Bluffs Beach and a dense alder thicket for a half mile. Then it's a brief dune ramble past sand verbena and native grasses to wild, wave-worn Ossagon Rocks.

It's a blast to let the cool ocean mist fill your lungs as light sprays of wave water shower over you. A rare treat to feel like you're a part of the big rocks that are endlessly cleansed and recleansed by the wave action.

To complete this varied hike, consider a couple miles worth of barefoot strolling along a pristine section of smooth, clean Gold Bluffs Beach. Completely concealed from Highway 101 by massive redwood forests, this portion of Gold Bluffs Beach heading south allows you to pretend it's your own private strip of wet sand.

Hike 7

Prairie Creek Trail
in Prairie Creek Redwoods State Park

LENGTH: 9 miles round-trip; 5.5 miles round-trip to Zig Zag Trail No. 1.

DIFFICULTY: easy.

TOTAL ELEVATION GAIN: 200 feet.

WATER: available from Prairie Creek (purify); or bring your own.

SEASON: all—more creek access for photographing changing colors of the bigleaf and vine maples in the fall; prettier and more powerful creek in the winter, especially after a hard rain; more people along the trail in summer; most silence and seclusion on a weekday in winter.

MAP: Prairie Creek Redwoods State Park or USGS topo Fern Canyon.

INFORMATION: Prairie Creek Redwoods State Park, (707) 488-2171 or (707) 464-6101 ext. 5300.

DIRECTIONS TO TRAILHEAD: From the town of Orick (41 miles north of Eureka), drive farther north on Highway 101 for about 7 miles, then turn onto Newton B. Drury Road. Follow it to Prairie Creek Redwoods State Park Visitor Center parking lot. The trail begins as the Nature Trail at a large trail sign in front of the visitor's center.

All creeks are spiritual and rhythmic, and most creeks are beautiful. Prairie Creek is as spiritually liberating and gorgeous as it gets, bar none.

Prairie Creek Trail hugs this wondrous creek the entire way, bestowing an up-close and personal feel that most other creek trails can't match. Spectacular bigleaf maple trees and grand redwoods are guardians over Prairie Creek, the namesake of the park it blesses.

The bulk of this hike chapter unveils the special spots, scenic highlights, and overall virtues of Prairie Creek, but be aware of the one tradeoff—the sound of cars touring on nearby Newton B. Drury Road can offset the appeal some. A few years ago, this road was super-busy Highway 101, meaning that Prairie Creek Trail hikers heard continuous car noise. Highway 101 has since been rerouted a few miles inland, leaving this old highway segment (Newton B. Drury Road) for park tourists. Go on a weekday in the fall or winter, when there are much fewer tourists driving the road, and this journey will likely become a favorite.

From the get-go, clear and rapid Prairie Creek bends and twists

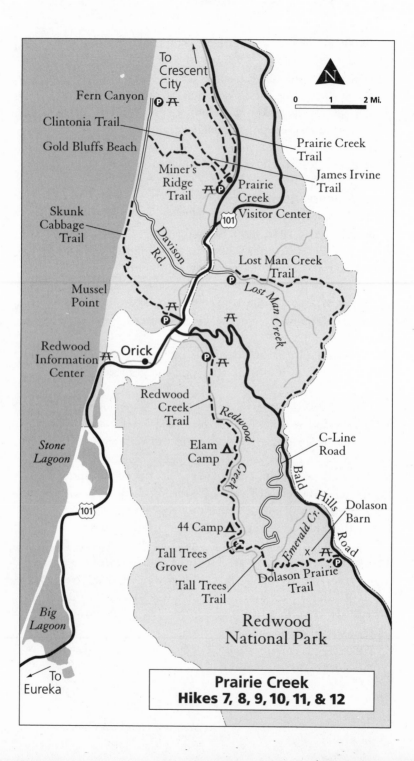

To
Crescent
City

Fern Canyon

Clintonia Trail

Gold Bluffs Beach

Prairie Creek
Trail

Miner's
Ridge
Trail

Prairie
Creek

James Irvine
Trail

Visitor Center

Skunk
Cabbage
Trail

101

Davison Rd.

Lost Man Creek
Trail

Lost Man Creek

Mussel
Point

Redwood
Information
Center

Orick

Redwood
Creek
Trail

Redwood Creek

C-Line
Road

Elam
Camp

Stone
Lagoon

101

Bald Hills Road

Dolason
Barn

44 Camp

Emerald Cr.

Tall Trees
Grove

Tall Trees
Trail

Dolason Prairie
Trail

Big
Lagoon

To
Eureka

Redwood
National
Park

0   1   2 Mi.

N

Prairie Creek
Hikes 7, 8, 9, 10, 11, & 12

gracefully in some areas and dramatically in others. Old-growth redwoods are particularly dominant over the first couple of miles—farther on, Sitka spruces join the overstory.

After a half mile, the leaf- and needle-carpeted path takes you into an alluvial flat where clusters of this hike's largest redwoods tower over the creek. Several sunny, open sites decorate this area, and on them bigleaf maples sway in the breeze and glisten in the light. These native deciduous trees often furnish filtered sunlight here for the lush sword fern gardens underneath.

Near a rustic redwood footbridge, 20-foot-tall vine maple trees are nestled next to a lone bigleaf maple giant. Look for the toppled redwood tree trunk over wooden steps farther along Prairie Creek Trail. Note the California huckleberry shrubs growing in the rotted matter high up on the leaning trunk.

In early summer, swift currents flow into deep pools, which are often suitable for swimming. Although most of the journey is spent in shaded creekside forest, there are lots of sunny spots for warming the blood, having a picnic and/or a short and refreshing nap. Watch for many kinds of birds darting and swooping over Prairie Creek. If you missed good photo opportunities toward the beginning, many more colorful vine and bigleaf maples leaning over the creek await before and after the signed trail junction with Zig Zag Trail 1 at 2.8 miles.

At this interval, and at signed Zig Zag Trail 2 (at 4.5 miles), a hiker can add variety to the hike by returning via the West Ridge Trail (the Zig Zag Trails are short connectors). Account for a few ups and downs, and look forward to being in a dark and virgin forest mainly of Douglas fir and redwood, but also some Sitka spruce and hemlock conifers mixed in.

Hike 8

Miner's Ridge Trail, Gold Bluffs Beach, Fern Canyon, and James Irvine Trail

> **LENGTH:** 9.5 miles as described; 6 miles round-trip by using the Clintonia connector trail.
> **DIFFICULTY:** moderate.

TOTAL ELEVATION GAIN: 800 feet.

WATER: available from Prairie, Godwood, and Home Creeks.

SEASON: all—beware of washouts and slippery spots after heavy winter rains.

MAP: USGS topos Fern Canyon and Orick, or Prairie Creek Redwoods State Park map. See p. 20.

INFORMATION: Prairie Creek Redwoods State Park, (707) 488-2171 or (707) 464-6101.

DIRECTIONS TO TRAILHEAD: From Orick (41 miles north of Eureka), drive farther north on Highway 101 for about 7 miles, then turn onto Newton B. Drury Road. Follow it to Prairie Creek Redwoods State Park. The trail begins as the Nature Trail at a large trail sign in front of the visitor's center.

The best way to be an elf frolicking in an enchanted, primeval forest is to take this journey past virgin redwoods to a pristine beach. Except for Tall Trees Grove (Hike 11), the redwoods don't get any bigger than the ones along the Miner's Ridge and James Irvine Trails. Once you get deep into the forest, which is right off the bat, these giants are everywhere, and it stays that way most of the way.

To start, cross rushing Prairie Creek over a sturdy wooden bridge, then hang two quick lefts before getting onto the signed Miner's Ridge Trail. The good thing about this trail is that you get the bulk of your climbing out of the way from the get-go. The curving footpath follows a narrow spine of the Miner's Ridge, which affords ample sights down into both canyonsides of a fern, salal, and huckleberry understory lined with redwoods sporting massive trunks.

You have to peer up into the sky to detect the redwood needle foliage. This immense redwood grove proves that these distinctive conifers can take on many amazing shapes and forms. One cluster of five huge redwoods near the beginning of the trail appears to be joined at the trunk to become in effect one multiple-trunked redwood giant.

Countless redwood specimens along this stretch may eventually contend for widest redwood trunk or tallest tree in the world. Lightning frequently wreaks havoc here. Many large trunks have

Although the females tend to be protective during calving season, the Roosevelt elk stags are docile.

been blackened and scarred from the bottom to near the top, still holding sprays of foliage way up high. Lightning has drastically gouged some of these redwoods, reducing them to wood sculptures.

At 2.2 miles, you come to the Clintonia connector trail, a 1-mile jaunt that snakes through a dark, peaceful forest to the James Irvine Trail, serving as a shortcut if one's pressed for time. To reach Gold Bluffs Beach, continue straight along wooden walkways that cross a series of babbling brooks that merge with Squashan Creek.

On crossing dusty Davison Road, and then passing through the campground, the beach unfolds. The beach was named long ago for prospectors who discovered a few gold flakes in the sand, got stoked enough to set up gold-mining camps, then became disappointed when the big Gold Rush never happened here.

While beachcombing north, look for the herd of Roosevelt elk. After about a mile, veer right near Home Creek and follow the red alder forest into fern-coated Fern Canyon (turn to Hike 6 for full description of this lush, shady garden of ferns). Sword and five-finger ferns are the most common along this half-mile trail within misty, dark Fern Canyon, with a sprinkling of bracken and lady ferns.

Soon the trail ascends the canyon, and you'll take a right at the ridgetop onto the signed James Irvine Trail. After 0.3 mile, you reach a footbridge where a waterfall topples 20 feet in Home Creek. The closer one gets to the Clintonia connector trail, the bigger the Douglas fir grow amid the bigger redwoods.

Once past the connector trail, the fir diminish and again you're traipsing past shady groves of mainly ancient redwoods. Often the only sound heard is the rhythm of your footsteps drumming on a carpet of littered needles.

After passing a fern-lined section of trickling Home Creek, you climb briefly to some huge rotted redwood stumps with huckleberry shrubs growing on top of them. The trail then levels along the flat forest floor for almost a mile past a couple of tiny brooks to a point where Godwood Creek joins the trail.

Since Godwood Creek is small, and towering redwoods line its banks, only a partial riparian habitat exists. Profuse patches of sword fern and occasional red alder comprise the landscape. Cloverlike redwood sorrel (actually an oxalis) hugs the ground the rest of the way.

Hike 9

Lost Man Creek Trail in Redwood National Park

LENGTH: 3.4 miles round-trip.
DIFFICULTY: easy.
TOTAL ELEVATION GAIN: 200 feet.
WATER: available from Lost Man Creek (purify); bring your own.
SEASON: all—the creek is wild and exciting in the early spring, especially after a hard rain (look for some cascades); good chance of having the trail to yourself in the winter; trailside mushrooms in the autumn.
MAP: Redwood National Park map or USGS topo Orick.

Vine maples are small native trees that flourish—like this one—on the banks of Lost Man Creek.

INFORMATION: Redwood National Park, (707) 464-6101 or (707) 488-3461.

DIRECTIONS TO TRAILHEAD: From the town of Orick (41 miles north of Eureka on Highway 101), drive farther north on 101 for 3 miles, then turn right onto Lost Man Creek Road. The large parking area and trailhead is a short distance away.

When time and/or energy is in short supply, this hike will energize the spirit and make time stand still. Naturally moving water has a special way of spreading good vibes, and this stroll along meandering Lost Man Creek is apt to bring good cheer. The virgin redwoods here reach high into the sky, not a whole lot bigger than during the days when the Yurok Indians roamed this wild, dense section of Northern California coast.

It's rare for a roving wanderer to be able to pull off Highway 101 and within a few minutes be deep in the midst of lush, pristine, and secluded country. This land is already dark along the creekside, beneath conifers and deciduous trees—here during a deep fog you're wonderfully ensconced in a dark gray dream scene.

The redwoods maintain a comfortable existence within the moist environs of the Lost Man Creek canyon. The area gets frequent fog and lots of rainfall. Those factors, combined with shelter from the wind, deep shade, and a perpetual blanket of organic mulch from needles, twigs, and leaves, present the ideal conditions redwoods favor.

It's no surprise to see a newt munching on a long and slimy banana slug along this old dirt road called Lost Man Creek Trail that hugs Lost Man Creek. The spotted owl and the marbled murrelet are more likely to be witnessed during dawn and dusk. The varied thrush, with its squeaky call, and the gregarious Steller jay are more likely to be spotted during the day. Lost Man Creek was the site of the World Heritage Site park dedication back in 1980. Lost Man Creek Trail takes off next to the gate and picnic tables and rises slightly for a short while with Lost Man Creek usually within earshot and eyeshot. Contrasting with nearby Prairie Creek (Hike

7), more of a rock-bottomed stream, predominantly dirt-bottomed Lost Man Creek tends to be darker and deeper.

Large alders reach for the sun over fast-flowing Lost Man Creek, particularly between the two large log bridges. Scattered old-growth redwoods dominate the riparian landscape over the first mile or so, with many more young redwoods along with Sitka spruce and tan oak in the mix.

At 1.2 miles, a pretty tributary flows into Lost Man Creek, with a thriving thicket of salal on the left and a cluster of vine maple trees on the right.

Lost Man Creek Trail, a well-maintained gravel service road, stays mostly flat for another half mile before the heavy-duty climbing ensues where the trail veers up and away from the creek. By this time, the primary highlights have been appreciated.

For a thorough aerobic workout guaranteed to make you sweat, keep climbing anywhere from a short distance to Bald Hills Road, now 8 miles to the east. The ascent goes through forest logged long ago. It's recommended to trudge up a little way at least—it improves the blood flow, clears the cobwebs from the mind, and reveals a changing landscape and plant habitat.

Hike 10

Skunk Cabbage Creek to Gold Bluffs Beach in Redwood National Park

LENGTH: 10 miles round-trip as described; 5.2 miles round-trip to Mussel Point.

DIFFICULTY: moderate.

TOTAL ELEVATION GAIN: 1,100 feet.

WATER: available from Skunk Cabbage Creek (purify); bring your own.

SEASON: all—mucky trail sections sometimes in winter and spring; best weather for clear views in autumn.

MAP: Redwood National Park map or USGS topos Orick and Fern Canyon. See p. 20.

INFORMATION: Redwood National Park, (707) 464-6101.

DIRECTIONS TO TRAILHEAD: Get to the tiny town of Orick on Highway 101 first, which is between Eureka (south) and Crescent City (north). From the Redwood Creek Bridge in Orick, drive north for 1.5 miles, then turn west (at M.122.69 marker). Travel 0.8 mile until the road dead-ends at the trailhead parking area.

Sometimes hikers feel like "been there, done that" regarding typical coast excursions. If that case arises, take this trek—it's weird in a good way.

First of all, almost half the journey is spent in a moist alder/ spruce forest, and there aren't too many of those around Northern California. Secondly, although it's called Skunk Cabbage Trail, all the native skunk cabbage is hidden along the nearby banks of Skunk Cabbage Creek, meaning a hiker has to exit the trail to admire this close relative of the corn lily. Third of all, the hike's mid portion is on a coastline slope so lush in vegetation that Tarzan would dig it.

What a radical change it is to break out of the jungle and suddenly burst onto wide-open Gold Bluffs Beach! Long, strange trips tend to feature drama—this one fits the bill, especially when you get to check out the ocean from various perches up to 500 feet above it.

At the onset, you're surrounded by slender, white-barked trunks —a tall grove of red alder trees hovers above both sides of Skunk Cabbage Trail. Soon after crossing a lovely old wooden footbridge and three wooden planks, the mostly flat trail enters a lush sword fern garden, canopied by moss-coated Sitka spruce. Alaska's state tree, these stalwart conifers grow here near its southernmost native range. Look close and hard, you're bound to spot an occasional and massive redwood specimen, lucky to be growing old and spared from the logging that went on here long ago.

Meandering Skunk Cabbage Trail crosses sedge-clogged babbling brooks time and again. The eclectic array of alder and spruce stands at leaning attention above the cool, moist forest floor. Their poles reach gracefully to the sky to snag sunlight. The soothing and rhythmic murmur of Skunk Cabbage Creek comes into play in brief spurts, the creek itself concealed in dense plants. At 2.0 miles, the footpath snakes upward, a friendly reminder that ocean vistas are soon to come. Most creeks this close to the sea usually pour into it— Skunk Cabbage Creek flows away from it. Just prior to reaching the creek's head at a scenic red alder-shaded flat, the inspirational roar of the surf stirs the spirit while your hard-working lungs fill with that clean sea air.

From the signed trail junction, you can gaze down on the ocean far below, watching its waves steadily cleanse a cluster of sea stacks, then rinse across a smooth, sandy beach. A signed spur trail leads to this secluded beach, which is tucked against Mussel Point. For total privacy and great shoreline views, take this side trip. You may be satisfied enough to hang out a long while, and then head back, thus cutting the journey in half.

Back on the main trail, the purr of the surf is constant and comforting during a brief climb and then a longer descent. The narrow path here cuts through dense jungle, so check for ticks. After dropping in and out of a pair of fern-coated canyons, a thicket of salal signals the dramatic finale of jungle and the meeting point of Gold Bluffs Beach.

Before strolling over the driftwood to the gray sands of Gold Bluffs Beach, make note of the large sign that says "Skunk Cabbage Section." Look for this marker later to regain the return route.

This portion of Gold Bluffs Beach is very wide and so unknown to the public, you may be the only soul roaming it. Driftwood, long ago a part of some distant forest, is deposited by winter storms onto the beach and neighboring grassy sand dunes. This dune strip separates the surf from the densely vegetated inland banks along this promenade.

Although this beach goes on unimpeded for almost 10 miles to Ossagon Rocks (Hike 6), most people turn back after a mile or so. Or they traipse across the dunes after 2 miles to reach their car shuttle at the Prairie Creek Redwoods State Park campgrounds entrance station/parking lot, thus cutting the hike in half.

Hike 11

Redwood Creek to Tall Trees Grove in Redwood National Park

LENGTH: 18 miles round-trip as described; 9.5 miles one way, climbing to C-Line Road (see directions to trailhead).

DIFFICULTY: moderate.

TOTAL ELEVATION GAIN: 500 feet.

WATER: available from Redwood Creek (purify); bring lots of your own.

SEASON: late spring through fall; call ahead to see if creek can be waded during bridgeless wet season; fewer people in the fall; meadow flowers in the spring.

MAP: Redwood National Park brochure or USGS topos Orick, Rodgers Peak, and Bald Hills. See p. 20.

INFORMATION: Redwood National Park, (707) 464-6101.

DIRECTIONS TO TRAILHEAD: For one way, with arranged shuttle: drive to Redwood Information Center to obtain a permit and combination to the locked gate. It's located on Highway 101 a mile south of Orick, which is 40 miles north of Eureka. Then drive just north of Orick and turn east onto Bald Hills Road (it's 0.1 mile north of the Redwood Creek Bridge). Your driver then travels 7 miles to a locked gate (the combination unlocks it), which is C-Line Road. Drive 6 miles on this dirt road to the Tall Trees trailhead. For round-trip: turn east onto Bald Hills Road just north of Orick, turn right after a quarter mile, then park after a half mile at the large Redwood Creek Trail parking lot.

For zesty individuals in the mood for the wild and the wonderful, this all-day hike/backpack trip along the banks of Redwood Creek is sure to please. It starts in a streamside forest of alder and bay, passes meadow strips that are green in the spring and brown in the summer, then lingers long in redwood/riparian forests.

The journey's ultimate goal is to be a dwarf under one of the world's tallest trees (a 358-foot-tall redwood), but getting there is where the action is. There are plenty of chances to ditch Redwood Creek Trail and explore Redwood Creek intimately by "barhopping" (alternating between traipsing across the creek's numerous gravel bars and wading in shallow creek sections). These long, flat islands composed of clean pebbles and an occasional willow are ideal for camping on (register first).

Wide Redwood Creek, which flows past Orick and then into the ocean, is with you virtually the whole way. That's the good news. The bad news is that this creek often swells to uncrossable depths during the rainy season (inquire), and portions of the trail are overcrowded with lush plants. Wear long pants to avoid ticks (especially in late spring) and stinging nettle.

At the start, red alder and California bay laurel trees partially shade the flat trail past a seasonal creek featuring a giant bigleaf maple at 0.4 mile. Salmonberry and blackberry bushes thrive here, and you can harvest the flavorful berries in late spring and early summer.

At 1.6 miles you reach a gravel flat covered with wild mustard, foxglove, and lupine flowers. Cross the Redwood Creek bridge here. If the movable bridge is gone, find then wade the widest creek portion. To regain the trail, spot the red, diamond-shaped marker on the creek's south shoreline.

The clear waters of Redwood Creek look serene from several vantage points above it, beginning at 2 miles. The bigleaf maples that canopy redwood sorrel and ferns are huge here, but they're dwarfed by the stately redwoods. At 2.7 miles, note the twin towers —two lightning-charred redwoods joined at the trunk. At 3 miles, there's a statuesque moss-covered maple that adorns an ideal picnic site near a scenic gravel bar.

You get to cross a series of gorgeous seasonal streams and perennial creeks that drain into Redwood Creek, beginning at 4.2 miles and continuing to Tall Trees Grove. Rushing Bond Creek is crossed at 5.6 miles, followed by Forty Four Creek, decorated with lush, shaded, steep canyon walls a mile farther.

Redwood Creek Trail then climbs gently away from the creek for about a mile, eventually granting a great view down on the creek and an inaugural sighting of the world's tallest redwoods from Tall

Trees Overlook. After a half mile, the trail returns to Redwood Creek at an alluvial flat where the creek bends beneath gargantuan redwoods. Cross this shallow and wide creek section and step into a stately grove of ancient redwoods with cathedral-like elegance called Tall Trees Grove. This magnificent 0.7-mile-long stroll past lush ferns and under giant redwoods leads to the tallest measured tree in the world. At 14 feet in diameter, this specimen is about 600 years old. This and the other redwoods flourish here because of the organically rich soil, sheltered canyon bottom, plentiful rainfall, and moderate temperatures.

If a car shuttle is arranged, climb out of the grove via the Tall Trees Trail to the terminus of C-Line Road. To add several more miles to the trip, consider doing nearby Hike 12 in reverse. Otherwise, retrace your steps to the trailhead.

Hike 12

Dolason Prairie Bald Hills to Tall Trees Grove in Redwood National Park

LENGTH: 12 miles round-trip as described; 6 miles one way for car shuttle; 2.4 miles round-trip to Dolason Barn.

DIFFICULTY: strenuous on the return trip; otherwise moderate.

TOTAL ELEVATION GAIN: 2,100 feet.

WATER: available from Redwood Creek and Emerald Creek (purify); bring lots of your own.

SEASON: all—spring features green grasses and colorful wildflowers; fewer people if any in winter.

MAP: USGS topo Bald Hills or Redwood National Park map. See p. 20.

INFORMATION: Redwood National Park, (707) 464-6101.

DIRECTIONS TO TRAILHEAD: Get to the tiny town of Orick first, which is on Highway 101 between Crescent City (north) and Eureka (south). A tenth of a mile north of the Redwood Creek Bridge, turn east on Bald Hills Road. After a few miles, C-Line Road appears on the right. This 6-mile-long dirt road can be used for car shuttle purposes to cut the hiking distance in half, but you must first get a permit and gate lock combination from the Redwood Information Center near Orick—call (707) 464-6101. To get to Dolason Prairie Trailhead, continue on Bald Hills Road (11 miles from Highway 101).

This uniquely different monster ramble tends to be preferred by park naturalists and rangers. That's because few folks know about it and it offers lots of special plant types. Of course, Tall Trees Grove with one of the world's tallest trees and several that come close to its height is the ultimate destination on this odyssey. Along the way, there's prairie allowing wide-ranging views of the distant ocean and nearby forested mountainsides. Oregon oak woodlands, groves of rhododendrons nestled under mammoth redwoods and creek beauty round out the bonuses.

On the first part of the journey, the Dolason Prairie Trail cuts briefly through a section of prairie (sometimes overgrown, check for ticks) then into a dense forest of tall Douglas fir. At 0.5 mile, the trail temporarily becomes an old gravel road, darting right and escorting you past a unique mix of Doug firs in many sizes and shapes, including lots of living Christmas tree sizes.

A quarter mile farther, the trail returns to footpath status next to some patches of coyote brush and bracken fern. After 0.4 mile of woods-shaded descent, a large prairie is reached, featuring views of the far-off ocean beyond nearby Dolason Barn. Thousands of sheep once pastured on these prairies, wintering around sheep sheds like this triangular "half barn" built in 1914. These prairies were preserved long ago via burns by the Native American Indians, and these days invasive nonnative plants and conifers continue to be restrained by controlled burns.

The slender footpath cuts through the prairie, consisting of yard-tall perennial grasses, and soon connects with the wildlife edge between prairie and forest. Look for a stand of Oregon white oak here. Very few of these deciduous native oaks (resembling valley oaks, but smaller) grow along the Northern California coast.

Thankfully, the route was designed to weave in and out of coastal prairie and Douglas fir woodlands for a good mile, making for the double bonus of expansive views into the Redwood Creek canyon, and the peaceful seclusion of strolling in a conifer forest.

Eventually the trail plunges into cool forest where ancient redwoods join fir in towering over tan oak, California bay laurel, huckleberry shrubs, and sword fern. Farther down, rhododendrons (striking flowers in May), and the occasional Oregon grape shrubs comprise the understory. This needle-littered and leaf-scattered section of the Dolason Prairie Trail seems to wander aimlessly, allowing a soul to pretend to be hopelessly and perfectly lost.

At 4.5 miles, a gorgeous view of rocky-bottomed Emerald Creek awaits from a bridge 100 feet above. From this perch, one can gaze down on a cluster of large redwood logs strewn haphazardly above the clear waters.

By following the trail junction signs for Tall Trees Grove, the next couple of miles is spent in old-growth redwood forest, the final leg in an alluvial flat near Redwood Creek called Tall Trees Grove. The creek is wide and gorgeous here, and the redwood trees in this grove seem to inspire energy for the thigh-burning trudge back up to the car. It's almost a custom to have your picture taken in front of Tall Tree (358 feet—bring a flash). By combining this journey with Hike 11 (along Redwood Creek), one gets an outrageous 14-mile one-way backpacking trip (get permit).

Hike 13

Mussel Rocks and Palmer's Point
in Patrick's Point State Park

LENGTH: 5 miles, including all the spur trails.
DIFFICULTY: easy to moderate.
TOTAL ELEVATION GAIN: 500 feet.
WATER: from campground faucets along the way.
SEASON: all—summer has more people and fog.
MAP: USGS topo Trinidad, or Patrick's Point State Park map.
INFORMATION: Patrick's Point State Park, (707) 677-3570 or (707) 445-6547.

DIRECTIONS TO TRAILHEAD: From Eureka on Highway 101, it's about 25 miles north to Trinidad and another 5 miles to Patrick's Point Drive. Follow it to Patrick's Point State Park, then drive to the paved Agate Beach parking lot.

The numerous destinations on this hike come via spur trails. It'll take some careful and frequent map studying, but the object is to get greedy and get on as many of these side paths as possible. Most of the place-name spur trails furnish commanding vistas of the shiny Pacific Ocean and dark, wave-worn sea stacks, while others also include sprawling Agate Beach.

The mostly flat and densely shaded Rim Trail, described as a counterclockwise route to lessen wind in your face, is accompanied by the sea's rhythmic roar most of the way. A few of the destinations

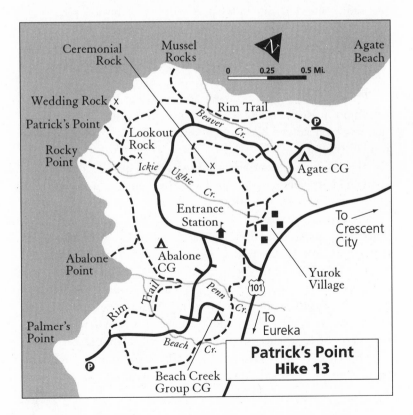

serve as highlights of this journey and consist of dramatic drops of up to 100 feet to the water's edge.

The plunge to foamy and frothing Mussel Rocks is one of these. This is a boulder-strewn stretch of rugged coastline, suitable for boulder hopping or perching like a seabird on a big old rock to watch the waves pound the steep, sea-slicked sea stacks.

Coast silktassel shrubbery and young Sitka spruce escort you down the Wedding Rock spur trail to a three-way fork. Continuing straight means a brief climb to the Wedding Rock lookout. The other two side trails quickly lead to boulders and the water's edge.

The flat and brief stroll to Patrick's Point (wheelchair accessible by parking at the Wedding Rock lot) ducks under some bishop pine, passes ceanothus and California huckleberry, then climaxes at cliff railings.

The switchbacking climb up Lookout Rock begins under towering red alders and concludes past windswept bishop pines. The views, partially shrouded by plants, may not compare with this trip's other lookouts, but the serenity makes it special. Imagine, this is an old sea stack like Ceremonial Rock, left high and dry when the ocean receded.

The best way to feel the salty and misty sea breeze is to spend hang time at Rocky Point. This is the second westernmost destination on this headland hike, and allows one to trace the countryside just left behind.

The 100-foot descent along the Abalone Point Trail leads past ferns and horsetails to a peaceful cove. The highlight here is the view of Palmer's Point past countless pillarlike rocks wedged in the ocean.

On leaving this wheelchair stretch of the Rim Trail, you begin in a grove of gargantuan Sitka spruces, cross narrow Beach Creek, densely surrounded by lush greenery, then alternate between red alder and upright spruce groves to the Palmer's Point spur trail next to an open field. Although you can't go to the end of steep Palmer's Point, one can gaze northward to study Abalone Point and neighboring cove along with Rocky Point, and southward to the secluded and inaccessible beaches steeply below Patrick's Point Drive.

The native plant garden is still signed, but has run wild at last report. Many of the small flowers have long disappeared, but several shrub specimens remain identified through signage, such as salal, Pacific wax myrtle, western azalea, rhododendron, ninebark, snowberry, vine maple, Pacific dogwood, and flowering currant.

The Yurok Indian Village next door invites a visit. Situated on a grassy flat, it features a cluster of short, teepeelike dwellings made of redwood with round holes to crawl through to get inside. Many of the Yurok Indians used Patrick's Point as a seasonal camp, hunting deer, elk, and sea mammals, and fishing for sturgeon and salmon. A number of protected archaeological sites exist here. Celebrations and tribal dances are frequently performed here by Native Americans, and many school groups studying California history visit the village.

A stone stairway escorts you steeply up Ceremonial Rock. After passing a couple of two- or three-story-tall rock outcrops draped with ivy, a rewarding vista awaits of green fields and Agate Beach to the northeast and gothic groves of Sitka spruce behind you. Another side trail loops around this 100-foot-high chunk of rock, leading to the green field, ideal for snagging sun and picnicking.

The 0.2-mile-long Octopus Trees Trail reveals an amazing Sitka spruce forest. Some of these giants feature gnarled, twisted, or multiple trunks. Some of these trees grew roots over logs that have long rotted away, leaving behind octopuslike tentacles as roots. Other spruces actually have ferns thriving in rotted litter accumulations on high branches.

Lost Coast

Mendocino and Sonoma Counties

Hike 14

Lost Coast Trail—Mattole River to Shelter Cove

LENGTH: 25 miles one way (arrange car shuttle); 6 miles round-trip to Punta Gorda Lighthouse; 12 miles round-trip to Cooskie Creek.

DIFFICULTY: moderate.

TOTAL ELEVATION GAIN: 800 feet.

WATER: available from Mattole River, Cooskie Creek, Randall Creek, Spanish Creek, Shipman Creek, and other streams (purify); or bring lots of your own.

SEASON: all—wildflowers in the spring; more likely to get fog-free, less windy weather in the autumn; sometimes totally devoid of people in the winter; your feet may get wet crossing swollen creeks after winter rains.

MAP: USGS topos Petrolia, Cooskie Creek, Shubrick Peak, and Shelter Cove; or King Range National Conservation Area brochure.

INFORMATION: Bureau of Land Management (BLM), (707) 822-7648.

DIRECTIONS TO TRAILHEAD: From Eureka, drive 60 miles south on Highway 101 to Redway. Take the South Fork/ Honeydew exit, then go west on Wilder Ridge Road. After 23 miles (in Honeydew), turn right on Mattole Road and drive 15 miles to Lighthouse Road (50 feet south of the Mattole River Bridge in Petrolia). Turn left and follow the road 5 miles to the parking area. Find the trailhead just past Mattole Campground.

Guaranteed to inspire, this section of the Lost Coast Trail, which traces California's most remote coastline, features the best of many worlds. It's a splendid blend of rugged bluffs and black sandy beaches, offering a hiker vast shoreline views alternating with closeup rendezvous with the ocean. The scenic and memorable place-names are constant along the way, from Punta Gorda Lighthouse and Spanish Flat to Big Flat Creek and finally the quaint community of Shelter Cove.

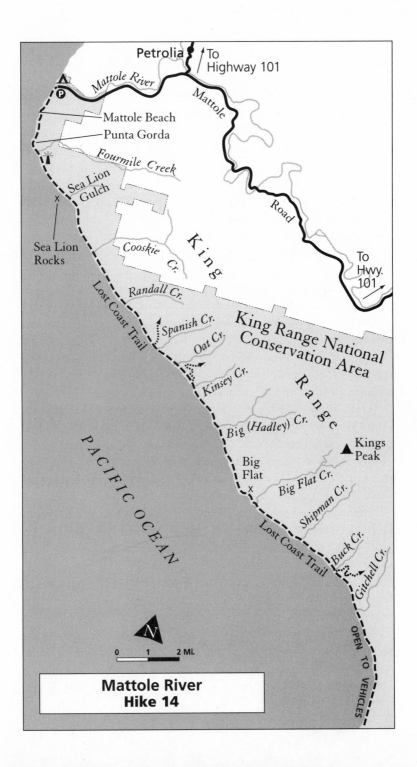

Petrolia

To Highway 101

Mattole River

Mattole

Road

To Hwy. 101

Mattole Beach

Punta Gorda

Fourmile Creek

Sea Lion Gulch

Sea Lion Rocks

King

Cooskie Cr.

Randall Cr.

Lost Coast Trail

Spanish Cr.

Oat Cr.

King Range National Conservation Area

Kinsey Cr.

Range

Big (Hadley) Cr.

Kings Peak

Big Flat

Big Flat Cr.

Shipman Cr.

Lost Coast Trail

Buck Cr.

Gitchell Cr.

PACIFIC OCEAN

N

0   1   2 Mi.

OPEN TO VEHICLES

Mattole River
Hike 14

If you plan a car shuttle in Shelter Cove, the gusty north winds will blow comfortably on your back, and the photographic trek passes quickly as a weekend getaway. There are loads of isolated campsites (get a campfire permit from BLM) and lots of ways to avoid a 5-mile-long trail stretch open to vehicles toward the hike's end. You can simply turn back at Cooskie Creek (6 miles in), or Randall Creek (8.5 miles in). Consider hiking 10 miles to Spanish Flat, then climbing 2,000 feet on the 2.5-mile-long Spanish Ridge Trail, then returning via the Ridge Trail.

There's a good reason this area is called the Lost Coast. Drastically isolated by time and the forces of nature, it's shielded on all sides purely by natural boundaries. It's a wonder how all the grazing sheep, rickety fences, and abandoned huts and houses got there in the first place. Sure, you'll see these signs of human activity in spots, but you'll see many more pristine hillocks, shiny clean beaches, steep bluffs, stark canyons, colorful meadow strips, and babbling creeks that empty into the ocean. This is the land where souls search for and find serenity and rebirth.

To start, it's well worth heading north a quarter mile to the wide mouth of the Mattole River. There's always a wider variety of waterbirds where freshwater and saltwater unite.

From Mattole River, consider tying your shoes to your pack and do the barefoot boogie south across the wide expanses of fine-grained Mattole Beach. For that sinking feeling, follow the foam from the receding tide. For firmer sand, stay slightly above the tide line. Note that more and more sea stacks interrupt the surf, and the beach narrows, the farther one roams this beach.

Eventually, an old ranch road climbs up a bluff, rounds Punta Gorda (which is Spanish for "massive point") and then displays the nearby Punta Gorda Lighthouse. A half mile farther a side trail darts to the abandoned ruins of the squat lighthouse, built soon after the *SS Columbia* crashed into the rocks here in 1907, killing 87 people. Check for a remnant of another crashed vessel embedded in the beach below.

Via the beach or an old jeep road, Sea Lion Rocks punctuates the surf zone just offshore from steep Sea Lion Gulch at 4 miles. From the wind-protected mouth of the cascading creek, you can check for the Steller sea lions wallowing on and/or barking from Sea Lion Rocks.

The Lost Coast Headlands are wild, rugged, and remote.

Over the next 4 miles there are Lost Coast Trail sections that may be blocked by extreme high tides or smothered with slippery boulders. Consider waiting for the tide to recede, and wear good gripping shoes. The rough going at times is all doable and magnificent in a wild way. A driftwood sweat lodge adorns the broad mouth of Cooskie Creek (remote camps are located a couple hundred yards upstream). A mile farther miniature waterfalls tumble onto the beach. Reynolds Rock juts offshore a ways further. Another camp is situated along nearby wooded Randall Creek.

Farther on you cross a couple of seasonal creeks bordered by native wildflowers in the spring, soon followed by grassy Spanish Flat (a popular camp spot). Wildflowers have returned to this site, where a sawmill once operated.

Other important place-names soon appearing include Spanish Creek Canyon (several campsites in or near this deep canyon), followed by pioneer Paul Smith's cabin, rocky and cascading Oat Creek, Etter Cabin (at 14 miles), and densely forested Big Flat Creek.

The stretch of wild coastline between Shipman Creek at 18 miles and Gitchell Creek at 21 miles is considered by many as this journey's main highlight. With many places to camp, lots of time can be spent gazing at the steep and lush cliffs, featuring springs and seeps that sustain hanging gardens of wildflowers. Driftwood camps, tidepools, and dense woods highlight Shipman Creek. Rocky beaches and steep-flowing creeks can be admired before and after Buck Creek. A 3,000-climb up Buck Creek Trail furnishes commanding ocean vistas and connects with King Crest Trail (Hike 15).

Hike 15

Lost Coast—Kings Peak
in King Range National Conservation Area

LENGTH: 10.5 miles round-trip.
DIFFICULTY: moderate but time consuming; intermittently strenuous.
TOTAL ELEVATION GAIN: 2,700 feet.

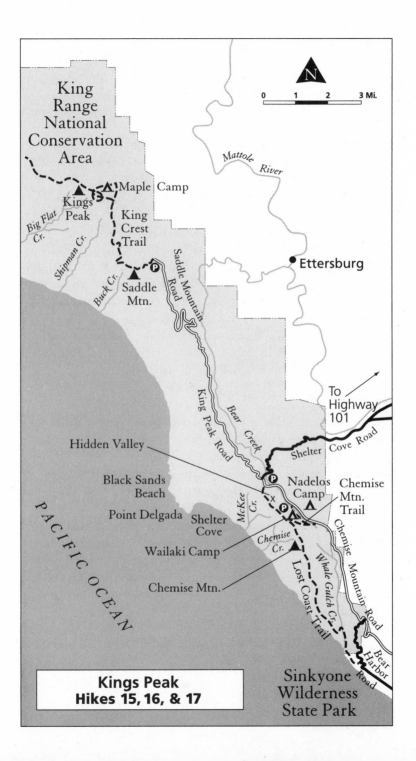

King
Range
National
Conservation
Area

Maple Camp

Kings
Peak

King
Crest
Trail

Big Flat Cr.

Shipman Cr.

Buck Cr.

Saddle
Mtn.

Saddle Mountain Road

Mattole River

● Ettersburg

King Peak Road

Bear Creek

To
Highway
101

Shelter Cove Road

Hidden Valley

Black Sands
Beach

Point Delgada

Shelter
Cove

Wailaki Camp

Chemise Mtn.

PACIFIC OCEAN

McKee Cr.

Nadelos
Camp

Chemise
Mtn.
Trail

Chemise Cr.

Lost Coast Trail

Whale Gulch Cr.

Chemise Mountain Road

Bear Harbor Road

Sinkyone
Wilderness
State Park

0   1   2   3 Mi.

**Kings Peak
Hikes 15, 16, & 17**

WATER: none; bring at least 2 quarts per hiker.

SEASON: all—call ahead for access and trail conditions; ideal on a clear winter's day when the snow-capped Trinity Alps, Lassen Peak, and Yolla Bolly Mountains can be seen.

MAP: BLM map or USGS topos Cooskie Creek and Shubrick Peak.

INFORMATION: Bureau of Land Management, (707) 825-2300.

DIRECTIONS TO TRAILHEAD: Get to Garberville first, which is on Highway 101 about halfway between Fort Bragg and (about 60 miles south of) Eureka. Follow the signs to the nearby town of Redway, make sure there's plenty of gas in the tank, then turn on Briceland Road. Follow all signs for Shelter Cove for 18 miles, then turn right onto Kings Peak Road. After 6.3 miles on this good dirt road, turn left on Saddle Mountain Road, which is steep, narrow, and winding but decent enough. (Call ahead during wet months to make sure the road isn't washed out.) Go right at an unsigned junction at 1.1 mile, then continue 2.4 miles and park in the dirt lot near the rusty gate. Cross the gate on foot, sign the registry under some tan oak and madrone trees, then continue down and then up on a wide dirt road.

The tippy top of this lofty peak is barely big enough yet flat enough for a handful of people to sleep on, but it's high enough and perfectly positioned to make someone feel on top of the world. The major mission of this hike is to reach this special spot, which, at 4,086 feet in elevation, happens to be the highest point on the continental U.S. shoreline.

Along this isolated journey, you pass through old-growth Douglas fir forests, dense chaparral, even a rare madrone forest. Most of the way, a nice view awaits around virtually every bend. For the most outrageous, far-reaching views of ocean and rugged mountains, do this trip on a clear day, a day or two after a cleansing rain. This way you're apt to admire the Trinity Alps and Lassen Peak in the distance from a rare vantage point atop Kings Peak. For the ultimate romantic endeavor, take your soul mate on a clear late after-

Thickets of ceanothus and clusters of boulders decorate Kings Peak.

noon, a day or two before a full moon, and time things so you're together on top as the moon rises.

The King Crest Trail at first winds and climbs moderately beneath woodland shade consisting mainly of Douglas fir, large and handsome madrones, and healthy and large tan oak trees (there are a few tall sugar pines hidden in the mix).

At 0.5 mile, the wide dirt road meets with the signed Buck Creek Trail (a path that plunges to meet the Lost Coast Trail on a black sand beach—see Hike 14), then commences a long but moderate descent, heading mostly west. You soon reach a vista of the shiny Pacific Ocean from the edge of a steep, imposing canyon draining into Shipman Creek. A wondrous canyon live oak specimen frames the view between three gothic Douglas firs. The steep, thick-wooded canyonsides spilling into the Shipman Creek drainage can be traced some 3,000 feet in elevation drop to the ocean's edge.

At a less impressive vista and clearing 0.3 mile farther, the King

Crest Trail resumes climbing and soon shows off views of rolling countryside to the east and a pretty strip of sandy beach covered along the Lost Coast Trail. As this ridge route continues its now less shaded ascent, the views improve, alternating between east and west. The plant communities switch between occasionally dense forest and manzanita/short canyon live oak chaparral.

At 3.2 miles, the trail rounds a bend and promptly becomes a slender footpath, then briefly breaks into a handsome forest of tall madrones that display twisted trunks and stripped bark revealing pinkish-brown interiors. In summer, many of these evergreen trees' leaves are shed, turning yellowish and crunching loudly in rhythm to your footsteps.

Once out of the madrone forest, the journey's serious climbing ensues, at first densely shaded and viewless. When the manzanita thickets appear, the best views yet of the ongoing mountains to the east unfold dramatically. By now, at just over 4 miles into the trek, it becomes quite clear that the soon-to-be-conquered Kings Peak will be a panoramic nirvana.

At 4.6 miles a side trail darts to the right and leads to Maple Camp (a good hangout destination for backpackers). The final half mile or so continues climbing on this curving ridge, past ceanothus and manzanita.

From atop this surprisingly small knob comprising Kings Peak, it's easy to pretend you're the only soul in the world. Kings Peak is pure boondocks—a long way from nowhere. Scream and shout all you want. The noise will disperse into nothingness, perhaps to be heard by a wily coyote or alert cougar.

The views to the west of the vast ocean are peaceful and inspiring, whether there's a puffy fog blanket moving in or a purple haze over the horizon. A tiny segment of Big Flat Creek can be seen, along with a small beach section directly west.

The bluffs in Sinkyone Wilderness are visible to the south. Snow Mountain and the Yolla Bolly Mountains perch majestically over the sprawling hills to the east. The dark and steep south-facing slopes of the King Range hide the ocean and Punta Gorda Lighthouse (Hike 14) to the northwest.

Hike 16

Hidden Valley to Whale Gulch
via Chemise Mountain in King Range

LENGTH: 14 miles round-trip as described; 15 miles round-trip to Jones Beach Environmental Camp; 5 miles round-trip to Chemise Mountain.

DIFFICULTY: strenuous, especially returning back up Chemise Mountain.

TOTAL ELEVATION GAIN: 4,000 feet total; 1,200 feet round-trip to Chemise Mountain.

WATER: none; bring 1 quart per 3 miles of hiking.

SEASON: all—ideal in winter when Hidden Valley is green and the high peaks to the east are snow clad; call ahead for access and trail conditions.

MAP: BLM map or USGS topo Shelter Cove. See p. 45.

INFORMATION: Bureau of Land Management, (707) 825-2300.

DIRECTIONS TO TRAILHEAD: Get to Garberville first, which is on Highway 101 about halfway between Fort Bragg and Eureka (it's about 60 miles south of Eureka). Follow the signs to the nearby town of Redway, make sure there's enough gas in the tank, then turn on Briceland Road. Follow all signs for Shelter Cove for 17.7 miles, then turn left onto Chemise Mountain Road. After a quarter mile, go right into the dirt trailhead parking lot.

To a black bear, a brown pelican or somebody visiting, King Range, Sinkyone Wilderness, and the Lost Coast are so interconnected, in many ways they're one and the same. This ambitious journey illustrates this notion splendidly.

It starts in King Range's Hidden Valley, which is mostly covered with the same grasses embedded in the slopes in and north of Usal Camp (see Hike 20) in the southernmost section of Sinkyone Wilderness. The ensuing climb begins in a dark and shady forest mainly of Douglas fir, by far the most prominent tree in this entire rugged and remote area. The vista from Chemise Mountain reveals ridge after ridge in King Range and Sinkyone Wilderness, each one as dark and as steep as the other. In fact, these are California's steepest coastal mountains.

From atop Chemise Mountain, the path turns into the Lost Coast Trail, departs Humboldt County, passes into Mendocino County, and eventually drops into Whale Gulch and the northern boundary of Sinkyone Wilderness State Park.

Of all the journeys in this book, this one is probably the most remote and requires the most planning. Registering to camp, bringing enough water, calling ahead to make sure parts of the trail past Chemise Mountain aren't too overgrown and that Whale Gulch is crossable—all these things may need to be addressed. Bringing a good map (see earlier notes) and leaving an itinerary back home are good ideas. If time and/or energy is short, consider Hike 17 to Chemise Mountain or carefully arrange a car shuttle on County Road 435 (also Needle Rock Road) at the gate above Jones Beach.

At the onset, an old dirt road promptly leads past red alder trees and young Douglas firs to a perennially moist section of Hidden Valley. Ferns, horsetails, and Oregon grape (not a grape but a beautiful native shrub) thrive along with perennial grasses here.

Consider taking the short spur trail at 0.2 mile into the middle of Hidden Valley. In springtime, the annual oatgrass is green, and the poppies and lupine are in bloom. In summer and fall, all but the previously mentioned moist section of the meadow are bone dry and gray. Roosevelt elk occasionally graze or sleep here.

The Chemise Mountain Trail soon veers inland, right into a Douglas fir strip so dense you feel like you're journeying into a tunnel. After a number of steep switchbacks followed by a brief drop, you pass into a flat festooned with gothic Douglas fir giants.

Moderate climbing ensues to a flat clearing, displaying sweeping scenes of the sea and steep mountains that appear to rise out of the surf. At 2 miles, the trail arcs along the ridge at a signed trail junction, and soon switches from a burned section of Douglas fir forest into a hardwood forest of mostly tan oak, with some madrone and California bay laurel trees woven into the overstory tapestry.

Suddenly the scene switches to chaparral mainly of knobcone pine and manzanita thickets in a flat just prior to reaching the 2,598-foot summit of Chemise Mountain. Spot the overgrown side trail under a huge madrone, and negotiate it for 50 yards to a perch. With a little leaning and scurrying, you can admire King Crest (Hike 15) to the north and the numerous ridges of Sinkyone Wilderness plunging into the sea.

The upper portion of what is now called the Lost Coast Trail beyond Chemise Mountain illustrates the ruggedness of the area. Rocks line the slender trail, and some sections of the upper ridge are narrow. A couple of steps to either side puts a hiker at the ridge edge. Young Douglas fir emerge from impenetrable thickets of manzanita. Knobcone pines and whitethorn ceanothus thrive in the sunny sections along with sporadic chemise. In the more sheltered spots a wide array of native flora including tan oak, young canyon live oak, bay laurel, madrone, coast silktassel, poison oak, and bracken fern densely occupies the territory. The trail drops, then climbs two knobs with southward views before descending the ridge.

After briefly passing through a hardwood forest, you enter a deeper Douglas fir forest where huckleberry and California wild rose grow. At 3.2 miles past Chemise Mountain, you come to a grassy clearing where a nearby spur trail promptly leads to a meadow. Overgrown trail sections follow below the 1,000-foot elevation level, along with a couple more short climbs and the eventual and sometimes tricky crossing of Whale Gulch Creek. The rest of this trek is described in Hike 18, if you want to proceed further.

Hike 17

Nadelos Camp to Chemise Mountain in King Range National Conservation Area

LENGTH: 3.8 miles round-trip as described; 5.8 miles round-trip by returning via Hidden Valley (see Hike 16).

DIFFICULTY: easy to moderate.

TOTAL ELEVATION GAIN: 700 feet.

WATER: from faucets at Nadelos Camp and nearby Wailaki Camp.

SEASON: all—ideal in winter when the high peaks are snow clad; can get hot (low 90s F) in the summer.

MAP: BLM map or USGS topo Shelter Cove. See p. 45.

INFORMATION: Bureau of Land Management, (707) 825-2300.

DIRECTIONS TO TRAILHEAD: Get to Garberville first, which is on Highway 101 about halfway between Fort Bragg and Eureka (it's about 60 miles south of Eureka). Follow the signs to the nearby town of Redway, make sure there's plenty of gas in the tank, then turn on Briceland Road. Follow all signs for Shelter Cove for 17.7 miles, then go left onto Chemise Mountain Road. Travel 1.4 miles and park in the lot at Nadelos Camp.

Backpack trips and grueling day hikes are the norm in the Lost Coast, but this trip allows a hiker to get a big slice of pure country for a modest time and energy investment. What I suggest for the Lost Coast is this—do as many of the much longer King Range and Sinkyone Wilderness hikes described in this book as time allows, then squeeze in this three-hour wonder.

Nadelos Camp has outhouses, a creek that runs through it, and water faucets, and is also centrally located to serve as a prime base camp for hiking many of the Lost Coast hikes described in this book. This journey takes off from Nadelos Camp (8 sites) and crams in a lot of highlights, from pristine views to extreme isolation.

As an added bonus, the trail begins in a riparian habitat, switches to Douglas fir, then a hardwood forest, and climaxes in a chaparral community. At the trek's beginning, a good footpath leaves Nadelos Camp and ambles along Bear Creek. It soon leads to a horsetail marsh crossing on a wooden walkway. The easy walking along small and quiet Bear Creek continues under the shade of tan oak.

A steady and moderate climb departs the creek after taking the right trailfork just behind Wailaki Camp (13 sites). The always neat and clean evergreen shrubs such as huckleberry, Oregon grape, and salal adorn the trailside up to and beyond a three-way trail junction (head straight).

You soon pass through a burned forest section from the Chemise Mountain/Finley Creek fire of 1973, then reach the Hidden Valley trail junction (note the trail on the right makes an ideal loop trip coming back down Chemise Mountain).

After making a left turn climbing Chemise Mountain, you soon pass into a hardwood forest mainly of tan oak, but also madrone and California bay laurel. Farther on, Douglas fir rejoins the forest in a section devastated by heavy winds (note the numerous uprooted trees with their expansive root systems).

The Chemise Mountain Trail levels for 0.2 mile in chaparral, consisting primarily of short knobcone pines and manzanita, with occasional whitethorn ceanothus and yerba santa in the mix. To snag wondrous oceanic views or sweeping scenes of the ongoing rugged mountains spreading to the east, you often have to play peekaboo with the shrub and small tree limbs, but it's well worth it.

To discover the overgrown spur trail along this flat ridgetop called Chemise Mountain, spot and then duck under a huge madrone tree with a twisted trunk on the left. After about 50 yards of trail negotiating, you'll reach a cramped space featuring the best views on the mountain of King Crest and the Sinkyone Wilderness. A Chemise Mountain geodetic survey reference mark is embedded in a rock here, placed during World War II.

The most inspiring views are of the numerous steep canyonsides comprising Sinkyone Wilderness State Park to the south, beyond whitethorn ceanothus and young canyon live oak. The Douglas-fir-clad mountains to the east are topped by the Yolla Bolly Mountains in the distance. Like all mountaintop hikes, choosing a clear day is optimal. Although these far-reaching views are superb, they don't rival those found atop King Crest (see Hike 15).

From up here, one can note the numerous creek bottoms that run a fast and steep course directly into the ocean. A combination of steep slopes, unstable soil and high rainfall continue to create talus piles, rock slides, and steep cliffs. These occur more to the west, but the densely vegetated steep slopes prevent erosion much better than the few nonvegetated spots. Note how the beaches tend to be intermittent and narrow, interspersed with steep and rocky points that jut into the surf.

Hike 18

Lost Coast—Needle Rock, Jones Beach, and Whale Gulch in Sinkyone Wilderness State Park

LENGTH: 4.5 miles round-trip as described; Jones Beach Camp —2.8 miles round-trip.

DIFFICULTY: easy.

TOTAL ELEVATION GAIN: 300 feet.

WATER: available from creeks (purify) or bring your own.

SEASON: all—call ahead for trailhead accessibility and trail conditions, especially during the wet months; less fog in the fall.

MAP: Sinkyone Wilderness State Park map or USGS topo Bear Harbor.

INFORMATION: Sinkyone Wilderness State Park, (707) 986-7711 or (707) 445-6547.

DIRECTIONS TO TRAILHEAD: Get to Garberville first, which is on Highway 101, halfway between Fort Bragg and Eureka. Drive to the nearby town of Redway, then turn on Briceland Road. Travel 12 miles then turn left and go through the tiny town of Whitethorn. After about 4 miles, go straight at the "Four Corners" junction, then proceed another 3.6 miles (the dirt road is called County Road 435) to the Visitor Center, which doubles as the trailhead. The trail takes off behind the old barn.

Call this hike a superb introduction to the Lost Coast—a good way to get to know Sinkyone Wilderness in an easy nutshell. If the rugged and remote Lost Coast is your goal, and you've got young kids or limited time, this hike is the ticket for attaining a closer understanding of how the Lost Coast got its name. Trust me, everybody has a slightly different opinion or theory on that.

This is the land where the brown pelicans soar in the summer sunset and the Roosevelt elk roam in the grasslands. This is the land where many of the shore cliffs plunge perpendicularly up to 1,000 feet into the infinite sea. This is the land where nearby Kings Peak rises more than 4,000 feet above the ocean floor in less than 3 miles distance.

Lost Coast's Cape Mendocino to the north, California's westernmost point, along with the active San Andreas Fault lying just offshore, combine with the steep canyons to create a sensational scenario of irregularity and unpredictability.

The Lost Coast is so isolated, you may feel you have the place to

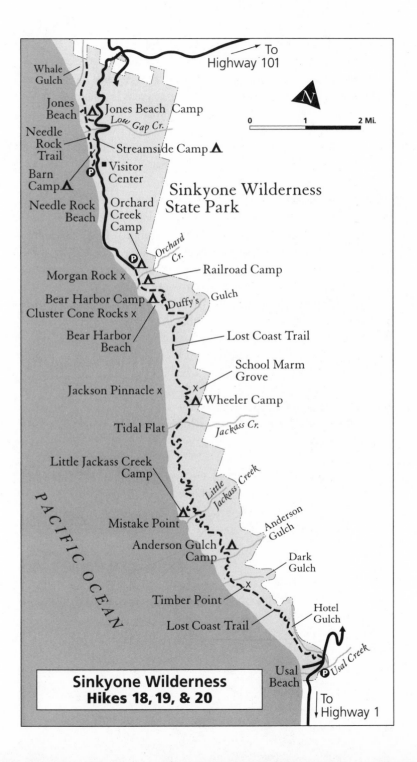

To
Highway 101

Whale
Gulch

Jones
Beach
Jones Beach Camp
Low Gap Cr.

Needle
Rock
Trail
Streamside Camp

Barn
Camp
Visitor
Center

Needle Rock
Beach
Orchard
Creek
Camp

Sinkyone Wilderness
State Park

Orchard
Cr.

Railroad Camp

Morgan Rock x

Bear Harbor Camp
Cluster Cone Rocks x
Duffy's   Gulch

Bear Harbor
Beach

Lost Coast Trail

School Marm
Grove

Jackson Pinnacle x
x
Wheeler Camp

Tidal Flat
Jackass Cr.

Little Jackass Creek
Camp

Little Jackass Creek

Mistake Point

Anderson Gulch
Camp
Anderson
Gulch

Dark
Gulch

Timber Point
x

Lost Coast Trail

Hotel
Gulch

PACIFIC OCEAN

Usal
Beach
Usal Creek

To
Highway 1

0   1   2 Mi.

N

Sinkyone Wilderness
Hikes 18, 19, & 20

yourself, making it hard to imagine that not too long ago humans impacted the area considerably. Many of this hike's marine terraces and grasslands once pastured cattle and sheep. Most of the Lost Coast's dirt roads were once graded for logging operations. What look like jeep trails or wagon roads are actually abandoned railroad rights-of-way. Most of the footpaths used to be gaming trails converted into pack mule pathways for hauling tanbark to San Francisco tanneries.

At the onset, the trail promptly goes by Barn Camp (shaded by alder and fir trees with an ocean view), then heads straight for a bluff looking down on the waves trying to get through Needle Rock's tunnel. After reversing 200 yards inland, the trail pulls up alongside a small, red-alder-lined stream (Streamside Camp, where one of the three sites features a wondrous ocean vista), then veers west again.

Sustained views of the vast sea are yours for the taking, as the Needle Rock Trail passes through more open grasslands dotted with bush lupine, coffeeberry, and coyote brush.

On getting to a eucalyptus grove at 1.4 miles (Jones Beach Camp), take the short and scant spur trail past an unshaded camp to the bluff's edge overlooking Jones Beach. The cliff face is extremely steep and eroded, but serves as an ideal perch for listening to the black pebbles being swept about by the receding waves. A patch of summer-blooming wildflowers, including white yarrow, blankets one of the slopes above the beach. Pelicans frequently divebomb into the sea here.

After doubling back then crossing a creek, take the 0.2-mile-long sideshow jaunt down to black pebble-covered Jones Beach. At high tide, many of the waves rinse against the steep and jagged rocky banks. Some strewn driftwood tree bases partially dam the beach outlet stream. Back on the trail proper, the jungly scene of adjacent Whale Gulch contrasts with the open grasslands you've just roamed. Look for large Roosevelt elk wading in the swampy sections of Whale Gulch. A shallow bog is lined with red alder sedges and rushes and partially covered with algae.

Just past the swamp, a large pocket beach known as Whale Gulch Beach awaits. The trail here darts inland and up a much steeper section of alder-clogged Whale Gulch, connecting with

Lost Coast is typified by steep banks, gorgeous dark beaches, and narrow canyons.

Hike 16. These two hikes combined make for a great Lost Coast backpacking trip.

Hike 19

Lost Coast—Bear Harbor to Wheeler Camp in Sinkyone Wilderness State Park

LENGTH: Wheeler Camp—9 miles round-trip; Orchard Creek Camp to Duffy's Gulch—4.5 miles round-trip.
DIFFICULTY: moderate.
TOTAL ELEVATION GAIN: 1,400 feet.
WATER: available from a variety of creeks (purify); or bring lots of your own.

SEASON: all—call ahead for winter and spring trailhead access and trail conditions; it's less foggy in the fall.
MAP: Sinkyone Wilderness State Park map or USGS topo Bear Harbor (the trail was finished in 1986, and therefore not on the much older topo). See p. 55.
INFORMATION: Sinkyone Wilderness State Park, (707) 986-7711 or (707) 445-6547.
DIRECTIONS TO TRAILHEAD: Get to Garberville first, which is on Highway 101 about halfway between Fort Bragg and (about 60 miles south of) Eureka. Drive to the nearby town of Redway, then turn on Briceland Road. Travel 12 miles, then turn left and go through the tiny town of Whitethorn. After 4 miles, go straight at the "Four Corners" junction, then proceed another 3.6 miles (the dirt road is now called County Road 435) to the Visitor Center. The next 2.4 miles to the Bear Harbor Trailhead are even more narrow, winding, and potholed than the past 3 miles.

All the prime goodies Sinkyone Wilderness State Park has to offer —rugged coastline views, pristine beaches, great backpack camps, flashes of wildflowers, stately redwood groves, steep canyons, and relaxing seclusion—can be attained from this hike. As added bonuses, this hike puts you close to other journeys in this book and is easier than starting from the south section of Sinkyone Wilderness at Usal Camp (Hike 20).

Also, this section of the Lost Coast Trail best illustrates the local logging and railroad history of Sinkyone Wilderness, revealing traces and remnants of a logging ghost town and the remains of an unusual railroad line. The trek commences near Railroad Camp, where, by scouting up Railroad Canyon, one can spot a few faint traces of the railbed. A few rusty rails hang from the cliffs at Bear Harbor, the only remaining indications of two disasters that ruined the railroad—the huge Pacific storm of 1899 and the San Francisco earthquake of 1906.

After leaving your car at the large dirt lot, cross an old wooden bridge over Orchard Creek nestled under a grove of towering red alders. The footpath stays flat, shaded by some gargantuan eucalyptus trees growing along slim Orchard Creek. After passing Railroad

Camp on the left at 0.2 mile, the trail continues along the creek, breaking into an open meadow strip decorated by horsetails.

Cross Orchard Creek at the small black sand beach at Bear Harbor, then scramble up the small knoll for spectacular views up and down the Lost Coastline. It's an excellent perch for watching big waves exploding against Cluster Cone Rocks (steep rocky sea stacks resembling Tibetan mountaintops).

Plan on wandering southward along Bear Harbor Beach for a half mile to the "no pass" rocky point. Floating brown kelp and the whitewater foam intermingle lazily in the harbor. After the beach trek, double back past the driftwood-strewn Orchard Creek outlet next to the beachfront Bear Harbor Camp (an environmental camp with views of Bear Harbor, nestled under tall red alders and alongside Orchard Creek), and regain the Lost Coast Trail.

The next 0.3 mile marches inland in full sun next to a gulch lush with cow parsnips, sword ferns, and huge red alders. California bay laurel trees show up as the canyon narrows and gets more shaded. The footpath soon crosses the stream and begins a series of shaded switchbacks up the canyon. Redwood sorrel and profuse sword fern comprise the understory, canopied by tall California bay laurel and occasional Douglas fir. Higher up, California huckleberry becomes the highlighted shrub.

The crossing of Duffy's Gulch is a shaded scene worth resting at. The tiny and peaceful brook topples gracefully over moss-covered boulders. A massive bigleaf maple tree shares the overstory with old-growth redwoods. Ferns decorate the stream, including sword, lady, five-finger, and leather ferns.

The Lost Coast Trail departs the gulch here and heads directly toward the steep bluffs overlooking the ocean. On reaching the bluffs, you pass through an open grasslands section, awash in springtime with lupines, poppies, and blue-eyed grass. Just before alternating between dark forests and more grasslands, the trail briefly passes through a blackberry thicket, followed by a garden of orange bush monkeyflower and coyote brush. The key view here is northward of Bear Harbor and Cluster Cone Rocks.

A redwood forest appears at 3.3 miles, just before reaching School Marm Grove, named after the former Wheeler Schoolhouse nearby. Old-growth redwoods dominate this cool and peaceful grove, which contains two camps—the first sits under two huge redwoods and a clearing, while the second camp is situated just downstream near the North Fork of Jackass Creek.

What's left of the logging town of Wheeler, established in 1950 then deserted a decade later, is revealed past the creek. Look for remnants of an old bridge, crumbling cement foundations and side roads over the next quarter mile to where the sawmill once stood at the confluence of the two creek forks. Venture west here past large red alders and admire a scenic black sand beach at Tidal Flat.

The Lost Coast Trail continues south from here for another 12 miles, promptly climbing in and out of a series of steep canyons covering 4 miles—the most strenuous section of Sinkyone Wilderness's trail system. If a car shuttle is arranged at Usal Camp, more Lost Coast Trail descriptions and the Usal trailhead details are covered in Hike 20.

Hike 20

Lost Coast—Usal Camp to Little Jackass Creek Camp in Sinkyone Wilderness State Park

LENGTH: Little Jackass Creek—15 miles round-trip; Anderson Gulch Camp—10 miles round-trip; Wheeler Camp—12.5 miles one way; Bear Harbor—16.5 miles one way.

DIFFICULTY: moderate to strenuous.

TOTAL ELEVATION GAIN: 2,600 feet for the Little Jackass Creek round-trip; 5,300 feet one way to Bear Harbor.

WATER: available from a variety of creeks (purify); or bring lots of your own

SEASON: all—call ahead for winter and spring access and trail conditions; less fog in the fall.

MAP: Sinkyone Wilderness State Park map or USGS topo Bear Harbor. See p. 55.

INFORMATION: Sinkyone Wilderness State Park, (707) 986-7711 or (707) 445-6547.

DIRECTIONS TO TRAILHEAD: From the tiny town of Leggett on Highway 101 (between Eureka north and Fort Bragg

Deep into the Lost Coast journey from Usal Camp, scenery like this is the norm.

south), take Highway 1 and drive west several miles to within a mile or so of the ocean. Look closely for County Road 431 (Usal Road) on the right at highway marker 90.88. Go north on this road way up, then way down, for 6 miles to the Usal Camp trailhead.

Call this the journey that so many people dream about doing but so few actually get the chance. Chalk it up to the long drive, the sometimes-hard-to-find trailhead, the sheer remoteness of the region, or the sweat it takes to finish. Get past these challenges and you find out firsthand why most who've hiked beyond Usal Camp into what is called the New Lost Coast consider it the closest thing to isolated paradise.

When facing the Pacific Ocean on any of this trip's many black sand beaches, it's easy to pretend you're happily stranded on a secluded island, perhaps never to be found. The numerous creeks on this trek that angle steeply and climax in the sea are so fern-encased, one could imagine gremlins or hobbits amusedly watching you in hiding. The flowers are aglow across the steep and grassy hillsides in spring, and the breathtaking coastline views constantly fade, with the promise of a prompt return.

Settled in the 1860s, then logged and ranched, this wilderness was named after the Sinkyone Indians, who originally occupied this rugged territory. For thousands of years the Sinkyone tribe established villages alongside the creeks and rivers, and used their backwoods skills to hunt and eat Roosevelt elk, black-tailed deer, grizzly, and black bears. They made redwood canoes for hunting sea lions and seals. The women used the abundant supply of ferns to make hats and baskets. Redwood and madrone wood were used to build lean-tos and circular houses. Each Sinkyone Indian village featured sweat lodges and ceremonial dances.

If you're in no hurry and would rather get an early morning start, self-registering for an overnighter at Usal Camp (15 sites, picnic tables and outhouses) is ideal. Usal Beach is big enough for barefoot Frisbee, and the nearby meadow, partially shaded by Douglas fir and tan oak trees, is graced by smooth-flowing Usal Creek.

From the get-go, the Lost Coast Trail climbs incessantly via switchbacks, covering 800 feet of climbing in just over a mile, mostly in shaded Douglas fir forest. Consider this hefty escalation as a warm-up, merely shapes of things to come later.

The trail stays mostly level across exposed annual grasslands featuring blooming lupines in the spring. The views to the west are sustained here, revealing a staggered file of bluffs and cliffs that plunge almost perpendicularly (up to 1,000 feet in places) to the sea. A couple of miles into the hike you can look up through grassy clearings and spot Hotel Gulch Road (also called the horse trail), which should be noted for variety's sake as a good return route (just scramble up the grassy slope wherever you spot this old dirt road).

Past view-laden Timber Point, some serious up and down climbing ensues, in and out of ferny Dark and Anderson Gulches, shaded mostly by Douglas fir and tan oak. Although you get a good view of the mouth of Anderson Gulch from Anderson Camp, Mistake Point and Little Jackass Creek offer more. The views of the perpendicular Anderson Cliffs to the north from Mistake Point are photogenic, and there's a pretty pocket beach often featuring barking sea lions near Little Jackass Creek Camp. Two shaded campsites are situated at the edge of Sally Bell Grove, which contains majestic old-growth redwoods. Two other trail camps are located close to the beach.

The heaviest-duty hiking stretch is from here to Wheeler Camp near Jackass Creek. If time and energy permit, consider this 4.5-mile sweaty workout, filled with gorgeous seaward and coastline views (take a couple of the side trails westward to Anderson Cliffs) and climaxed by a wildflower-sprinkled hanging valley with a vernal pool.

If you have a car shuttle arranged at Bear Harbor, see access info along with descriptions of the final 4 miles as detailed in Hike 19.

Hike 21

Lake Cleone and Laguna Point in MacKerricher State Park

> **LENGTH:** 6.4 miles as described; 1 mile around Lake Cleone; 2.4 miles round-trip to Laguna Point.
> **DIFFICULTY:** easy.
> **TOTAL ELEVATION GAIN:** 200 feet.
> **WATER:** stock up from park faucets.
> **SEASON:** any—winter has more whales and seals and fewer people.
> **MAP:** USGS topo Inglenook.
> **INFORMATION:** MacKerricher State Park, (707) 937-5804.
> **DIRECTIONS TO TRAILHEAD:** From Highway 1, drive 3 miles north from Fort Bragg and turn west into the signed MacKerricher State Park in the tiny town of Cleone. Park in the small paved lot near the main office (next to the gray-whale skeleton exhibit).

This hike covers marshlands, two lakes, and lots of sand dunes, providing plenty of opportunities to explore Ten Mile Beach. Binoculars are ideal for studying shorebirds, harbor seals, and California gray whales from high coastal bluffs.

Lake Cleone is a rare coastal lake, once a tidal lagoon before a road was built, cutting it off from the sea. Geese and other water birds frequently visit this lake. Ten Mile Beach stretches northward to Ten Mile River, backed by one of the longest sand dunes along the California coast.

The unsigned trail takes off next to a "No Dogs/No Bikes" sign, and soon you go left on the signed La Laguna Trail. Red alders canopy 200 yards worth of wooden walkway, featuring a maze of aquatic plants thriving in a mix of mini marshes and ponds off of Mill Creek.

The first glimpses of Lake Cleone are westward, with a cattail marsh in the foreground at 0.3 mile under a small stand of 50-foot-high bishop pines.

The trail approaches a paved access road at 0.8 mile, where Mill Creek becomes Lake Cleone's outlet and flows into the Pacific

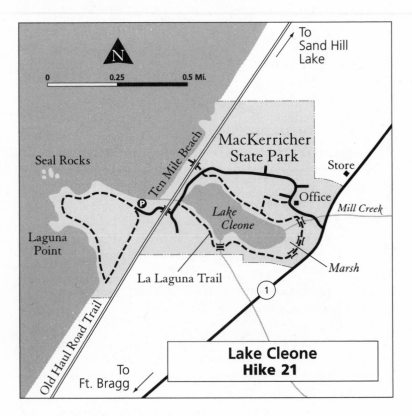

Ocean. Scurry past ice plant here to a pile of huge driftwood to view the surf at Ten Mile Beach.

Find the beach parking lot to the south next to a grove of small, wind-sculpted shore pines, then pick up the signed trail that leads to the harbor-seal-watching station. You can hear the pounding surf while you walk on wooden planks that duck under a Monterey cypress grove.

Choose from a number of perches along this high bluff trail (most of it is wheelchair accessible) to study the harbor seals flopping around on Seal Rocks a couple hundred feet offshore. Wintertime is ideal for spotting the California gray whale taking a dive out of the water, if you're lucky. Wander over to Laguna Point, the site of a Pomo Indian encampment for several thousand years.

After completing this grasslands loop, access the Old Haul Road Trail (see book map) at 2.0 miles on the journey, where you can scout Ten Mile Beach stretching northward for up to 5 miles. A curvaceous and wild shoreline this beautiful deserves to be appreciated farther away from the crowds. The 2-mile trek to Sand Hill Lake accomplishes this.

After negotiating past two washed-out road sections along the continuous sand dunes that parallel the trail, you'll reach marshy Sand Hill Lake. This unique ecosystem supports a variety of spiders endemic to this sensitive area, and rare plants such as marsh pennywort.

On your return, pick up the wood planks on the north end of Lake Cleone for the 0.4-mile clockwise stroll past ferns, tan oak, red alder, and head-high Pacific wax myrtle shrubs to your car.

Hike 22

Ecological Staircase in Jug Handle State Reserve

LENGTH: 5.5 miles round-trip.
DIFFICULTY: easy.
TOTAL ELEVATION GAIN: 500 feet.
WATER: bring your own.
SEASON: all—most likely to get best views of Jug Handle Cove in the autumn; blufftop wildflowers in the spring.

MAP: Jug Handle State Reserve self-guided brochure or USGS topos Fort Bragg and Mendocino.
INFORMATION: Jug Handle State Reserve, (707) 937-5804.
DIRECTIONS TO TRAILHEAD: From Fort Bragg, drive south for 5 miles on Highway 1, then turn west into signed Jug Handle State Reserve. The trail starts by an interpretive signboard and self-guided brochure (snag one) machine near the parking lot.

People plugged into science and nature are apt to be keenly interested in this hike's rare natural phenomenon—five ancient terraces called the "ecological staircase." Your mission is to climb it, each "terrace" being about 100 feet higher and 100,000 years older than the one below it.

Incessant wave action continues to gradually uplift the watershed

of Jug Handle Creek, depositing sediments once on the ocean's bottom. The result, solidly summarized and explained in the self-guided brochure available near the parking lot, is the ecological staircase.

The Ecological Staircase Trail climbs these rare terraces to a flat field of dwarfed native conifers called a pygmy forest. Other pygmy forests can be studied at Van Damme State Park (Hike 24) and Salt Point State Park (Hike 27); both are farther south on Highway 1.

Although uncommon, there are other wave-formed terraces among California coastal locales. The terraces at Jug Handle State Reserve, however, are more evident and less eroded.

To start, Ecological Staircase Nature Trail leads west onto some grassy blufftops overlooking the mouth of Jug Handle Creek, where a sixth terrace is beginning to form. The fantastic view also encompasses a cluster of wave-pounded sea stacks that puncture Jug Handle Bay, framed by a small pocket beach. A spur trail descends to this intimate beach. Windswept bishop pines, Monterey pines, and Sitka spruces are scattered across the bluffs. The southernmost extent of the native Sitka spruce is a mere mile from here.

The path continues along these bluffs, then ducks under the highway bridge and soon into forest where some grand fir trees grow along with bishop and Monterey pines. By now, you're apt to be absorbed in reading about the numbered posts corresponding to the brochure. Keep it handy as you reach each terrace, culminating in the pygmy forest. For more info on this incredible group of full-grown dwarfed conifers, consult Hikes 24 and 27.

Hike 23

Russian Gulch Falls and Devil's Punch Bowl

LENGTH: 9.5 miles total; 3.5 miles one way to falls; 1 mile round-trip on Headlands Trails.
DIFFICULTY: moderate.
TOTAL ELEVATION GAIN: 800 feet.
WATER: available from Russian Gulch Creek.
SEASON: any—the falls and creek are more powerful in winter.
MAP: USGS topo Mendocino or park map.

INFORMATION: Russian Gulch State Park, (707) 937-5804.

DIRECTIONS TO TRAILHEAD: From Fort Bragg, travel south for 6 miles on Highway 1 to the signed Russian Gulch State Park entrance. Follow the signs to the trailhead.

Wander into a deep second-growth redwood forest along a narrow canyon leading to a popular waterfall that sprays cool moisture in your face. Spend a couple of miles meandering past little fern gullies that trickle into Russian Gulch Creek, then cap your journey checking out a cove highlighted by wave-worn Devil's Punch Bowl.

The signed North Trail, at the east end of the campground, takes you on a 0.5-mile moderate climb through a dark and quiet redwood forest dotted with small tan oak trees. Occasional redwood sorrel hugs the narrow dirt path, while western sword ferns and taller California huckleberry shrubs are more abundant.

A small stand of bishop pines and Mendocino cypress appear on the crest at a four-way junction, where you continue straight (again 0.2 mile farther). Look for a wooden bench for resting to the right, and a gargantuan, triple-trunked, lightning-charred redwood on the left.

Soon after a short descent, an old wooden footbridge crosses a tiny meandering stream, the North Trail's only water source available in the winter and spring months. A bit farther, marvel at how a California huckleberry bush thrives inside a 6-foot-tall and wide redwood stump carved out by lightning. Decayed needle litter and rotting wood have gradually formed enough soil to support the plant.

The trail then drops quickly to a handful of picnic benches next to Russian Gulch Creek at 2.6 miles. To prolong the trip's anticipation of the finale (Russian Gulch Falls), bear right here at the signed junction and promptly cross a redwood-railed footbridge over the creek. The Falls Loop Trail then climbs gently along one of the creek's tributaries 0.8 mile before veering north in thick forest another 1.7 miles to the falls.

The prime benefit of the extra 2.5 miles is the pleasant reunion with Russian Gulch Creek 100 yards before reaching the falls. You can hear the powerful noise all during this brief descent, which crescendoes as stone steps bring you to a rewarding view from atop

To
Ft. Bragg

Devil's
Punch
Bowl
Overlook

X

Park HQ

Fern Canyon Trail

Russian Gulch
Falls

Russian Gulch Creek

Russian Gulch
State Park

Falls Loop Trail

PACIFIC OCEAN

To
Mendocino

Jackson
State
Forest

0   0.5   1 Mi.

N

1

**Russian Gulch State Park
Hike 23**

the 36-foot-high falls. They're nearly as wide as tall, especially when the creek runs higher during wintertime, and they cascade next to an array of huge fallen logs into a small, misting pool.

After your feast and meditation at the falls, continue your counterclockwise direction and immediately catch hawk's-eye views of the narrow and winding creek—it's never out of sight along the gradually descending 1-mile stroll to your reunion with the picnic tables.

You can now retrace your steps on the North Trail, or opt for the shorter and more flat Fern Canyon Trail (paved for bicycle use). Although this trail is the most popular, it does provide fresh scenery, with creekside accompaniment under the shade of redwoods, red alders, and bigleaf maples.

This park features a short hiking bonus—a mile's worth of trails that explore the headlands and the Devil's Punch Bowl. This 200-foot-long sea-cut tunnel collapsed at its inland end to create a 60-

foot-deep hole measuring about a hundred feet across. Its steep walls are coated with lots of plants, including wildflowers. Watch and wait for the big waves to crash around the punch bowl's interior, accompanied by an impressive array of throaty echoes.

Hike 24

Fern Canyon to Pygmy Forest in Van Damme State Park

LENGTH: 8 miles round-trip as described; 3.5 miles round-trip doing just the loop starting from Airport Road.

DIFFICULTY: easy.

TOTAL ELEVATION GAIN: 500 feet.

WATER: available from Little River (purify); bring your own.

SEASON: all—Little River is more exciting in late winter, when you may get wet feet crossing it and its side streams; large crowds in summer.

MAP: Van Damme State Park brochure or USGS topo Mendocino.

INFORMATION: Van Damme State Park, (707) 445-6547 or (707) 937-5804.

DIRECTIONS TO TRAILHEAD: Van Damme State Park is 3 miles south of Mendocino on Highway 1. Travel the paved park road 0.8 mile past the campground to the trailhead. Campers can begin near Campground 26. For a shorter hike, drive 3.5 miles east on Airport Road, which is less than a mile south of the signed Van Damme State Park entrance.

This journey illustrates two extremes in nature. You start in fern-rich environs along lush and redwood-shaded Little River, but wind up marveling at perfectly miniature cypress and pine monarchs in bonsai forms.

Wander into the Pygmy Forest, and tower over conifers perhaps three times your age. As intriguing as the nearby redwood forests are stately, the unique Pygmy Forest is no fluke. Nature has decreed that these grownup conifers that fascinate kids shall be stunted and dwarfed. It took tens of thousands of years for the

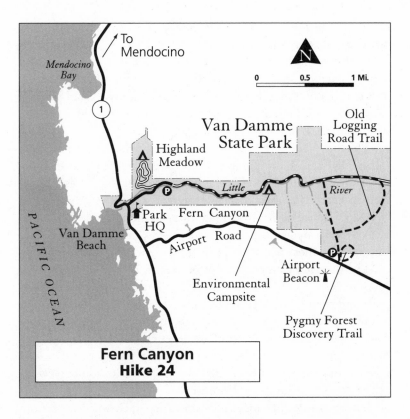

Map labels:
To Mendocino
Mendocino Bay
N
0   0.5   1 Mi.
1
Van Damme State Park
Old Logging Road Trail
Highland Meadow
Little
River
Park HQ
Fern Canyon
PACIFIC OCEAN
Van Damme Beach
Airport Road
Environmental Campsite
Airport Beacon
Pygmy Forest Discovery Trail
Fern Canyon
Hike 24

ocean to recede here, helping to create a highly acidic but nutrient-poor soil called podzol. The conifer roots can't penetrate into the dense hardpan beneath this gray soil, thus drastically limiting tree size in the forest.

The initial 2 miles of aptly named Fern Canyon Trail is an old, paved logging road, crossing Little River several times. An impressive variety of ferns—sword, five-finger, lady, licorice, and deer ferns—coat the dark side canyons and rock walls bordering Little River. In spots, tangled patches of elderberry, salmonberry, and Oregon grape bushes thrive near the fast-flowing small river. Redwoods and Douglas fir rise above bigleaf maples, tan oaks, and red alder trees, rounding out the lush and colorful riparian habitat.

A half mile past the 10 environmental campsites is a trail junction at 2.3 miles—go either way, soon bearing right at a trail junction signed for Pygmy Forest. The trail, now an old dirt road, continues climbing into drier country, where bishop pines dominate over scattered chinquapin bushes.

In this 1.5-mile ramble, the transition away from the jungled Little River to the stark Pygmy Forest is gradual but noticeable. You're actually climbing past a series of geologically created terraces, each about a hundred feet higher and a hundred thousand years older than the one below.

The final stage is the Pygmy Forest itself, where a 0.3-mile-long self-guided nature trail (grab the brochure here) loops through the forest on an elevated wooden walkway. Almost as acidic as vinegar, the soil here is the most acidic in the world. This soil condition is caused by rains that form puddles, carrying minerals downward to add to the hardpan. The poor drainage steeps the scant forest litter into a sort of "herb tea" that makes the podzol soil even more acidic.

The dwarfed conifers capable of existing in this often swampy forest include the rare Mendocino cypress and Bolander pine, bishop pine, and even Douglas fir on the outer perimeters. Although most of the conifers here are 2 to 3 feet high, most are mature adults that bear cones. Thickness in trunk is a better indicator of age than height. Four native shrubs, all in the same family as manzanita (heath family) that thrive here include California huckleberry, western azalea, salal, and rhododendron.

If a car shuttle is arranged at nearby Airport Road, your hike can be concluded at 4 miles.

Hike 25

Lake Davis and Alder Creek
in Manchester State Beach Park

LENGTH: 5.4 miles total; 1.2 miles round-trip to Lake Davis; 3.4 miles round-trip to Alder Creek.

DIFFICULTY: easy.

TOTAL ELEVATION GAIN: 200 feet.

WATER: available at Alder Creek.

SEASON: any—best wildflower display in spring.

MAP: USGS topo Point Arena.

INFORMATION: Manchester Beach State Park, (707) 937-5804.

DIRECTIONS TO TRAILHEAD: Drive north for 7 miles on Highway 1 from Point Arena and turn left on Kinney Road at the signed Manchester State Beach entrance. Just past the KOA campgrounds, turn right, promptly make another right at a sign that reads, "Walk-in campgrounds," and park in the small grassy lot 0.1 mile farther.

If you like radiant sunsets that set the coast all aglow, then plan on visiting Manchester State Beach Park and hope to get lucky at twilight time.

Get on the mowed grassland trail, which promptly goes through a long grove of Monterey cypress trees growing in an east-west direction to provide needed protection for the campers from the fierce north winds, which are more frequent in the summer. Consider obtaining a wind report in advance before striking out on this view-filled but fully exposed flat hike.

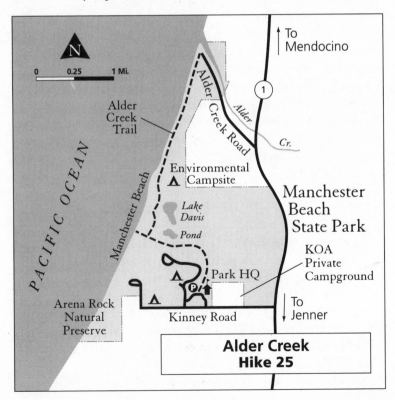

This virtually treeless trek is dominated over the first half mile by coyote brush, with occasional bush lupine, ceanothus, and coffeeberry interspersed. The Alder Creek Trail then switches abruptly to sand at a small freshwater pond blanketed in the middle by dense cattails.

Follow the strewn driftwood another 100 yards, then go with the footprints in the sand to an easy access to Manchester State Beach. At high tide, the crashing surf creates a reckless scene, foaming over the immense driftwood strip that coats this beach. This spot serves well for taking far-reaching oceanic views and for barefoot driftwood hopping.

If visibility is far enough, Navarro Point can be checked out to the north and Point Arena to the south. The coastal terrace and dunes near Point Arena were once inhabited by Bokeya Pomo natives whose main village was just up the Garcia River a mile or so inland. Descendants of these natives still collect traditional foods along the beach such as snails, surf fish, seaweed, and abalone.

After you're done at the beach, regain the trail and head north a couple hundred yards to reach slim, shallow Lake Davis near a secluded beach section. You'll see the trail sign where the lake's creek empties into the sea. At high tide, and/or when the creek is swollen by winter rains, you may need to skillfully time a barefoot crossing.

Follow the trail a good hundred yards to a signed junction, then turn right into signed Seagull Environmental Camp, enclosed in a shaded and peaceful Monterey cypress grove, featuring some uncommonly thick and twisted trunks. The trail then becomes an old fire road, which passes an outhouse and more campsites, then an old, dilapidated, abandoned house. Spring and summer wildflowers such as California poppy, wild strawberry, and baby blue-eyes carpet the surrounding grassy area.

The fire road meets the paved Alder Road at 1.7 miles, near where the road ends in a parking lot. This area is where the San Andreas Fault goes out to sea and is also the mouth of Alder Creek, decked out with large gravel bars and enclosed in steep coastal bluffs. The swirling Alder Creek, where river otters sometimes frolic, looks more like a river during the wet months.

While visiting this popular site, you're blessed with three options. Elongate the hike by crossing the creek if it's safe, then head north for a mile or so along a pristine section of Manchester State Beach under towering coastal cliffs. Consider retracing your steps on the fire road, or hang a left and explore the most secluded portion of the beach back to the mouth of Lake Davis's creek.

Manchester State Beach is notorious for lots of shipwrecks that occurred in the late 1800s. Now it's known for profuse piles of driftwood, where jackrabbits scurry.

This park contains a couple of small trails that originate at the west end of the main campground and lead to southern access of the beach. By heading south, beachcombers can appreciate 5 miles of sandy beach, featuring the nearby Arena Rock Natural Preserve, which protects a wide array of underwater plants and animals native to this coastal area. Majestic tundra swans winter near the Garcia River farther south below the Point Arena Lighthouse. In operation since 1870, the lighthouse is open daily, and can be climbed for great views of this rocky point.

Hike 26

Gualala River and Gualala Point

LENGTH: 5.7 miles as described; 2 miles round-trip to the mouth of the Gualala River; 3 miles round-trip to Whale Watch Point.
DIFFICULTY: easy.
TOTAL ELEVATION GAIN: 200 feet.
WATER: available from Gualala River.
SEASON: any; best for whale watching in the winter; best for grasslands wildflowers in the spring.
MAP: USGS topo Gualala.
INFORMATION: Gualala Point Regional Park, (707) 785-2377.
DIRECTIONS TO TRAILHEAD: From the tiny town of Gualala (14 miles south of Point Arena and 49 miles south of Mendocino), drive south on Highway 1 for a quarter mile, turn west into the signed park entrance, then park at the visitor's center.

It's a rare treat to go beachcombing where a glance to the east reveals Gualala River and a head turn to the west displays the Pacific Ocean.

This journey begins with just that, then covers a couple miles worth of prime coastal blufftops past two points, and finally winds through a lush, creekside jungle.

After looking at the exhibits in the wind-powered center for visitors, take the unsigned grassy trail next to the restrooms, and promptly reach a spur trail on the right. It ducks under some handsome California laurel trees to a wind- and sun-protected picnic spot with table overlooking the Gualala River.

Bush lupines and occasional coyote brush escort you on this 0.5-mile grasslands stroll to Gualala Beach. The massive rock outcrops comprising Point Arena attract attention to the north, during the next half mile covering the flat, wide, and mostly bare beach to the mouth of the Gualala River. On a clear day, the ocean here always looks bluer when contrasted with the sandy brown waters of the river. Both are contained in simultaneous views, punctuated by a steep rocky bluff below some posh beachfront mansions. A handful of miniature waterfalls splash down the bluffs.

Most coastal creeks and rivers empty into the sea after a westward journey. Gualala River follows the San Andreas Fault instead, meandering mostly from south to north.

On completing the beach and river bank loop, follow the wheelchair-accessible trail winding west. Then pick up the narrow Coastal Bluffs Trail behind the drinking fountain and restrooms. The trail ducks in and out of Monterey cypress groves, which provide shelter and spur trails that promptly lead to inspirational ocean vistas, including a larger vista called Whale Watch Point.

During winter and early spring, the California gray whales can be spotted during their incredible journey from Alaska to Baja California. The fewer the whitecaps, the easier it is to scan the ocean to spot these whales. Look for the distinctive white spray puffs, which are exhalations. The whales then dive underneath for several minutes at a time before resurfacing some distance away from the last point seen.

Back on the trail, you'll briefly break into open grasslands, then go straight through a fence opening at a signed junction (a left turn here leads to the parking area, abbreviating the trip by more than 2 miles). The Coastal Bluffs Trail then proceeds on the seaside of a neighborhood of mansions, occasionally dotted with deer. Soon

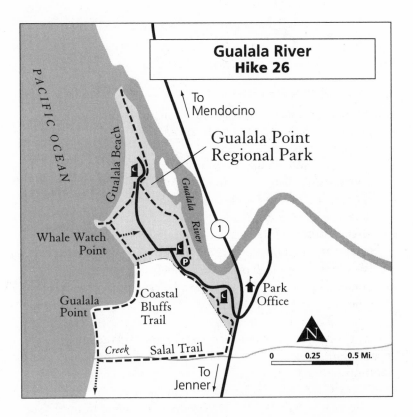

To
Mendocino

PACIFIC OCEAN

Gualala Point
Regional Park

Gualala Beach

Gualala River

①

Whale Watch
Point

Gualala
Point

Coastal
Bluffs
Trail

P

Park
Office

N

Creek   Salal Trail

0   0.25   0.5 Mi.

To
Jenner

you'll look down on a secluded cove surrounded by brown rocks and
cliffs and highlighted by a sandy beach where waves roll in gently.

A little farther on, Gualala Point beckons a visit to watch spectacular waves pound the big rocks. There are several flat rocks to sit on.

The trail then crosses a creek and reaches a signed trail junction
at 4.5 miles. Continuing straight on, the Coastal Bluffs Trail proceeds
2.2 miles to Walk On Beach (several short trails lead from Highway
1 south of here down to this beach).

The signed Salal Trail contrasts drastically with the Coastal
Bluffs Trail. It's lush and shady, hugging the small creek past red
alders and Pacific wax myrtle. A small pool makes for a good rest
spot, decorated with tall redwoods. The trail then crosses a paved
road, then eventually veers left and parallels the golf course along
Highway 1.

Hike 27

Pygmy Forest and Stump Beach Trail
in Salt Point State Park

LENGTH: 5.8 miles as described; 3.2 miles round-trip to coastal prairie; 4 miles round-trip to Pygmy Forest.
DIFFICULTY: easy to moderate.
TOTAL ELEVATION GAIN: 600 feet.
WATER: available from Warren and Miller Creeks.
SEASON: any—best wildflowers on prairie in spring.
MAP: USGS topo Plantation.
INFORMATION: Salt Point State Park, (707) 847-3221.
DIRECTIONS TO TRAILHEAD: On Highway 1, Salt Point State Park is 19 miles north of Jenner or about 80 miles south of Fort Bragg. Turn at the signed east entrance, drive about 0.2 mile, then park in the paved lot.

Enjoy the openness of a unique coastal prairie and the smallness of a pygmy forest, then visit a small beach before wandering along a blufftop adorned with jagged points and ancient sandstone outcrops to Gerstle Cove, which is loaded with underwater life.

The nearby Salt Point area was once the home to the Kashia Pomo Indians, who gathered abalone and salt here.

This hike as described covers many of the key highlights of Salt Point Park. That, and lots of variety, is the good news. The tradeoff is that once the hike is done at wheelchair-accessible Gerstle Cove, you'll have to hoof it up to your car, unless shuttle arrangements are made.

The Pygmy Forest Trail commences just beyond a statuesque bishop pine hovering over a mature and beautiful madrone tree. From the onset, this old dirt road takes care of the major climbing part of the journey right off the bat. The shade and wind protection are comforting, and the scenery is pleasing, with bishop pine, Douglas fir, madrone, tan oak, manzanita, California huckleberry, and Pacific wax myrtle decorating trailside.

Ignore the first two trail junctions on the left—you can connect with either of them later if you want to abbreviate the journey. Make a mental note of the signed trail junction at 1.2 miles—you'll use the

Salt Point State Park

To
Ft. Bragg

Miller Creek

Stream

Pygmy
Forest

Prairie

Stump
Beach
Cove

Stump
Beach
Trail

North Trail

Warren Creek

Pygmy
Forest Trail

Group
Campground

Stream

Salt Point

Visitor Center

Gerstle
Cove

Gerstle
Cove
Campground

N

0   0.5   1 Mi.

**Salt Point State Park
Hike 27**

To
Jenner

trail on the left to get to the Pygmy Forest. For now, continue straight and enter a rare and natural coastal prairie 0.2 mile farther on. Walled on all sides by a deep forest of bishop pine, Douglas fir, tan oak, and madrone, this peaceful prairie is particularly striking when the wildflowers bloom abundantly during spring.

Once you've returned to the previously mentioned trail junction and turned right, you'll be treated to some huge and gorgeous madrones and manzanitas (both with appealing, smooth, stripped bark in the heath family) along this 0.6-mile jaunt on a flat and narrow footpath to the Pygmy Forest.

Notice how the ground you walk on changes the instant you enter the Pygmy Forest. The soil becomes lighter and firmer, and the trees become stunted pygmies over the next quarter mile. This is due to a shallow hardpan that prevents roots and water from penetrating. The hardpan here tends to be deeper than at another pygmy forest also on coastal upland in Van Damme State Park (see Hike 24). Therefore the dwarfed trees at Salt Point State Park range from 6 to 20 feet tall, but some trees at Van Damme State Park may be just as mature at only 2 feet high. Mendocino cypress and bishop pine are the dominant conifers in Salt Point State Park's pygmy forest, where heath-family shrubs such as California huckleberry, California rhododendron, and salal thrive at normal heights.

A huge redwood on the left and some towering tan oaks ahead signal an abrupt end to the Pygmy Forest. After a brief descent, continue straight on the signed North Trail. You'll parallel Warren Creek briefly, then stay on the North Trail at another signed junction (a left turn here goes 0.5 mile to your car). Prior to reaching Highway 1, you'll be rewarded with uncommon and refreshing glimpses of the ocean through a conifer forest still standing but ravaged by a past fire. Without this ecological happening, the view would have been shrouded.

After crossing Highway 1, it's well worth the hop, skip, and a jump down to photogenic Stump Beach Cove, featuring the park's only sandy beach. Miller Creek meanders enticingly near this small beach, surrounded by steep coastal bluffs laden with mudstones, conglomerates, and trace fossils. If time, energy, and desire still exist, you can pick up the trail heading north past a couple of gulches with waterfalls along the blufftop for 1.6 miles to Fisk Mill Cove.

Our journey exits pelican-inhabited Stump Beach Cove, back up the stone steps and then in a beeline to the ocean and Stump Beach Trail. Your back stays against those cold north winds on clear days 1.2 miles to Gerstle Cove. This stretch covers perhaps the most geologically interesting stretch of coastal bluffs in California.

This blufftop trail passes five rocky points before culminating with Salt Point, guarding Gerstle Cove to the south. These points are pounded by big waves, carving natural sculptures into these rock faces that resemble ribs, ridges, pits, and knobs. Your mission is to spot as many sea stacks and sea arches to the west and as many massive blocks of sandstone to the east as possible.

The Gerstle Cove overlook gives a good look at the cove itself and the coarse-grained sandstone rocks that surround it. The abundant marine life is completely protected in the underwater reserve at Gerstle Cove.

Coyote brush shrub, Douglas fir, bishop pine, and native coastal prairie near Pygmy Forest.

Hike 28

Austin Creek and Gilliam Creek Trails

LENGTH: 9.2 miles round-trip as described; 4.9 miles round-trip if you skip the Gilliam Creek Backpack Camp loop.

DIFFICULTY: moderate.

TOTAL ELEVATION GAIN: 900 feet.

WATER: available from East Austin and Gilliam Creeks; purify.

SEASON: all—can get to over 100ºF in summer; creeks may be swollen after heavy rains in winter—so call ahead; best in spring when green and full of wildflowers.

MAP: Armstrong Redwoods State Reserve map or USGS topo Guerneville.

INFORMATION: Austin Creek State Recreation Area, (707) 869-2015.

DIRECTIONS TO TRAILHEAD: From Highway 101 just north of

Santa Rosa, take Highway 116 and travel 16 miles west to Guerneville. Turn north at the town's only stop sign onto Armstrong Woods Road and drive 2.2 miles to Armstrong Redwoods State Park. Continue on the paved road as it gets steep, narrow, and winding for 3.3 miles, park in the lot, then walk down to start at the gate. To reach Guerneville from Highway 1, turn east on Highway 116 south of Jenner and drive 11 miles.

This is a hike with a view, in mostly open oak woodland where the western fence lizard scurries. Although the wide-open Pacific Ocean hides over those rugged coastal mountains, and urban activity abounds a mere few miles away, this is a quiet journey that gives a sense of total isolation. Once underway, you won't hear a car or see a fence, power pole, or any other human artifact. And to think these rolling foothills actually fit snugly against a huge redwood for-

est in neighboring Armstrong Redwoods State Reserve, where the crowds are.

From the startup on the East Austin Creek Trail, you get great open views to the west of lush coastal mountains. They continue as this service road descends in an open oak woodland of black oak, coast live oak, and blue oak, with occasional madrones accenting the landscape. In springtime the grasses are lush green, interspersed with blooming brodiaea, clover, lupine, iris, buttercup, monkey-flower, and filaree.

At 1.3 miles the trail plunges into a shady riparian zone of bigleaf maple, California bay laurel, and Douglas fir that canopy nearby Gilliam Creek. You soon reach the wooden bridge that crosses it at a three-way intersection where Schoolhouse Creek empties into Gilliam Creek. By crossing here, you can reach Tom King Trail Camp, nestled next to Thompson Creek, after a 1.3-mile walk via the service road, or Mannings Flat Trail Camp between two of East Austin Creek's tributaries in 2.7 miles.

I recommend the shady and flat 1.3-mile stroll along Gilliam Creek to Gilliam Creek Trail Camp. Here you can duck your toe where Gilliam Creek finishes into East Austin Creek and explore a very wide and flat stretch of the latter creek. This way you can make a nice clockwise loop by connecting with the East Austin Creek Trail back to the previously mentioned wooden bridge.

All three of these camps are ideal for a secluded year-round back-packing trip. They have wood stoves, pit toilets, and tables. Be sure to get a camping permit at the park office.

In these remote regions, you're more likely to hear or see deer, raccoons, skunks, and squirrels. In rare cases, gray foxes, bobcats, wild turkeys, and wild pigs may be spotted. Great blue herons, white-tailed kites, and red-shouldered hawks patrol Austin and Gilliam Creeks, while California quail hide in the bushes.

Back at the wooden bridge and three-way intersection, go right onto a section of the Gilliam Creek Trail you've yet to delve into to complete a figure-eight loop trip. Strewn with lichen-covered boulders, the first 0.4 mile hugs charming Schoolhouse Creek. You'll cross this narrow and peaceful creek (compared to the louder Gilliam Creek) three times before this footpath abruptly climbs where Schoolhouse Creek branches in two. You'll briefly parallel the

north branch, then pass through a chaparral community of manzanita, toyon, and chamise. The climb then persists through oak
woodland to a gap and three-way trail junction. A right turn puts
you on the Pool Ridge Trail, and going straight connects with the
East Ridge Trail; both trails combined cover Hike 29. To return to
your car, take a left onto Bullfrog Pond Trail for a mile's worth of
ridge walking filled with views similar to this journey's beginning.

Hike 29

*Pool Ridge and East Ridge Trails in Armstrong
Redwoods State Reserve*

LENGTH: 5.3 miles round-trip; about 1 mile total on the self-
guided trail.
DIFFICULTY: moderate.
TOTAL ELEVATION GAIN: 1,100 feet.
WATER: bring plenty of your own.
SEASON: all—most seclusion is during winter.
MAP: Armstrong Redwoods State Reserve map or USGS
topo Guerneville. See p. 82.
INFORMATION: Armstrong Redwoods State Reserve, (707)
869-2015.
DIRECTIONS TO TRAILHEAD: From Highway 1, turn east on
Highway 116 south of Jenner and drive 11 miles to
Guerneville. Turn north at the town's only stop sign onto
Armstrong Woods Road and drive 2.2 miles to Armstrong
Redwoods State Reserve. From Highway 101 just north of
Santa Rosa, take River Road and travel 16 miles west to
Guerneville.

It's easy to pretend you're a hobbit or dwarf underneath the giant
redwoods in magical Armstrong Redwoods State Park. Redwoods
are the tallest living thing in the world, and these redwoods here
rival Muir Woods and Tall Trees Grove as areas in California with
the largest redwoods. This loop hike first features quality time beneath the giants, then after some quiet woods walking, a chance to
glance down on a blanket of big redwood tops.

The trip begins on the level Pioneer Trail (pick up the self-guided nature trail brochure at the nearby visitor center), a short loop past some redwoods that are as tall as a football field is long. Spot the 310-foot-tall Parson Jones tree right off, and a little farther on, the Colonel Armstrong redwood, which is almost as tall. Both are around 14 feet in diameter and 1,400 years old.

After completing the entire loop, double back to, and then get on, the Pool Ridge Trail at either northernmost junctions from the nature trail. The eastern stretch follows Fife Creek's main branch past bigleaf maples and California bay laurel to a picnic area, before cutting west. The western portion of the trail stays in old-growth redwoods along with tanbark oak for the first quarter mile, then continues with the shriveling west branch of Fife Creek before leaving it and heading east.

On both of these Pool Ridge Trail connectors, the redwoods gradually shrink in size and number as large Douglas firs become more common. When you're not being a hobbit, looking up at both giant conifers, look down to the ground. In winter, liverworts, lichens, mushrooms, and mosses coat the rich earth. In spring, look for redwood sorrel in bloom (with big, cloverlike leaves), redwood orchid, and trillium.

The middle portion of this trail climbs steeply in sections and is level at times, alternating between shade and sunny sites (where the manzanita grows tall). A couple of open, grassy slopes plunge into the lush canyonside to the west.

The final half mile of the Pool Ridge Trail climbs moderately through woods in deep shade. The occasional sprawling canyonside views to the east are beyond Douglas fir, madrone, and California bay laurel. Just prior to reaching the trail junction at the gap, look for an amazing California bay laurel on the right of the trail. The main trunk is growing diagonally down the canyonside, and its scaffold branches reach to the sky.

At 2.4 miles you come to a three-way trail junction next to the paved park road. Going left on the Gilliam Creek Trail heads into Austin Creek State Recreation Area (see Hike 28), an oak woodlands hike completely different from this hike and suitable for day hiking or backpacking. To complete this hike, turn right onto the signed East Ridge Trail. Soon after crossing the park road, the trail comes to another fork. A left turn means 400 feet of climbing in two-thirds of a mile to a service road at 1,600 feet in elevation, where you get great views of canyonsides, redwood forests, and lush coastal mountains.

A right turn returns you to the parking area after 2.8 miles spanning 200 feet of elevation gently downhill in shady woods along the east ridge, sporting good lookouts of canyonsides and old-growth redwoods. The East Ridge Trail gets more foot traffic than the Pool Ridge Trail.

Hike 30
Goat Rock and Blind Beach to Peaked Hill and Shell Beach

LENGTH: 4.5 miles round-trip.
DIFFICULTY: easy.
TOTAL ELEVATION GAIN: 400 feet.
WATER: none, bring your own.
SEASON: all—spring has the most wildflowers; fall has the least wind.
MAP: Send 80 cents to SOS, P.O. Box 221, Duncan Mills, CA 95430.
INFORMATION: Sonoma Coast State Beach, (707) 875-3483.
DIRECTIONS TO TRAILHEAD: From Highway 101 just north of Santa Rosa, take Highway 116 west 27 miles to Highway 1 just south of Jenner. Turn south on Highway 1 and drive 0.8 mile (you'll cross the Russian River Bridge), then turn west onto Goat Rock Road. Take this paved and winding road for 1.9 miles, then turn left into a large parking lot overlooking Goat Rock. The indistinct trail parallels the road south for a couple hundred yards.

There's a lot of lofty landmarks with enticing names stuffed into this beaches and bluffs hike. How can anyone resist whale watching on Peaked Hill, checking out harbor seals at the mouth of the Russian River, or wandering aimlessly on Blind Beach?

Goat Rock, Blind, Shell, and Wright's Beaches are in the Sonoma Coast Beach system, and are not part of the better known state parks.

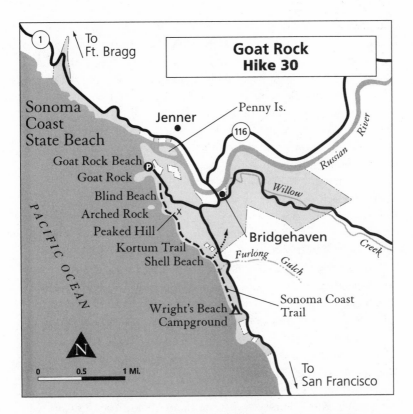

That, coupled with the fact that these beaches are shielded by tall bluffs or nestled away in rocky coves and not visible by people in cars on Highway 1, make them less visited and more secluded.

Before or after your hike, drive down to Goat Rock Beach and spot ospreys nesting in the nearby treetops. Observe the brown pelicans at their home on Penny Island decorating the mouth of the Russian River, among the largest rivers along the coast. From a parking lot down near Goat Rock, you can access Goat Rock Beach and Whale Point to the north or stroll Blind Beach while admiring Arched Rock to the south. The hike described next begins higher up, at the asphalt parking lot mentioned in the directions to the trailhead, and heads south along the bluffs.

You'll soon reach and get on the signed Kortum Trail and pass along a grassy slope briefly heading away from the Pacific Ocean past yarrow, bracken fern, cow parsnip (huge leaves and white flowers in the spring), and coyote brush. In the spring you're apt to notice wildflowers such as lupine, sea fig, and Indian paintbrush.

The slender footpath, a strip of compacted grass here, climbs earnestly for a couple hundred feet, and passes a cluster of lichen-coated large boulders, then reaches the shoulder of Peaked Hill. You get eastward views here of the smooth and rolling coastal hills that epitomize this stretch of the Sonoma coastline.

Take the three minutes to climb the knob known as Peaked Hill for an exhilarating panorama. Steep on all sides, 120-foot-tall Goat Rock punctuates the coastline to the south along with Arched Rock's large tunnel. A large, old, weathered barn is stationed across the swooping plain near the highway. By gazing south, you can spy Rock Point and Mussel Point farther in the distance near Bodega Head (see Hike 31).

Back on the trail, follow it past an old fence with an entry way, then veer southwest for a mile's worth of flat walking on a wide-open plain. It goes near a couple of giant rock formations, and stays close to the steep bluffs, providing many views of the sea.

Eventually you'll cross a ravine, then take the spur trail down to Shell Beach for some decent beachcombing. For further hiking, you can continue south on the trail (now called the Sonoma Coast Trail) 2 more miles to Wright's Beach and its campground. The trail promptly veers inland past private homes, becomes a gravel road, and follows Highway 1 closely for awhile—not quite the wilderness experience compared to Blind Beach to Shell Beach.

For the return trip, be inventive—choose from the maze of makeshift trails, perhaps mixing in some more beach walking. If those pesky north winds get in your face big time, it'll be quick work getting back to the car.

Hike 31

Bodega Dunes and South Salmon Creek Beach to Bodega Head

LENGTH: 8.4 miles round-trip as described; 2.5 miles round-trip to South Salmon Creek Beach; 4.5 miles round-trip to Mussel Point.

DIFFICULTY: moderate.

TOTAL ELEVATION GAIN: 600 feet.

WATER: none, bring your own.

SEASON: all—exceptional wildflowers around Bodega Head in spring; winter is particularly secluded.

MAP: send 80 cents to SOS, P.O. Box 221, Duncan Mills, CA 95430, or obtain from Bodega Dunes Campground entrance station.

INFORMATION: Sonoma Coast State Beach, (707) 875-3483.

DIRECTIONS TO TRAILHEAD: Take the East Washington Avenue exit from Highway 101 in Petaluma, then go west on Bodega Avenue and drive 25 miles to Bodega Bay (10 miles south of Highway 116) on Highway 1. At the north end of town, turn west onto the road signed for Bodega Dunes Campground. Turn right at the entrance station and

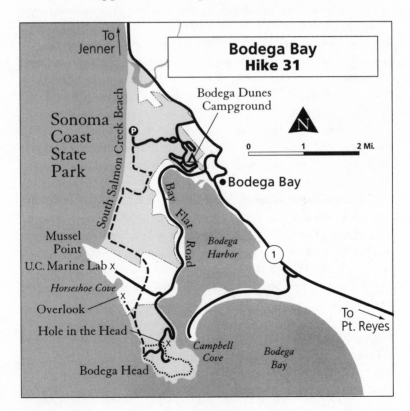

follow the paved road 1 mile to its end, a large parking lot. Walk 100 yards south on the road, then pick up the wide, sandy trail next to a dinky gate.

Tall, expansive sand dunes are perfect for kids who want to play army, and for those who want to feel hidden and secluded on an ocean walk. This journey lets the soul roam in dunes, along a scenic beach and then capture staggering views of Bodega Harbor and the sea stacks below Bodega Head.

There's so much to admire here, it's well worth camping at Bodega Dunes Campground and making two separate outings from the hike described next. One hike can cover the dunes and beach. The other can include the short loop trail that spans several vista points overlooking the Pacific Ocean from atop the massive granite knob comprising Bodega Head.

From the onset, the deep and loose sand works out your thigh and calf muscles splendidly to the soft purr of the ocean. The rolling sand dunes on the right, featuring a few knolls up to 30 feet tall, are securely stabilized by a sand-gripping, nonnative bunchgrass called European beachgrass. These yard-tall yellow and green plants nod gently in the breeze, interspersed here with coyote brush and yellow-flowered bush lupine.

By continuing straight, past the first arrow-signed junction, you'll soon skirt a couple of mansions, promptly followed by an expansive vista at 0.5 mile of Bodega Harbor and the metropolis of fishing boat docks below.

The next side trail heading west (0.3 mile long) bisects the dunes and displays inaugural views of the ocean beyond a gentle slope covered with ice plant. To have a dune-flanked beach strand virtually to one's self, make a beeline for driftwood-littered South Salmon Creek Beach. The next two-thirds of a mile can easily be spent daydreaming while traipsing south to the comforting rhythm of the waves. Just be sure to cross and climb the sandy dunes before reaching Mussel Point.

To regain the trail proper, one undergoes a light but sweaty work-out, each footstep sinking in the sand steadily climbing the sprawling dunes. To reach the hilltop is to gain a reward—a vista eastward past a flat and sandy field of Bodega Harbor and Bodega Bay.

The steep bluffs near Bodega Head plunge to a cozy pocket beach.

The next half mile gets a tad tricky at times. Merely negotiate the maze of occasionally indistinct trails (follow the wooden posts) as best as possible, and keep heading south toward the power lines that parallel the paved road (it dead-ends at the modernized University of California Marine Laboratory facilities used for teaching and research). Pick up the signed trail at the point where the yellow road line ends.

Inspiring views of Bodega Bay and Bodega Harbor accompany a moderate 0.7-mile climb along a narrow strip of trail often clogged by bush lupine, white-flowered yarrow, and thistle. Consider putting on long pants here or checking for ticks when done hiking.

At 3.3 miles, take the 0.2-mile-long spur trail that shows off the harbor to the east and the ocean to the west. From atop some scattered boulders on Horseshoe Cove Overlook, a fabulous panorama awaits. With a gradual sweep of the head, you can fully appreciate the aforementioned water scenes, along with Point Reyes seashore to the south and tiny and lovely Horseshoe Cove Beach to the north, topped by the expansive U.C. Marine Lab.

The 0.8-mile stroll down to Bodega Head is the highlight of the journey. The Bodega Head shoreline below is wild and rugged, as waves dash against the dazzling array of sea stacks, then sweep gently over two tiny beach pockets. From March into July, a feast of flowers adorns the steep slope that plunges to the shore.

*Marin County
and San Francisco Bay Area*

Hike 32

Tomales Point in Point Reyes National Seashore

LENGTH: 9.3 miles round-trip; hike can easily be shortened to any desired length beyond 3 miles.

DIFFICULTY: easy to moderate.

TOTAL ELEVATION GAIN: 800 feet.

WATER: none; bring plenty of your own.

SEASON: all—most likely to get best views in the fall; wildflowers in spring; fewer hikers on a winter weekday.

MAP: Point Reyes National Seashore brochure or USGS topo Tomales.

INFORMATION: Point Reyes National Seashore, (415) 663-1092.

DIRECTIONS TO TRAILHEAD: From Highway 101 north of the Golden Gate Bridge, take Sir Francis Drake Boulevard west for about 20 miles to the tiny town of Olema (turn right on Highway 1). Olema is 13 miles north of Stinson Beach. From Highway 1, you soon turn west on Sir Francis Drake Highway. After 8.5 miles, turn right on Pierce Point Road, then drive 9.2 miles to the Tomales Point trailhead.

On this journey, hikers get to decide which treat delights the senses the most—observing a herd of tule elk, or being a tiny speck on Tomales Point checking out superb bay and ocean views.

Elk or jackrabbit, pelican or hawk, this solitary strip of land, which forms the northern tip of Point Reyes Peninsula, is loaded with wildlife. With Tomales Bay on the east side, the vast sea on the west and freshwater ponds in between, birds and land animals have it made. This same scenario translates into dreamy views for the wayfarer.

Resembling deer but much larger, the elk tend to gather in the evening near a watering hole set in a valley a couple miles into the journey. By the 1860s, hunters had eliminated Point Reyes Peninsula's large elk population, but a century later the National Park Service relocated some elk onto Tomales Point from Owens Valley.

The hike starts at the Upper Pierce Dairy Ranch (which pro-

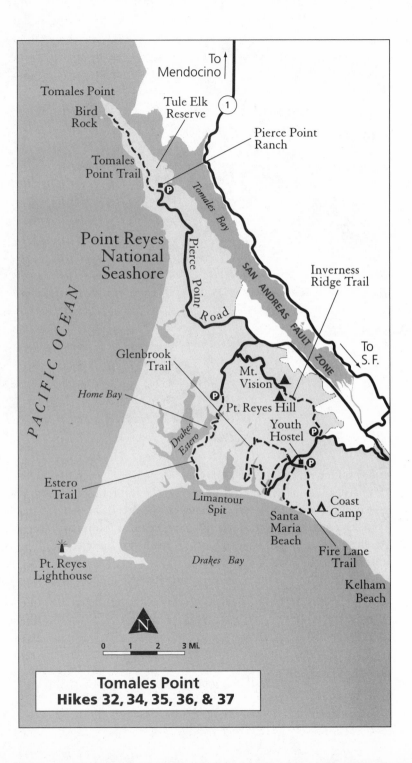

To
Mendocino

Tomales Point
Bird Rock
Tule Elk Reserve
Pierce Point Ranch
Tomales Point Trail
1

Point Reyes National Seashore

Tomales Bay

Pierce Point Road

SAN ANDREAS FAULT ZONE

Inverness Ridge Trail

To S.F.

PACIFIC OCEAN

Glenbrook Trail

Home Bay

Mt. Vision

Pt. Reyes Hill

Drakes Estero

Youth Hostel

Estero Trail

Limantour Spit

Coast Camp

Santa Maria Beach

Fire Lane Trail

Pt. Reyes Lighthouse

Drakes Bay

Kelham Beach

N

0   1   2   3 Mi.

Tomales Point
Hikes 32, 34, 35, 36, & 37

The northernmost section of McClure's Beach.

duced butter in the mid 1800s), where the old Pierce family house and barn still stands. The trail, an old ranch road for awhile, climbs a fifth of a mile to photogenic scenes of the ocean on the left and Tomales Bay on the right. Gaze down on clean and shiny McClure's Beach (a recommended half-mile side trip from the trailhead) 0.1 mile farther.

Tomales Point Trail climbs gently eastward, soon unveiling White Gulch and Hog Island on Tomales Bay. If it's springtime, California poppies, tidy tips, and yellow bush lupine adorn the green hillsides and ravines.

At 1.4 miles, a 7-foot-tall boulder punctuates a view-filled crest. A view of Bodega Bay where it joins Tomales Bay at Avalis Beach shows up a half mile farther. Good photos of Bodega Bay through tall bush lupine are yours for the taking, especially from 2.6 miles and beyond.

Curious souls can extend the trip by exploring any of the many elk spur trails that cross the main trail here. Meanwhile, views of the small town of Dillon Beach appear from just above a small pond at 2.8 miles, where the elk commonly congregate.

The wide and worn Tomales Point Trail becomes a sometimes indistinct footpath at 3.1 miles, where another gentle ascent ensues. A crest featuring sweeping vistas to the west of the ocean is reached 0.2 mile farther.

The tread switches to sand a bit farther, where a sign indicates Tomales Point. Keep on the faint path to Tomales Point proper, or pick and choose your way west, then pick a perch for studying the pelicans and cormorants that cling to aptly named Bird Rock just offshore. You're bound to feel you accomplished a major mission when the northernmost tip of Tomales Point is reached. The views ahead of Bodega Head are stunning. The ocean's waves cruising against the point steeply below can also be admired. The actual point here consists mainly of granite outcrops and cliffs, a rare occurrence along the Northern California coast.

Hike 33

Indian Beach and Jepson Memorial Grove in Tomales Bay State Park

LENGTH: 4.2 miles round-trip as described; 3 miles round-trip combining the Indian Beach Nature Trail and Jepson Trail; 1 mile round-trip on the Indian Beach Nature Trail.

DIFFICULTY: easy.

TOTAL ELEVATION GAIN: 400 feet.

WATER: available from faucets at Heart's Desire Beach parking lot.

SEASON: all—often less windy and foggy than most immediate coast areas in the summer, but also warmer.

MAP: Tomales Bay State Park map or USGS topo Tomales.

INFORMATION: Tomales Bay State Park, (415) 669-1140 or (415) 456-1286.

DIRECTIONS TO TRAILHEAD: Take the Sir Francis Drake Boulevard exit off Highway 101 in San Rafael, and drive west about 20 miles to the town of Olema (which is 13 miles north of Stinson Beach on Highway 1). After turning right on Highway 1 and going a short distance, make a left onto Sir Francis Drake. Travel 8.3 miles, then turn right onto Pierce Ranch Road. After 1.2 miles, go right onto the signed road indicating Tomales Bay State Park, and park in the large paved lot 1.5 miles farther, at Heart's Desire Beach.

To truly get the feel of Tomales Bay, one should traipse the trails of Tomales Bay State Park, past gentle and surfless beaches and amidst virgin groves of craggy bishop pines. Indian and Pebble Beaches are tiny, isolated, and cozy, nestled next to the western waterfront of Tomales Bay.

From a distance, as in being atop Point Reyes Hill (Hike 35) or Mount Wittenberg, one could almost think Tomales Bay looks like a big blue lake. Then again, a lake wouldn't have sharks and rays, as saltwater Tomales Bay does.

To see it up close and personal, get on the Indian Beach Nature Trail and follow this interpretive trail (showing the plants the Miwok Indians used for food and medicine) to Indian Beach. The shaded and tranquil trail features a wide variety of flora including toyon, coffeeberry, California hazelnut, California huckleberry, native wild blackberry, ferns, coast live oak (many with twisted and leaning trunks), California bay laurel, madrone, and bishop pine. The Miwoks survived on these plants, along with fish from Tomales Bay, for 3,500 years.

Indian Beach, which divides the bay and a marshy cove (at times nearly dry), features three old wooden teepees and is much more secluded than Heart's Desire Beach. A bishop pine forest with coast silktassel and gooseberry surrounds this pristine scene. The trail is littered with soil-protecting and -enriching leaves, needles, and twigs.

When done with this short walk, drive over to the other parking lot and get on the signed Jepson Trail. Named after botanist Willis Jepson, who founded the acclaimed native plant book called the *Jepson Manual,* this mile-long trail is a semishaded slender footpath that weaves and climbs into a rare and ancient bishop pine forest.

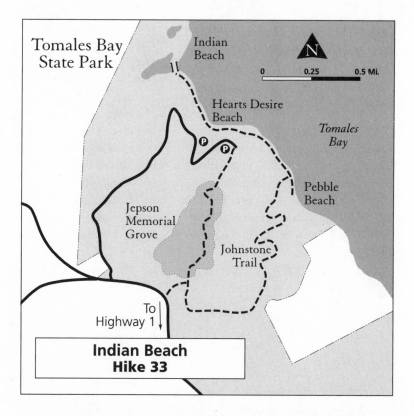

Indian
Beach

N

0   0.25   0.5 Mi.

Hearts Desire
Beach

*Tomales
Bay*

Jepson
Memorial
Grove

Pebble
Beach

Johnstone
Trail

To
Highway 1

**Indian Beach
Hike 33**

Most of the conifers in Jepson Memorial Grove are highlighted by
wind-worn and time-sculpted bare trunks resembling bent umbrel-
las, with the foliage flowing out from the tippy top only.

A variety of grasses decorate trailside, along with orange bush
monkeyflower, bracken, and sword fern and lots of coffeeberry.
Other understory shrubs that appear occasionally include California
huckleberry, California hazelnut, gooseberry, ceanothus, poison oak,
and salal. A prolific display of salal in the sun awaits at a three-way
trail junction at 0.9 mile, canopied by a handful of statuesque bishop
pine specimens. This yard-tall salal thicket sports white, bell-shaped
flowers in the spring next to orange bush monkeyflower and blue-
flowering ceanothus for a rich and colorful show.

After crossing a narrow, paved service road at 1 mile, the grassy
footpath (now the Johnstone Trail) descends gently past a chaparral
community of coyote brush and cow parsnips to another trail junc-

tion 0.1 mile farther. The 1.2-mile trek to Pebble Beach stays level for 0.2 mile in an open woodland/chaparral area decorated by occasional madrones, to the recrossing of the same service road. The trail then promptly plunges into shade, provided mainly by tan oak, but also some madrones, bishop pines, and knobcone pines.

You'll soon catch occasional glimpses of Tomales Bay below before descending to small and secluded Pebble Beach. The land you're on as well as the whole bay is drifting northwestward at about 2 feet per decade. This granite bedrock chunk of land geologically matches the Tehachapi Mountains more than 300 miles to the southeast. It took about 10 million years (my, how time marches slowly) for the Point Reyes peninsula to move from there to here. But during the San Francisco earthquake of 1906, the largest measured displacement along the San Andreas Fault happened at the head of Tomales Bay, where a section west of the fault moved 20 feet in relation to the east side of the fault.

Hike 34

Drake's Estero to Sunset Beach
in Point Reyes National Seashore

LENGTH: 7 miles round-trip as described; 4 miles round-trip to Drake's Estero; 2.2 miles round-trip to Home Bay.

DIFFICULTY: moderate.

TOTAL ELEVATION GAIN: 800 feet.

WATER: bring your own.

SEASON: all—most likely to get the best views in the fall.

MAP: Point Reyes National Seashore brochure or USGS topo Drake's Bay. See p. 95.

INFORMATION: Point Reyes National Seashore, (415) 663-1092.

DIRECTIONS TO TRAILHEAD: From Highway 101 north of the Golden Gate Bridge, take Sir Francis Drake Boulevard west for about 20 miles to the town of Olema (turn right on Highway 1). Olema is 13 miles north of Stinson Beach. You soon turn west onto Bear Valley Road, travel 9.8 miles to a sign marked "Estero Trailhead," then turn left and drive 0.9 mile to the trailhead.

The shore at Sunset Beach.

This is one of those hikes in which bird fanciers don't just pack field glasses, they wear them around their necks. That's because most of this journey's mileage covers Home and Drake's Bays, Drake's Estero (Spanish for estuary), and several ponds.

This combination of immense freshwater and saltwater bodies of water creates a rich and varied habitat for numerous kinds of waterfowl and shorebirds. Snag the impressive bird checklist of Point Reyes Peninsula at the large Bear Valley Visitor Center (a half mile west of Highway 1 on Bear Valley Road). Then you can identify the region's common flying friends such as blue herons, loons, ducks, godwits, willets, and widgeons.

To do this trek, you travel on the Drake Highway and explore Drake's Estero and Drake's Bay, all named for English sailor and bay discoverer Sir Francis Drake. Historians figure he most likely anchored his ship in Drake's Estero, then was greeted and fed by the peaceful and friendly Coast Miwok Indians, who inhabited these shores.

Estero Trail, an old ranch road, leads past rolling cattle ranch lands where native bunchgrasses and rushes combine with clovers and pasture grasses. After a half mile, it veers sharply seaward, climbing to grand views of Inverness Ridge (Hike 35) to the east.

The trail ventures near a thick grove of Monterey pines of near identical height, planted simultaneously as a Christmas tree farm. A third of a mile farther, the initial view of Home Bay appears next to a swampy pond. The trail continues climbing, now past colorful natives bush lupine and cow parsnips, with flocks of varied birds swooping over or landing on Home Bay's mudflats and water's edge.

Estero Trail soon levels in a pasture, then swerves southeast past twin ponds and then the inaugural sighting of Drake's estero.

A bit farther, the trail reaches a junction. A left turn eventually leads to Limantour Beach (Hike 36), but our route continues seaward (straight) past several clusters of rushes, which you peer above to attain glorious scenes of the estero below. In winter and spring, the rolling and grassy hillsides that encase the estero are blanketed in smooth green. During the dry months, these same gently sloping hills turn golden, especially in late afternoon, the splotches of green coming mainly from the occasional bishop pine.

The trail remains mostly level the rest of the way, where a pond at 3.4 miles precedes sparkling Sunset Beach. Harbor seals haul out on sand islands just offshore on mostly calm Drake's Bay. Historians theorize that the eroded, chalky white cliffs here reminded Drake the pirate of the equally famous cliffs of Dover. If there's a full moon on a clear night, consider experiencing dusk at aptly named Sunset Beach, then hiking back via the light of the moon.

Hike 35

Inverness Ridge to Point Reyes Hill

LENGTH: 6.4 miles round-trip as described; hike can be successfully shortened to any length.
DIFFICULTY: moderate.
TOTAL ELEVATION GAIN: 700 feet.
WATER: none; bring plenty of your own.
SEASON: all—most likely to get the best views in the fall.
MAP: Point Reyes National Seashore map or USGS topos Drake's Bay and Inverness. See p. 95.
INFORMATION: Point Reyes National Seashore, (415) 663-1092.
DIRECTIONS TO TRAILHEAD: From Highway 101 just north of San Francisco, take Sir Francis Drake Boulevard west some 20 miles to Olema (turn right on Highway 1). You soon make a left onto Bear Valley Road and promptly pass the turnoff to the Bear Valley Visitor Center (lots of maps and info on the Point Reyes area there). Drive 1.3 miles past the turnoff, then turn left on Limantour Road. After 4.5 miles, turn right at the Bayview Trailhead, the starting point for the Inverness Ridge hike.

To study the devastating impact of the Vision Fire of 1995, and to learn firsthand how nature is healing and repairing itself from this illegal campfire that quickly spread out of control, you should walk on Inverness Ridge. If you're quiet and lucky enough, you may spot some of the fast-moving animals such as deer or birds who successfully fled this fire and then eventually returned. While taking this journey, it becomes easier to imagine what the huge furnace of flames and billowing smoke clouds looked like as the fire engulfed Mount Vision southward to Limantour Spit (Hike 36).

The Inverness Ridge Trail, ironically a fire road, allows perhaps the most reflective and in-depth study of the ongoing effects of the Vision Fire. The views west of this sunny trail prove that nature is fortunately healing fast. The smooth and rolling hillsides are clothed in a colorful mosaic of greens, yellows, and browns.

The grasses and herbs that shot up first are in various stages of giving way to coastal scrub consisting primarily of coyote brush. The charred, ghostly limbs have decomposed as rapidly as the new growth of this resilient shrub sprouted from the base.

The bishop pines that line the trail and dot the hillsides resprout vigorously from seed after a fire. Judging by the numerous saplings and other rapidly growing juvenile bishop pines, one can figure that in time there may be more bishop pines here than before the fire.

The views of Drake's Bay, punctuated by the Point Reyes shoreline, are virtually constant over the first mile or so of this trek. They tend to outdo the occasional views to the east of Bolinas Ridge.

After a brief descent to a paved road at 0.7 mile (stay on the dirt road), the trail climbs west in earnest past California huckleberry and coffeeberry shrubs, and then veers inland to the junction with Drake's Trail at 1.3 miles. (For the rambunctious adventurer, add a few miles to the journey by descending Drake's Trail, eventually looping over to Point Reyes Hill after a climb up the Bucklin Trail).

Point Reyes Hill, shaped like an ice cream cone, looms in full view by now, as the trail descends briefly while heading straight for it through a fire-ravaged bishop pine forest. As you begin the final steadfast climb (at 2.0 miles) the trail becomes a slender footpath clogged with grasses (wear long pants or check for ticks afterward). The first scenes of Tomales Bay to the northeast soon unfold.

As soon as this blue and gray bay temporarily disappears from sight, the Pacific Ocean takes its place. Mount Wittenberg to the south stands guard over the colorful canyons and hills that unravel into the ocean.

The trail soon snakes up and around to reveal an even better view of Tomales Bay, then reaches Point Reyes Hill next to a navigational station (please do not enter these grounds). Point Reyes Hill, 1,336 feet, is more like a huge and flat knob, longer and wider than a football field, blanketed with coyote brush. It serves as an ideal lookout for admiring pretty scenes of the esteros, bay, and ocean.

You've come this far, so if time permits, why not snag Mount Vision, waiting to be conquered a mere 0.2 mile farther to the north?

Hike 36

Limantour Beach via Muddy Hollow and Estero Trails in Point Reyes National Seashore

LENGTH: 8.4 miles round-trip as described; 4.4 miles round-trip to Limantour Beach including Limantour Spit; 3.6 miles round-trip to Limantour Beach.

DIFFICULTY: moderate.

TOTAL ELEVATION GAIN: 500 feet.

WATER: available from faucets at Limantour Beach and from Glenbrook Creek; bring some of your own.

SEASON: all—best in winter and early spring when the creeks are high, the hills are green and the crowds are down; muddy sections after big rains.

MAP: Point Reyes National Seashore map or USGS topo Drake's Bay. See p. 95.

INFORMATION: Point Reyes National Seashore, (415) 663-1092.

DIRECTIONS TO TRAILHEAD: From Highway 101 in San Rafael, take Sir Francis Drake Boulevard west for about 20 miles to Olema (turn right on Highway 1). You soon make a left on Bear Valley Road and promptly pass the turnoff to the Bear Valley Visitor Center (lots of maps and info there). Drive 1.3 miles past the turnoff, then turn left on Limantour Road. After 5.7 miles, turn right onto a dirt road that promptly leads to the Muddy Hollow Trailhead, this hike's beginning.

Mindful missions tend to make for good hikes. The mission here is to follow a creek past two ponds straight to Limantour Beach, then loop back the long way, overlooking Estero de Limantour and crossing Glenbrook Creek twice. Like climbing a mountain to see what's on the other side, a journey to a special beach reaps exceptional rewards. Add the view-filled return trek past Estero de Limantour, then over grassy hillsides, and the mission is successfully accomplished.

The 1.8-mile-long Muddy Hollow Trail stays just out of sight and sound of a nearby stream the entire way, and marches directly to Limantour Beach. A riparian habitat accompanies this flat stroll in the sunshine, where large red alders eventually mesh into a marsh thicket of skinnier red alders.

A variety of annual grasses and perennial sedges gently sway in the slightest breeze. Scattered paintbrush adorn the trailside along with horsetail and numerous herbs, including poison hemlock. Eventually you pass a circular freshwater pond, the junction with the Estero Trail (described later as a good return loop), then your trail hugs the shoreline of a large freshwater marsh/pond. It features a calm creek that gracefully wanders into pond sections and next to mostly dry areas.

A couple of short spur trails over land fingers give a wayfaring wanderer chances to get in the middle of the marshy pond area to further explore the curvaceous creek and patches of grassy meadows.

The smooth, clean, and sandy Limantour Beach invites some barefoot meandering. The far-reaching views are improved by rolling and grassy hillsides to the east and north and Point Reyes beyond Drake's Bay to the west and southwest. Many miles and much good walking time can be had along the Limantour Beach strand.

A good side path follows the slender sand strip known as Limantour Spit. This fine ramble furnishes gorgeous seaside close-ups of the estero. You can return anytime along the beach; just exit the spit via the grassy sand dunes that border the beach.

The 2-mile-long Estero Trail begins by bisecting the two ponds passed earlier, and a jungle of tall perla grass and hemlock (check for ticks afterward). It then climbs 200 feet to a bare knoll. This serves as a good lookout over the marsh, pond, ocean, Limantour Beach,

Limantour Spit, and portions of Estero de Limantour. It eventually snakes its way down the hillside, crosses Glenbrook Creek near a marsh, then hangs close to a portion of the estero (a birdwatcher's paradise). It soon winds away, showcasing picturesque views to the west, and connecting with the Glenbrook Trail (bear right here, then right again a half mile farther).

The Muddy Hollow Fire Road promptly brings you to the final crossing of Glenbrook Creek (the bridge was destroyed by the Vision Fire), descending gently along a grassy hillside just above an un-named and meandering stream. After a mile, it passes the Bucklin Trail, which leads to Point Reyes Hill (see Hike 35). In another half mile, Muddy Hollow Fire Road goes by the Bayview Trail under a grove of fire-ravaged Monterey cypress trees, then crosses a creek, guarded by multiple-trunked red alder trees just prior to reaching the trailhead.

Hike 37

Coast Trail in Point Reyes National Seashore

LENGTH: 5.2 miles round-trip.
DIFFICULTY: easy.
TOTAL ELEVATION GAIN: 400 feet.
WATER: bring your own.
SEASON: all—best views in the fall; more wildflowers in spring; virtual seclusion on a weekday in winter, when gray whales can be spotted.
MAP: USGS topos Double Point and Inverness, or Point Reyes National Seashore park map. See p. 95.
INFORMATION: Point Reyes National Seashore, (415) 663-1092.
DIRECTIONS TO TRAILHEAD: From Highway 101 just north of San Francisco, take Sir Francis Drake Boulevard west some 20 miles to Olema (turn right on Highway 1). After a very short drive, make a left onto Bear Valley Road and promptly pass the turnoff to Bear Valley Visitor Center (featuring lots of maps, exhibits, and Point Reyes info there). Drive 1.3

miles past the turnoff, then turn left onto Limantour Road.
After 5.7 miles, turn left onto the access road for the signed
Point Reyes Hostel, travel two-tenths of a mile and then
park on the right side of the road just above the hostel. The
Coast Trail takes off from a gate just below the hostel.

If you could be a pelican, swooping over this hike's terrain, there'd be
a lot of historic reminders. Drake's Bay meets the gradually arcing
beach shoreline where Sir Francis Drake landed his ship then hung
out with the Miwok Indians. The continental drift—the constant
motion of the earth's crust—causes the rocks of this craggy coast to
match those of the Tehachapi Mountains 300 miles to the south. A
look down on the recovering vegetation from the Vision Fire of 1995
may perhaps stir continued hope that the land this hike wanders
through the middle of will always be unusual and beautiful.

If ever there was a chance to see as many as possible of the 361
known bird species that spread their wings over Point Reyes
National Seashore, this hike is it. The path leads into streamside riparian habitat, goes by a freshwater marsh, then above the beach,
and finally into coastal scrub and grasslands.

The first 1.8 miles of the Coast Trail follows a well-graded fire
road, which makes a direct yet gentle descent to Drake's Bay in the
Pacific Ocean. It stays in the bottom of a U-shaped valley, alongside
a discreet and meandering stream. Of noteworthy interest are the
contrasting effects of the Vision Fire—the coyote-brush-lined hillsides were charred heavily, while the willow- and alder-lined riparian habitat was left virtually intact.

The Coast Trail crosses the stream at 0.7 mile, beneath a throng
of red alder trees. Scattered ferns, coyote brush, and bush lupines
adorn the south side, while mint and horsetails intersperse with cattails offsetting a parade of white-trunked alders. The stream gradually widens into a cattail-dominated marsh/lake. Coast Trail winds
around it, then reveals inaugural views of the bay and the eastern
section of Limantour Beach (see Hike 36 for the scoop on this beach).

Our trail continues its leisurely promenade, heading east to the
rhythm of the ocean's waves. Seagulls soar over the low, perennial-
grass-covered bluffs. It's easy to appreciate the oceanic views on one
side and the soft fields stretching to the rolling bald hills on the other

side along this 1.1-mile coast strand stroll. This gentle and unassuming coastline scene differs drastically from the steep territory in the Lost Coast farther north or the Big Sur Coast down south.

The Coast Trail reaches a thistle thicket, then heads inland past coyote brush and a gorgeous, lone eucalyptus tree to a signed trailhead at 2.8 miles. An ideal backpacker stayover is 0.1 mile away along the Coast Trail (permit required). Coast Camp sits on an open, grassy bluff high above Santa Maria Beach, featuring picnic tables and an outhouse. An overnighter at Coast Camp could complete day one of a coastline backpack trip ending at Palomarin (see Hike 40) some 12 miles away.

This hike now heads inland and begins a moderate climb on the Fire Lane Trail. Along this grassy hillside climb, revealing must-see views of the ocean behind, the Fire Lane Trail switches from old dirt road to slender footpath. It soon reaches a grassy flat, displaying a cluster of smooth and rounded hilltops above a couple of small and mucky ponds.

This seldom visited, remote section of Point Reyes National Seashore is the land where the coyote roams and the hawk hovers. After a mile on this return route, bear left onto the signed Laguna Trail, which promptly displays Point Reyes Hill (see Hike 35). The black and ghostly skeletal outlines of Douglas firs loom over the grassy expanses.

After passing a cluster of steep and interesting rock outcrops, Laguna Trail descends moderately along the bottom of an open canyon and soon comes to the access road.

Hike 38

Arch Rock and Kelham Beach
in Point Reyes National Seashore

LENGTH: 8.8 miles round-trip as described; 3.8 miles round-trip to Divide Meadow.
DIFFICULTY: easy.
TOTAL ELEVATION GAIN: 500 feet.
WATER: seasonally available from Coast and Bear Valley Creeks (purify); best to bring your own.

SEASON: all—most likely to get best views in the fall; fewer people on winter weekdays.

MAP: Point Reyes National Seashore brochure or USGS topos Inverness and Double Point.

INFORMATION: Point Reyes National Seashore, (415) 663-1092.

DIRECTIONS TO TRAILHEAD: From Highway 101 in San Rafael, take Sir Francis Drake Boulevard west for about 20 miles to Olema (turn right on Highway 1). You soon make a left onto Bear Valley Road, drive 0.5 mile then go left at the turnoff to the Bear Valley Visitor Center.

When the mood strikes for a different hike, consider this creekside stroll to a stunning shoreline vista of rugged Point Reyes National Seashore.

For starters, you get to stand on a major movement and displacement area of the 1906 San Francisco earthquake (take the 0.5-mile-long Earthquake Trail over Olema Creek, across from the visitor center). It's neat to check out a traditional Miwok Indian village built just outside the visitor center, including a sweat lodge and family dwellings. Before setting out on the main trail, also stroll the self-guided, super-short Woodpecker Trail (leaves from visitor center), which reveals and explains a generous sampling of Point Reyes flora.

You also see close up a bizarre, San Andreas Fault–shaped drainage pattern in which Bear Valley Creek flows away from the ocean but nearby Coast Creek flows into it. As an added bonus, the main trail is flanked in spots with profuse supplies of berries from five different plant species.

Popular Bear Valley Trail, which doubles as an old wagon road and compressed-rock park road, begins just south of the Morgan Horse Ranch. It's a shaded 200-foot climb over a 1.5-mile span to Divide Meadow, under Douglas fir, tan oak, California bay laurel, and alder trees. Redwoods would typically grow in a sheltered Northern California coast region such as this, but the granitic soils of Point Reyes Peninsula tend to prohibit their presence. The Bear Valley Creek understory consists mainly of trailside herbs and native berry-producing plants such as California huckleberry, thimble-berry, elderberry, and salal.

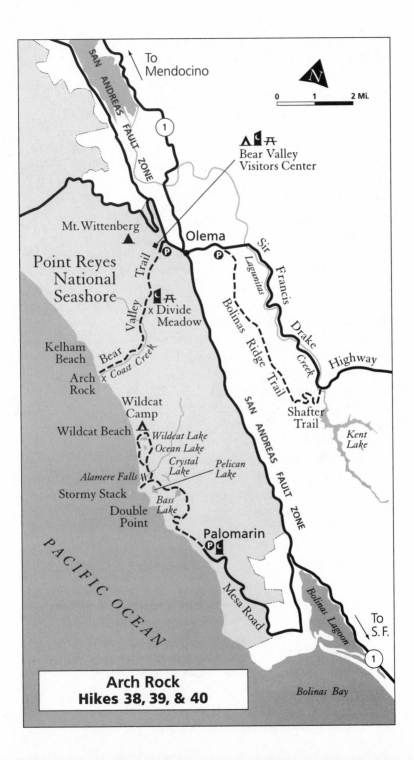

To Mendocino

N

0   1   2 Mi.

SAN ANDREAS FAULT ZONE

Bear Valley Visitors Center

Mt. Wittenberg

Olema

Point Reyes National Seashore

Sir Francis Drake Highway

Lagunitas Creek

Bear Valley Trail

Divide Meadow

Bolinas Ridge Trail

Kelham Beach

Coast Creek

Arch Rock

Wildcat Camp

SAN ANDREAS FAULT ZONE

Shafter Trail

Kent Lake

Wildcat Beach

Wildcat Lake
Ocean Lake
Crystal Lake

Pelican Lake

Alamere Falls

Stormy Stack

Double Point

Bass Lake

Palomarin

PACIFIC OCEAN

Mesa Road

Bolinas Lagoon

To S.F.

Bolinas Bay

Arch Rock
Hikes 38, 39, & 40

Aptly named Divide Meadow divides eastward-flowing Bear Valley Creek (which you now leave) from westward-moving Coast Creek (to be followed once you're done picnicking at the large meadow). This flat terrace sports an assortment of tall annual grasses that turn gold and gray when they dry up (by July).

Promptly on departing the meadow, the native tree diversity increases. Buckeye, willow, and coast live oak join the mix with alder, Douglas fir, and bay laurel. Cow parsnips (big umbels of white flowers in late spring) and a variety of ferns combine with intermittent peaks of the ocean as the wide trail gradually descends along Coast Creek, past some signed trail junctions (keep going straight).

At about 4 miles into the journey, riparian habitat is replaced by open, coastal scrub, where coyote brush accompanies immature Douglas fir. The first full-fledged view of the ocean soon appears, promptly followed by another signed trail junction, where you bear right for a third of a mile to chunky Arch Rock.

A brief scamper up this extrusive rock outcrop unveils far-ranging views of the rocky, bluff-lined coastline in both directions. Watch the scattered sea stacks attempt to block the waves that eventually cruise gently over Kelham Beach. Extending southwest and northeast of Arch Rock, at low tide this beach invites some barefoot straying. People like to crawl through Arch Rock's tunnel when it's low tide.

For a fabulous backpack trip (get permit first at Bear Valley Visitor Center), double back a couple hundred yards, and then go right at the signed trail junction. After 3.5 miles of scaling rolling, coastal scrub–clad bluffs on the Coast Trail, you'll reach Wildcat Beach (Hike 40).

Hike 39

Bolinas Ridge and Shafter Trails

LENGTH: 12.4 miles round-trip as described; 10 miles round-trip by skipping the Shafter trail; hike can be shortened to any length.

DIFFICULTY: moderate.

TOTAL ELEVATION GAIN: 1,300 feet; 700 feet if Shafter Trail is skipped.

WATER: none, bring your own.

SEASON: all—wildflowers in spring; most likely to get far-reaching, fog-free views in the fall.

MAP: USGS topos San Geronimo and Inverness. See p. 111.

INFORMATION: Golden Gate National Recreation Area, (415) 556-0561 or (415) 663-1092.

DIRECTIONS TO TRAILHEAD: From Golden Gate Bridge, drive north on Highway 101 and take the Sir Francis Drake Boulevard exit. Travel 17.5 miles on Sir Francis Drake Boulevard (3.4 miles past the Samuel P. Taylor State Park entrance station) and park on the south side of the road. From the tiny town of Olema on Highway 1, turn east on Sir Francis Drake Boulevard and drive 1 mile to the signed turnout.

The best way to take in the world-famous Point Reyes coast region is to climb among the barren foothills along Bolinas Ridge. The occasional well-placed native coast live oak trees, often accompanied by massive rock outcrops, furnish breathtakingly handsome foregrounds for Olema Valley, Tomales Bay, and Inverness Ridge.

Olema Valley, the epicenter of the San Francisco earthquake of 1906, and the geologic nuances of the San Andreas Fault, which runs through the entire Point Reyes area, can best be studied from Bolinas Ridge's numerous and divine vistas. You can't help but note the uncommonly straight and narrow shapes of Tomales Bay (about 12 miles long but only about a mile wide) and Olema Valley.

Most folks make the 700-foot climb over the first 2.5 miles, enjoy the views, then turn back. For better and more well-rounded hikes, consider one of two car shuttles—you can hike down to the Shafter Trailhead on Sir Francis Drake Boulevard (6.4 miles), or ramble on Bolinas Ridge Trail to its other trailhead on Bolinas-Fairfax Road (10 miles).

For the initial tenth of a mile, Bolinas Ridge Trail, an old dirt road, climbs past an old corral surrounded by cypress trees. It then breaks into bald, rolling hills covered with pasture weeds such as mustard, plantain, filaree, and oatgrass.

A lone boulder outcrop and a solo coast live oak specimen frame a picturesque view of Tomales Bay from a crest at 0.6 mile. A half mile farther, turn right at a signed trail junction and continue climbing the mostly bare, oak-dotted hillside. Here in the full sun, with little wind protection, these often massive evergreen oaks tend to grow wider than tall, with thick trunks.

You soon reach a ridgetop where the best views beckon to the west of dark-forested Inverness Ridge (Hike 35), which conceals the ocean. Along this stretch, glimpses of the slender, farm-lined Olema Valley appear intermittently.

A long grove of Douglas firs and coyote brush appears at 2.4 miles, followed by the first of two rush-lined ponds about a mile farther. The trail eventually gains its highest point near a cluster of five gigantic eucalyptus trees at 4.8 miles. For a better and much less visited vista, traipse another third of a mile to the junction of Shafter Trail, and scramble a few dozen yards to the west.

With a few hops, skips, and jumps in various directions, you can admire several major place-names. Mount Tamalpais, Bolinas Lagoon, and the Pacific Ocean sprawl to the south. More scenes of Inverness Ridge, Olema Valley, and Tomales Bay await to the west and northwest. Redwood-lined Lagunitas Creek to the east flows below a barren summit named Barnabe Peak (Hike 41).

Shafter Trail consists of a 1.3-mile-long plunge into a moist and shaded jungle of Douglas fir, tan oak, and California bay laurel to lovely Lagunitas Creek.

Hike 40

Pelican Lake and Wildcat Beach in Point Reyes National Seashore

LENGTH: 12 miles round-trip as described; 5.8 miles round-trip to Bass Lake.

DIFFICULTY: moderate.

TOTAL ELEVATION GAIN: 1,100 feet.

WATER: bring your own.

SEASON: all—most likely to get fog-free oceanic views in the fall; springtime wildflowers; Alamere Falls is big enough to cascade over the bluffs in winter and spring.

MAP: Point Reyes National Seashore brochure or USGS topo Double Point. See p. 111.

INFORMATION: Point Reyes National Seashore, (415) 663-1092.

DIRECTIONS TO TRAILHEAD: From Highway 1, 8.6 miles south of the town of Olema or 4.1 miles north of Stinson Beach, turn west on an unsigned paved road (farther on, it's signed "Olema/Bolinas Road"). It's just north of Bolinas Lagoon, where a Golden Gate National Recreation Area sign sits next to a big white house on Highway 1's east side. Drive 1.8 miles on Olema/Bolinas Road, then turn right on Mesa Road. Travel another 3.5 miles, bear right where the pavement ends, then drive 1.3 miles to signed Palomarin Trailhead.

This varied hike perhaps best epitomizes the remote foothills, secluded shoreline, and rugged beauty of Point Reyes National Seashore. After all, it leads past three hilltop ponds, four freshwater lakes, and a waterfall in quest of isolated and wonderful Wildcat Beach, with lots of splendid oceanic views along the way.

This southernmost section of Point Reyes National Seashore is chock full of wildlife. From Double Point, watch for the California gray whale in wintertime and California brown pelicans and cormorants lodging on Stormy Stacks jutting just offshore. Harbor seals typically haul out on the bay's pocket beach, as well as Wildcat Beach. Over the inland sections of the Coastal Trail, peer into the sky for osprey, hawk, and falcon soaring overhead. Large bass lurk in the lakes, which are often cruised over by waterfowl.

Coast Trail, an old farm road, promptly reaches a tall eucalyptus grove, then remains mostly level over the initial mile, featuring sprawling views of the nearby ocean. After swinging inland past gulches, canyons, and terraces, you ascend to a signed trail fork at 2.2 miles. Continue left on Coast Trail, which now cuts through a mixed forest of Douglas fir, bishop pine, and occasional blue oak. Spur trails dart left to three freshwater ponds in this area.

Swimmable Bass Lake shows up a quarter mile past the third small pond, then a westward view down on Pelican Lake, perched on a blufftop at 3.2 miles. The scene is enhanced by the ocean appearing through a rock hillside archway. The ensuing half mile sports view after view of Pelican Lake's emerald-gray waters. A scant trail descends to this approximately 10-acre lake from the north side of it.

Just past this side trail, another spur trail leads a third of a mile west to Double Point's northernmost twin shale outcropping. If it's early in the year, you can admire Alamere Falls (Coast Trail takes you by it later) toppling over the cliff onto serene Wildcat Beach.

Retrace your steps and soon reach a signed trail junction at 4.9 miles next to abundant coyote brush and orange bush monkeyflower. Note the trail on the left (return route), then continue straight on Coast Trail for a 1.3-mile promenade to Wildcat Beach. Here, it's normal to think you're the first person to discover this pristine, secluded beach. With Stormy Stack and Double Point highlighting the scene to the south, sloping bluffs behind, and Arch Rock (Hike 38) punctuating the view to the north, Wildcat Beach makes for a sublime vista point.

Just inland, Wildcat Camp roosts on a meadow overlooking strikingly gorgeous Wildcat Beach (backpackers, get permit first at Bear Valley Visitor Center—reservations suggested). This large camp facility offers benches, tables, and a spring-fed water spigot. Kelham Beach (also Hike 38) can be reached by continuing on the view-filled Coast Trail for 3.5 miles along bluffs and hillsides decorated with coastal scrub.

To head back, double back to the north shore of Wildcat Lake, then take the lower loop trail. This slender footpath is less than a quarter mile from Wildcat Beach, promptly climbing to a cluster of perches featuring great views of the coastline. Yarrow and poppy flowers adorn trailside, but brace for poison oak and thistle to intrude in spots. Gain an eastward view of Wildcat Lake, then drop next to rush-lined Ocean Lake before retracing previous trails to your car.

The climb to Barnabe Peak yields some far-reaching views.

Hike 41

Devil's Gulch Creek to Barnabe Peak in Samuel P. Taylor State Park

LENGTH: 7.2 miles round-trip as described; 2.4 miles round-trip to Stairstep Falls.

DIFFICULTY: moderate to strenuous.

TOTAL ELEVATION GAIN: 1,300 feet.

WATER: available from Devil's Gulch Creek and Lagunitas Creek (purify); or bring your own.

SEASON: all—watch the spawning run of silver salmon up Lagunitas Creek in winter; early spring is best for admiring Stairstep Falls.

MAP: Samuel P. Taylor State Park map or USGS topo San Geronimo.

INFORMATION: Samuel P. Taylor State Park, (415) 488-9897.

DIRECTIONS TO TRAILHEAD: From the north side of Golden Gate Bridge on Highway 101 in San Rafael, take the Sir Francis Drake Boulevard exit. Keep going west on Sir Francis Drake Boulevard 13 miles past Samuel P. Taylor State Park main entrance. Park on the south side near Lagunitas (Papermill) Creek, 0.9 mile past the park entrance. From Olema on Highway 1, travel about 6 miles east on Sir Francis Drake Boulevard. The trailhead is located across the boulevard, behind the gate (the trail's paved at first).

Taking gentle footsteps under redwood trees and in rhythm with a peaceful creek is a fast way to totally relax and get in tune with nature. The stroll along merrily winding Devil's Gulch Creek fits the bill. To get the adrenaline up and the blood flow high, the ensuing climb through shaded forest does the trick. To touch the soul with views of rolling hills and steep canyons, the journey's climax at 1,466-foot-high Barnabe Peak is just what the psychologist ordered.

There are also plenty of sideshow bonuses on this epic trek. Taking in steeply cascading Stairstep Falls in the winter and spring is one of them. Watching the silver salmon spawn up Lagunitas (Papermill) Creek in early winter is another treat. There's a deep swimming hole less than a half mile southwest of the trailhead on Sir Francis Drake Boulevard that's ideal for checking out the annual salmon run. There are also some modest waterfalls nearby for witnessing the remarkable feat of these salmon somehow getting up them. Cross the bridge here and follow the footpath leading to the sites of the old papermill and dam in use in the late 1800s.

At the onset, this shaded excursion along Devil's Gulch Creek proceeds under tall redwoods and picturesque coast live oak. California bay laurel trees, some reaching 80 feet into the sky, and occasional red alder also canopy this peaceful perennial creek. Some ancient alders hover over the banks and carpets of sword ferns comprise the understory. The occasional shrubs consist mainly of coffeeberry and hazelnut.

The footpath eventually climbs out of the canyon, follows above one of Devil's Gulch Creek's tributaries, crosses a footbridge, then winds back to the signed trail junction with Stairstep Falls.

After 0.2 mile on this spur trail, you reach aptly named Stairstep

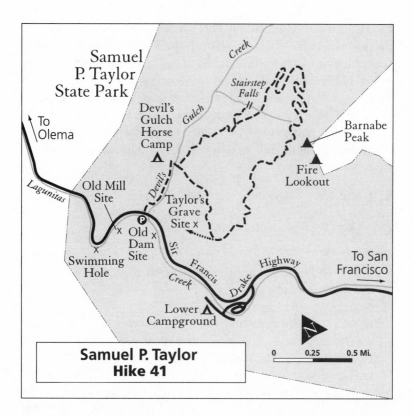

Samuel P. Taylor
State Park

To Olema

Devil's
Gulch
Horse
Camp

Gulch

Creek

Stairstep
Falls

Barnabe
Peak

Fire
Lookout

Lagunitas

Old Mill
Site

Devil's

Taylor's
Grave
Site

P

Old
Dam
Site

Swimming
Hole

Sir Francis

Creek

Drake Highway

To San
Francisco

Lower
Campground

N

**Samuel P. Taylor
Hike 41**

0   0.25   0.5 Mi.

Falls, which plunge 30 feet over dark, slick rock. The falls, splendidly powerful early in the year, are reduced to a mere trickle by late summer.

After doubling back, the main trail switchbacks up the hill through a dense hardwood forest of California bay laurel and bigleaf maple, with a few Douglas fir sprinkled in. After 2.5 miles of zigzags, climbing 1,100 feet in the process, you come to a grassy clearing, signed trail junction, and a superb view all at once. From here you can also see a fancy fire lookout station atop Barnabe Peak.

Climb the dirt road a quarter mile or so to snag Barnabe Peak and obtain even farther-reaching views, including the San Rafael area, Bolinas Ridge, Inverness Ridge, and portions of Tomales Bay, as well as Black Mountain to the north.

On a clear evening, especially with a full moon or near full moon, a romantic couple can treasure a precious sunset while strolling as lovers 2.5 miles down the old dirt service road. This return route drops elevation rapidly, past rolling and grassy hillsides—a stark contrast to the dense forest you climbed in on the protected north-facing slopes of Barnabe Peak. Face-first views of the rolling hills and sprawling redwood and fir forests linger long as you descend.

Veer right at the signed dirt road junction, and visit the grave site of the park's namesake, miner and mill owner Samuel P. Taylor. After that, continue right to return to Devil's Gulch Trail.

Hike 42

Bon Tempe and Alpine Lakes in the Mount Tamalpais Watershed

LENGTH: 6.8 miles round-trip as described; 2.8 miles round-trip to Alpine Lake.

DIFFICULTY: moderate.

TOTAL ELEVATION GAIN: 800 feet.

WATER: available from Bon Tempe and Alpine Lakes and East Fork Swede George Creek (purify); or bring your own.

SEASON: all—low lake levels in late summer reveal colorful shoreline; muddy sections on the Kent Trail after winter rains; wildflowers in spring.

MAP: Marin Municipal Water District brochure or USGS topo San Rafael.

INFORMATION: Sky Oaks Ranger Station at (415) 459-5267 or Marin Water District at (415) 924-4600.

DIRECTIONS TO TRAILHEAD: From San Rafael on Highway 101 (north of San Francisco), take the Sir Francis Drake Boulevard exit, then drive the short distance west to the town of Fairfax. Turn left on Claus Drive, then make an immediate left onto Broadway, followed by an immediate right onto Bolinas Drive. After 1.4 miles, go left onto Sky Oaks Road, then drive about 2 miles to the Lake Lagunitas parking lot.

Roaming this hike's four trails is like being in the midst of some gorgeous Tennessee wilderness. It's hard to figure that these lakes and

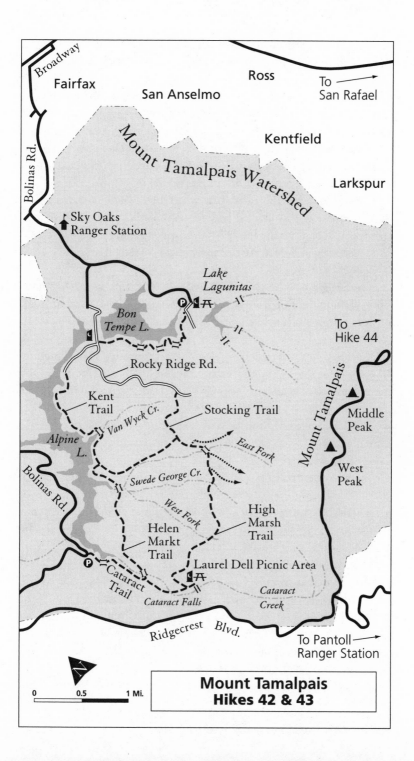

Broadway
Fairfax
San Anselmo
Ross
To San Rafael

Bolinas Rd.

Mount Tamalpais Watershed

Kentfield

Larkspur

Sky Oaks
Ranger Station

Lake
Lagunitas

Bon
Tempe L.

To
Hike 44

Rocky Ridge Rd.

Kent
Trail

Van Wyck Cr.

Stocking Trail

Alpine
L.

East Fork

Swede George Cr.

Mount Tamalpais

Middle
Peak

West
Peak

Bolinas Rd.

West Fork

Helen
Markt
Trail

High
Marsh
Trail

Laurel Dell Picnic Area

Cataract
Trail

Cataract Falls

Cataract
Creek

Ridgecrest   Blvd.

To Pantoll
Ranger Station

N

0   0.5   1 Mi.

Mount Tamalpais
Hikes 42 & 43

canyons tucked under the northwest flanks of mighty Mount Tamalpais are a mere 4 miles as the red-tailed hawk flies from the ocean's Bolinas Bay.

A grand journey features a wide variety of beauty and adventure, and this trek covering three reservoirs that supply water to Marin County citizens fits the bill. You'll be treated to generous views of Mount Tamalpais and Alpine and Bon Tempe Lakes, while wandering through grasslands, oak woodlands, dry chaparral, and moist forest to reach serpentine knolls and rugged ridgetops.

The diverse Mount Tamalpais watershed is a dynamic example of a unique environment. The lakes are periodically stocked with trout, which continually increases the osprey population. Foxes, bobcats, raccoons, and deer are numerous and coyotes are making a fast comeback.

To start, depart the scenic Lagunitas Lake Picnic Area, then head southwest on the Bon Tempe Trail, which provides an intimate look of Bon Tempe Lake while traversing up and down three of its small canyons.

At 1.4 miles the footpath reaches a three-way trail junction. Make note of Rocky Ridge Trail on the left (the return loop) and the Kent Trail straight ahead, then take a brief side trip to the right. This dirt road doubles as the dam road and the site for photos of Bon Tempe Lake with Mount Tamalpais looming above it. It's also the only place where you can admire Bon Tempe and Alpine Lakes up close, from one spot.

Back at the junction, get on Kent Trail, which is a dirt service road for half a mile, then a footpath. For a mile and a half, it weaves a remarkable route closely above Alpine Lake. You can't help but notice how oddly long and skinny Alpine Lake is. Unlike the nearby Pacific Ocean, Alpine Lake offers scarce shore access.

One minute you're stepping over rocks on the trail in sections of chaparral such as chamise, manzanita, ceanothus, and coyote brush, the next moment you're deep in a dark canyon. Here, the Douglas fir dominates over seasonal streambeds, with madrone and California bay laurel canopying California huckleberry shrubs. In other sections, oak woodlands take center stage, with perennial grass clumps interspersed between boulders.

At 2.8 miles, you reach the junction with Helen Markt Trail, which roams into redwoods above Alpine Lake for 1.6 miles to the Cataract Trail (Hike 43). Our trail now leaves Alpine Lake, continuing on the Kent Trail and commencing a vigorous climb of about 500 feet. The narrow footpath switches between the pristine riparian habitat of East Fork Swede George Creek and peaceful Douglas fir forest for nearly a mile to often unsigned Stocking Trail (take the first left).

The brief stint on this trail covers some serpentine rock sections before coming to Rocky Ridge Road Trail. Continuing straight shortens the hike by 1.8 miles. For sheer beauty and extra adventure, head left on the Rocky Ridge Trail for nice lake and surrounding forest views. It eventually reunites with Bon Tempe Lake, providing another chance to appreciate its charm while traveling in the opposite direction to the trailhead.

Hike 43

Cataract Falls and High Marsh Trail in the Mount Tamalpais Watershed

LENGTH: 7 miles round-trip as described; 2.4 miles round-trip to Cataract Falls.

DIFFICULTY: strenuous.

TOTAL ELEVATION GAIN: 1,500 feet.

WATER: available from Cataract Creek and East Fork Swede George Creek (purify); bring lots of your own.

SEASON: all—the falls can be a trickle in autumn, or a roaring powerhouse in the winter and spring; slick spots after a winter rain.

MAP: Marin Municipal Water District brochure, Mount Tamalpais State Park brochure or USGS topos Bolinas and San Rafael. See p. 121.

INFORMATION: Marin Municipal Water District, (415) 924-4600; or Mount Tamalpais State Park, (415) 388-2070.

DIRECTIONS TO TRAILHEAD: From San Rafael on Highway 101 (north of San Francisco), take the Sir Francis Drake Boulevard exit and make the short drive west into the town of Fairfax. Turn left on Claus Drive, then make an immediate left onto Broadway, followed by an immediate right onto scenic Bolinas Drive. Travel 8.2 steep and winding miles, cross Alpine Lake's dam, then park on the side of the road at the hairpin turn.

The thing that makes Mount Tamalpais so mighty is its series of ravines, ridges, and deep woods that seem magical when a hiker is enraptured in them. Among the seemingly countless trails that explore its lush slopes, this hike's four trails include the most gorgeous scenery, varied countryside, and major place-names of all.

It's truly the ultimate walk in the wild woods, where about the only things you don't encounter are fairies and elves. But you will associate with majestic redwoods, Mount Tam's most magnificent waterfall, dark canyons, hawk's-eye views of Bon Tempe and Alpine Lakes, and lots more.

The signed Cataract Trail commences a gentle climb, overlooking a slender and scenic arm of Alpine Lake. The shade is furnished courtesy of a mixed conifer and hardwood forest of redwood, tan oak, hazelnut, and bigleaf maple. Soon the well-built trail veers up and away from the lake, then the climb intensifies as patches of ferns and thickets of California huckleberry join the dense woods.

As you wander deeper into these wild yet soothing woods, make note of the Helen Markt Trail (at 0.6 mile) on the left (your return loop).

About a half mile farther along Cataract Creek, the ears sense the roar of Cataract Falls. The sound intensifies as the canyon steepens. The huge live oaks are so sheltered here, their trunks are draped with mosses and tiny ferns, rendering a mystic fairytale setting. An unsigned spur trail brings you up close to the falls, which are actually a series of cascades. Often in late fall, they continue to spill, slide, and plummet over smooth and slippery boulders into a cluster of puddles and pools. In the spring, these cascades are white with rushing water, so loud and powerful the human voice gets drowned out.

Nearby Laurel Dell picnic area at 1.5 miles makes for another ideal hangout spot. It's a large clearing, surrounded by handsome and stately live oak, Douglas fir, California bay laurel, and bigleaf maple trees at creekside (there are even tables and restrooms here).

To reach High Marsh Trail, depart Laurel Dell picnic site by retracing your steps northwest for a couple hundred yards along the main trail. Bear right at the "Y" trail junction and promptly break into a grassy clearing overlooking a grove of Douglas firs. The outline of Ridgecrest Boulevard (one of the most scenic country drives along the Northern California coast) can be traced along the distant grassy ridgetop to the southwest.

The High Marsh Trail keeps climbing, snaking above and then around two wooded canyons, then crests at a vantage point next to manzanita shrubs, featuring stunning views of San Pablo Bay.

The woodsy canyon hopping continues to a ridgetop, featuring a photogenic view of Bon Tempe Lake (see Hike 42). The trail then boldly penetrates into an otherwise impenetrable chaparral thicket of manzanita, ceanothus, toyon, and chamise. Soon the trail drops to and crosses a rocky stream, then continues its descent into a Douglas fir forest. Be sure to go left at the next four, often unsigned trail junctions (two before and two after the crossing of East Fork Swede George Creek).

Kent Trail drops and winds in the direction of Alpine Lake, alternating between dense forest and serene riparian habitat along East Fork Swede George Creek, which is within earshot and eyeshot much of the course.

When you get to just above Alpine Lake, there's a trail junction. A right turn stays on Kent Trail and reveals stunning closeup aerials of Alpine Lake (Hike 42) through wooded canyons and rocky chaparral sections. Our loop goes left onto Helen Markt Trail for nice but farther away views above a slimmer section of the lake, through redwood groves.

Hike 44
Mount Tamalpais—Rock Springs Trail to East Peak

LENGTH: 8.4 miles round-trip; 2.4 miles round trip to Mountain Theatre; 4.5 miles round-trip to Westpoint Inn.
DIFFICULTY: moderate.
TOTAL ELEVATION GAIN: 1,400 feet.
WATER: from faucets at Pantoll, Mountain Theatre and East Peak parking area.

SEASON: all year, muddy trail sections in winter.
MAP: State Park map or USGS topo San Rafael.
INFORMATION: Marin Municipal Water District, (415) 924-4600, or Mount Tamalpais State Park, (415) 388-2070.
DIRECTIONS TO TRAILHEAD: Take the Muir Woods/Mount Tamalpais exit off Highway 101 (5 miles north of the Golden Gate Bridge). Drive west for 3 miles on Highway 1, then turn right onto Panoramic Highway. Follow all the "Mount Tamalpais" signs on 6 winding but well-paved miles to Pantoll Ranger Station. Or, from Stinson Beach on Highway 1, turn east on Panoramic Highway then drive 3.8 miles to the Pantoll parking area. If it's packed (summer weekends), consider driving another 4 miles to Mount Tamalpais summit and doing this hike in reverse.

This hike invites you to take in a little theatre (Mountain Theatre) and visit an old inn (Westpoint) on the way to the tippy top of 2,571-foot Mount Tamalpais East Peak. Three trails climb gently to take you there, and the views keep varying of bays, islands, urban areas, and ocean.

Botany-minded individuals can have a field day on the slopes of biologically rich and diverse Mount Tamalpais. Comprised of a mix of open grasslands, steep canyons, and hardwood forests, the mountain is home to 12 species of oaks. Most coastal spots feature only a couple kinds of oaks. Mount Tamalpais hosts a number of hybrid oaks you're apt to see but may not identify, including the cross between interior live oak and black oak, the park's most common hybrid. A rare oak, *Quercus parvula* variety *tamalpaisensis* (a small tree), was discovered here in 1991.

You begin the journey on the Old Mine Trail along a hillside of small coast live oaks that canopy oatgrass and allow sweeping views of the sea and San Francisco Bay. You soon reach Mountain Theatre, featuring seat rows built from metamorphosed rocks. Check ahead for early summer plays, performed at this outdoor masterpiece theatre since 1913.

From here pick up Rock Springs Trail and spend the first half mile in dense shade with ferns and lots of California bay laurel, crossing three wooden bridges. Just over 2 miles into the trip,

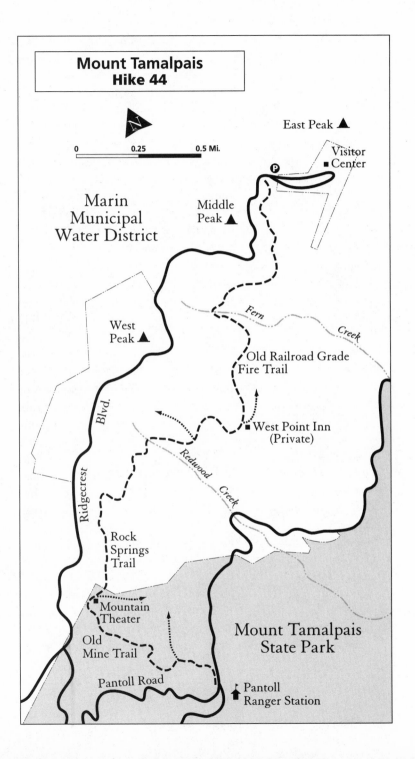

Mount Tamalpais
Hike 44

N

0	0.25	0.5 Mi.	

East Peak ▲

Visitor
■ Center

Ⓟ

Marin
Municipal
Water District

Middle
Peak ▲

West
Peak ▲

Fern

Creek

Old Railroad Grade
Fire Trail

Blvd.

West Point Inn
(Private)

Ridgecrest

Redwood   Creek

Rock
Springs
Trail

Mountain
Theater

Old
Mine Trail

Mount Tamalpais
State Park

Pantoll Road

Pantoll
Ranger Station

Westpoint Inn can be spotted tucked into the forest and framed by Angel Island and the Golden Gate Bridge.

Wander over and check out this stately stone lodge, a walk-in establishment that serves as shelter from a rainstorm. Find the signed Old Railroad Grade Fire Road Trail near this architecturally impressive and long-deserted structure, and continue the gradual climb.

Trailside is now decorated by the summer-flowering sticky orange monkeyflower bushes. The views eastward stay stupendous past a wooden water storage tank on the left. Admire San Pablo Bay and Mount Diablo, and be sure to stop at the sign noting Westpoint Inn at 3.6 miles, where a graceful Douglas fir showcases the Bay Bridge, towering skyscrapers, and Alcatraz Island.

The old dirt road stays mostly level over the final haul, as thick and dry chaparral disperses the frequently fierce north winds in your face. A variety of oaks, some Douglas fir, and yerba santa shrubs decorate the sweeping vistas now westward to the Pacific Ocean. When you reach the rusty gate, it's decision time. The summit parking lot is 0.1 mile east, where your shuttle car could be. If there's no transportation arranged, you can retreat right here or fish into your pocket or daypack for some change to buy snacks at the nearby snack bar. Plan on climbing 400 feet over the 0.4-mile path of embedded rocks to Mount Tamalpais East Peak.

From atop any of its clusters of big boulders, you can peer down on the shiny Pacific Ocean to the south. Turn your head counterclockwise and count the sailboats cruising San Francisco Bay, with its skyscraper backdrop. Mount Diablo dominates to the east, fronted by the Richmond Bridge over San Pablo Bay.

East Peak Summit's a good place to ponder what the Miwok tribe saw in the same views long ago. The Miwok Indians frequently visited Mount Tamalpais, surviving on shellfish, birds, and acorns from the prominent coast live oak.

The mountain itself was born when tectonic plates collided dramatically. The westward-moving North American plate clashed with the eastward-moving Farallon plate, heaving up seafloor rocks to create the chaotic jumble atop Tamalpais. The majority of rocks you're walking and sitting on consist of radiolarian chert, serpentine, sandstone, or quartz.

Hike 45

Stinson Beach, Dipsea, Steep Ravine, and Matt Davis Trails in Mount Tamalpais State Park

LENGTH: 6.8 miles round-trip.

DIFFICULTY: moderate to strenuous.

TOTAL ELEVATION GAIN: 1,500 feet.

WATER: available from Webb Creek (purify); Pantoll Ranger Station; or bring your own.

SEASON: all—grasslands wildflowers in spring; most likely to get best views in the autumn; slick trail spots in winter after a hard rain.

MAP: Mount Tamalpais State Park brochure or USGS topos San Rafael and Bolinas. See p. 127.

INFORMATION: Mount Tamalpais State Park, (415) 388-2070.

DIRECTIONS TO TRAILHEAD: From Highway 101 north of San Francisco, take the Stinson Beach exit (Highway 1). Continue to Stinson Beach, noting the signed Dipsea Trail at the intersection of Shoreline and Panoramic Highways, a few seconds prior to parking.

Wondrous Webb Creek sports a bounty of cathedral-like redwoods, qualifying it as one of the most fantastic streams along the Northern California coast. This hike's Steep Ravine Trail covers perhaps the most splendid section of this explosive yet peaceful creek.

The annual Dipsea Trail foot race has transformed the Dipsea Trail into a legend. But this hike's segment of the Dipsea Trail graduates from legendary to spectacular. It climbs through coastal scrub and grasslands blanketed with wildflowers in spring, displaying staggering and sweeping views of Stinson Beach and the ocean.

Three miles of the Matt Davis Trail are featured in this hike, the part with all the sensational, tree-framed views of the ocean. The well-made footpath averages 500 feet of descent per mile, providing a dramatic plunge toward the ocean.

Colorful and popular Stinson Beach lures beach drifters because of its long, wide sand strip and fine, rolling surf. An ideal way to cap this hefty hike is to spend hang time on this recreational beach.

The journey climbs two-thirds of the way up Mount Tamalpais, which is commonly mistaken for the remains of an extinct volcano. Instead, world-renowned Mount Tamalpais has been uplifted gradually by an ongoing process of folding and buckling within the earth's crust.

The coastal Miwok Indians who lived in the area for thousands of years furnished the mountain's namesake, which means, in Spanish, "the country of the Tamal Indians."

In 1896, construction of the "crookedest railroad in the world" began, and soon made Mount Tamalpais world famous. This railroad took tourists on a twisting and turning journey 8 miles to the summit from Mill Valley. The railroad era ended when the 1929 wildfire raged over the mountain, ruining most of the line.

At the onset, Dipsea Trail climbs briefly in shaded woods, breaking into coastal scrub highlighted by orange bush monkeyflower and lizard's-tail shrubs. As it traverses the slope, Dipsea Trail cuts through grassland sections that are green and dotted with poppies, lupines, and blue-eyed grass in the spring; soft yellow and brown in the late summer. As the climb continues, catch your breath with the breathtaking views of Stinson Beach and the ocean close behind.

Just beyond an unsigned dirt road, go left onto Steep Ravine Trail down at Webb Creek, 1.3 miles into the hike. Five wooden bridges take you across this shaded creek, which flows smoothly in spots and wildly in others. In the roaring parts, cascades glide over big boulders. The currents often glide gracefully into calm and cozy pools. Duck beneath numerous toppled redwood archways and eventually climb a 15-rung ladder. Large redwoods dominate the forest, towering over abundant sword fern and thimbleberry. The climb culminates at Pantoll Ranger Station at 3.4 miles, where you cross Panoramic Highway and commence a delightful descent to the ocean on the Matt Davis Trail. A mixed evergreen forest mainly of California bay laurel and Douglas fir leads to a crossing of a seasonal creek at 1.2 miles. While admiring glorious views of San Francisco Bay to the south, listen for the loud party sounds of the raucous Steller jays here, and watch for woodpeckers.

Continue straight at a signed trail junction 0.1 mile farther, then climb the nearby bare knoll for a sweeping vista of bay and sea.

Toward the end of a gorgeous grove of California bay laurel, go left at another signed trail junction. A bit farther sword fern and coast live oaks join the forest, followed by the harmonious hum of the ocean and Table Creek at trailside.

After a brief chaparral section, the trail drops into Wooded Gulch and soon ends at a paved street. To reach Stinson Beach, take the downhill roads at all street junctions.

Hike 46

Fern Creek and Ocean View Trails in Muir Woods

LENGTH: 4 miles round-trip.
DIFFICULTY: moderate.
TOTAL ELEVATION GAIN: 800 feet.
WATER: available from fountains near information stand.
SEASON: all—far fewer people on a winter weekday.
MAP: Muir Woods National Monument map or USGS topo San Rafael.
INFORMATION: Muir Woods, (415) 388-2596.
DIRECTIONS TO TRAILHEAD: From Highway 101 just north of San Francisco's Golden Gate Bridge, take the Highway 1 exit, then turn left on Shoreline Highway. After 2.5 miles, go right onto the Panoramic Highway. Travel 0.8 mile, then turn left on the lower road signed "Muir Woods." It's 1.5 miles to the parking lot. If it's full, park in permitted areas along the road below the main parking lot and annex parking lot.

All creeks are beautiful; some happen to be more outstanding, such as Fern Creek. It's a case of a good thing coming in a small package. This petite creek flows smoothly from a steep, wooded canyon into a sheltered valley floor full of immense redwoods. The journey starts along aptly named Redwood Creek at the bottom of this valley, darts up enchanting Fern Creek, passes through great groves of redwoods, and then eventually reaches a high spot near Panoramic Highway featuring ocean views.

Join the many interested visitors along the interpretive trail section covering the first quarter mile of this hike. The redwood grove here along Redwood Creek is among the largest and most gorgeous anywhere. The throngs of tourists virtually vanish in thin air the instant you embark on the Fern Trail, which promptly goes into a grove of tall redwoods (including a huge Douglas fir called Kent Memorial). These redwoods along with tanbark oak reach high into the sky, as this stream-hugging trail snakes up rocky-bottomed Fern Creek.

At 1.2 miles, the footpath comes to a long wooden bridge, where you begin climbing on the Lost Trail (bear right). After a few inspirational vistas down into the lush environs of Fern Creek, Lost Trail veers up and away and into a dark, peaceful, and primeval forest of California bay laurel and redwood.

After ascending several flights of wooden stairsteps, coast live oak and Douglas fir join the woodsy scene. After a half mile's worth of the quadriceps boogie on Lost Trail, the main climb eases as you come to a three-way signed trail junction (note the return loop on the right).

With all that climbing out of the way, why not invest in less than half a mile's worth of easy climbing to a cluster of hiker's vista points just below the Panoramic Highway? The far-reaching views encompass the ocean and a sea of redwoods.

To complete the loop, go back down the Ocean View Trail, also known as the Panoramic Trail. Although there are no more views, you drop in and out of two gulches lined with tall, thin redwoods. The mostly shaded trail descends moderately via switchbacks in woods highlighted by a few monster Douglas firs.

If you desire more beautiful creek hiking nearby, take a look at Hike 47, which explores Redwood Creek to Van Wyck Meadow.

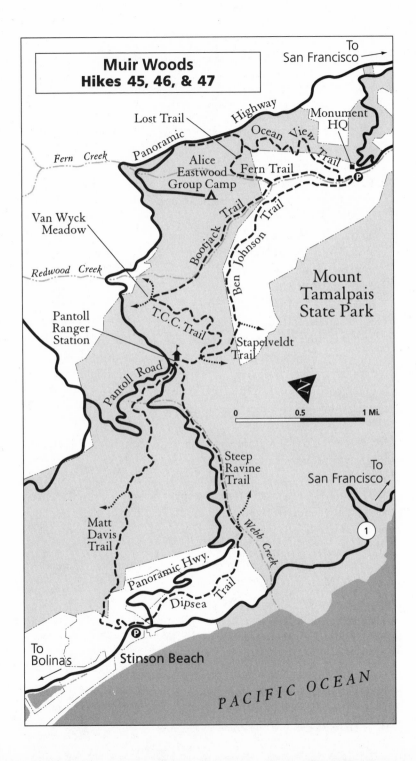

Muir Woods
Hikes 45, 46, & 47

Lost Trail

Highway

Panoramic

Ocean View Trail

Monument HQ

Fern Creek

Alice Eastwood Group Camp

Fern Trail

Van Wyck Meadow

Bootjack Trail

Ben Johnson Trail

Redwood Creek

Mount Tamalpais State Park

Pantoll Ranger Station

T.C.C. Trail

Stapelveldt Trail

Pantoll Road

N

0   0.5   1 Mi.

Steep Ravine Trail

To San Francisco

Matt Davis Trail

Webb Creek

Panoramic Hwy.

Dipsea Trail

To Bolinas

Stinson Beach

To San Francisco

1

PACIFIC OCEAN

Hike 47

Redwood Creek and Van Wyck Meadow in Muir Woods

LENGTH: 6 miles round-trip as described; 2 miles round-trip on the paved and level Main Trail.

DIFFICULTY: moderate.

TOTAL ELEVATION GAIN: 1,100 feet.

WATER: available from fountains at onset of hike.

SEASON: all—fewer people on winter weekdays; slick spots on the trails after a hard winter rain.

MAP: Muir Woods National Monument brochure or USGS topo San Rafael. See p. 133.

INFORMATION: Muir Woods, (415) 388-2596.

DIRECTIONS TO TRAILHEAD: From Highway 101 just north of San Francisco's Golden Gate Bridge, take the Highway 1 exit, then turn left on Shoreline Highway. After 2.5 miles, go right onto the Panoramic Highway. Travel 0.8 mile, then turn left on the lower road signed Muir Woods. It's 1.5 miles to the parking lot. If it's full, park in permitted areas along the road below the main and annex parking lots.

The Bay Area has few stands of large redwoods, but the protected old-growth redwoods in Muir Woods are not only the area's biggest by far, they're among the tallest groves in the San Francisco Bay Area.

This hike shows them off in two splendid ways—you'll seem so small as they loom over you along mystic Redwood Creek, but later you'll feel privileged peering down on a green cloth of those same redwoods.

Proclaimed a national monument by President Theodore Roosevelt, Muir Woods, at the insistence of William Kent, who donated the redwood canyon, was named after naturalist and writer John Muir. A famous conservationist who founded the Sierra Club, Muir raised the country's awareness of the importance of America's untouched natural areas such as Muir Woods.

It's hard to figure that the first section of the hike along Redwood

Creek is clogged with tourists, but once you cross the fourth bridge, solitude and tranquillity are virtually guaranteed. This is where the paved Muir Woods Main Trail suddenly becomes a well-made footpath called Bootjack Trail, which spirited souls take to unwind, recover, and reflect in a deep redwood forest.

To get there, you must take the mile-long Main Trail, which features wooden fences bordering noble and primeval redwoods along Redwood Creek. Helpful signposts contain interesting text about these graceful giants, including info on redwood burls, fire resistance, their ancient history, and much more. The brochure available at the trailhead provides lots more redwood info. Be sure to visit William Kent Memorial, which is a 273-foot-tall Douglas fir, the tallest tree in Muir Woods, located on the Fern Creek Trail (Hike 46).

Bootjack Trail is all about a sheltered redwood forest, a refreshingly secluded stretch of Redwood Creek, and serenity. The main sound you'll hear is the steady and comforting splash of the tumbling creek, which originates from along the upper flank of Mount Tamalpais's west peak.

After crossing a large wooden bridge, Bootjack Trail soon ascends steeply in deep Doug fir woods, with bracken and sword ferns decorating trailside beneath bigleaf maples. The trail reunites with Redwood Creek at a bouldery section at 1.9 miles, then climbs 0.4 mile farther to a grassy clearing called Van Wyck Meadow. A huge boulder stands out there, and it's fun to climb on. Coast live oak, California bay laurel, and Douglas fir ring this small meadow, which is a nice spot for a picnic.

The journey continues, departing Van Wyck Meadow with a left turn onto TCC Trail, which was built during World War I by the Tamalpais Conservation Club. It furnishes teasing peeps of Mount Tamalpais beyond low-hanging Douglas fir limbs as it stays mostly level and shaded across a series of quiet canyonsides.

At 3.7 miles a wooden bench and bridge signal two successive left turns onto the Stapelveldt Trail. During the descent, look for the pair of huge toppled redwoods forming an archway over the trail.

A couple hundred yards farther, go left onto Ben Johnson Trail, where you may hear the yacking Steller jay or perhaps the loud, barking call of a spotted owl, especially at dusk.

After about a mile of gradual descent, bear right onto the signed Hillside Trail. This level path treats you to several vistas overlooking the towering old-growth redwoods over Redwood Creek and the tourists, looking like slow-moving ants along the paved main trail below.

Hike 48

Muir Beach, Tennessee Beach, and Rodeo Beach on the Coastal Trail

LENGTH: 11 miles round-trip as described; 5.5 miles one way to Rodeo Beach if car shuttle is arranged; 6 miles round-trip to Tennessee Beach; 3.6 miles round-trip to Pirate's Cove.

DIFFICULTY: strenuous.

TOTAL ELEVATION GAIN: 2,800 feet.

WATER: Muir Beach faucets; bring a half gallon if you're doing the whole thing.

SEASON: all—more likely to get better views in the fall; the endless rolling hills are coated with green grasses and sprinkled with wildflowers in early spring.

MAP: Golden Gate National Recreation Area map or USGS topo Point Bonita.

INFORMATION: Golden Gate National Recreation Area at (415) 556-0560 or Marin Headlands at (415) 331-1540.

DIRECTIONS TO TRAILHEAD: From Highway 101 north of San Francisco's Golden Gate Bridge, take the Highway 1 exit, then turn left on the Shoreline Highway (also Highway 1). Follow it west all the way to the signed Muir Beach entrance and park in the huge lot. To reach Rodeo Beach (to be picked up), take the Alexander Avenue exit if going north just beyond the Golden Gate Bridge on Highway 101. If going south on Highway 101, take the exit signed for Rodeo Beach. Follow all signs indicating Marin Headlands and/or Rodeo Beach. The roads are Conzelman Road, McCullough Road, and Bunker Road, in that order.

In commerce and even in the outdoors, usually you get what you pay for. In the case of this epic endeavor up and down grassy hills to reach prime beaches, the big payment comes from your sweat, adrenaline, and heavy legs. Come braced for exertion, and you'll reap special rewards, like the privilege of looking down on breathtakingly beautiful beaches.

It takes energy to make energy—you'll smilingly know this on getting energized time after time after capping another exhausting hill revealing another award-winning coastal view.

The adventure begins at one of the Bay Area's most popular beaches, Muir Beach. It climaxes at another of the Bay Area's most popular beaches, Rodeo Beach. Along the way, there's the exciting discoveries of a few secretive and unnamed beaches.

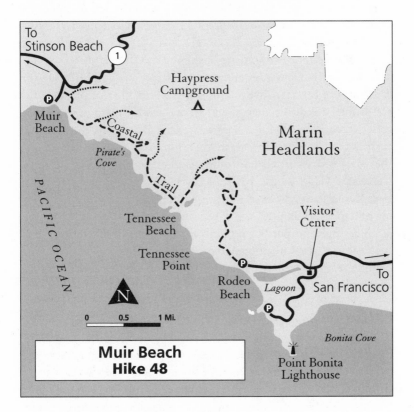

Much-visited Tennessee Beach is more or less the midpoint of the hike, and an excellent spot for a picnic. The glorious Tennessee Valley that drains into this beach is steep, photogenic, and well known, even way back in history. The steamship *Tennessee,* with 600 passengers aboard, was abandoned on a foggy night in 1853. It ran aground in the cove that encases Tennessee Beach, and the surf gradually blasted the ship to bits.

Coastal Trail begins as a dirt service road that promptly climbs to a knoll. From here the good views are mainly behind, of Muir Beach, its nearby moist pastures and looming Mount Tamalpais in the distance. Coyote Ridge and Green Gulch just east are also in full view.

From a westernmost overlook at an unsigned trail junction at 0.8 mile (our trail goes right), a sightseer gains a panorama of the aforementioned scenes plus Pirate's Cove down to the south. For now, Coastal Trail becomes a well-graded footpath, escorting you past a virtually undisturbed coastal scrub area partially covered with coyote brush, bush lupine, and orange bush monkeyflower.

The pristine views down the steep coastal scrub hillside into the rocky surf of Pirate's Cove (a spur trail leads to it before reaching the cove's inlet stream) are virtually continuous for about a mile. The trail descends briefly inland, crosses Pirate Cove's tiny inlet stream, then descends westward to another spur trail leading directly to the cove and its small and sandy pocket beach. This spot rivals Tennessee Cove in the beauty-and-views department. In fact, it bests Tennessee Cove overall because you're apt to have this secluded cove all to yourself.

A serious and persistent climb ensues from here (600 feet over half a mile), eased by ongoing ocean views and a cooling, soothing sea breeze. At 2.3 miles, a multiple trail junction is reached on a flat near a vista.

As Frank Sinatra used to croon, "the best is yet to come." The slender footpath hugs the extremely steep bluffs, and every precious step is a top-of-the-world experience. Have plenty of film on hand, especially for shooting the stark and rocky cliffs with San Francisco as a backdrop, as well as Tennessee Cove and Pirate's Cove shots.

The views down on Tennessee Valley and its lagoon are also a treasure to behold. It's best to check out all four promontories before descending steeply past poison oak down to brown and sandy

Tennessee Valley. The ridge in the distance must be climbed to get to Rodeo Beach.

Tennessee Beach. There's a secret, inaccessible beach highlighted by chocolate-brown sand, to be looked down on just before the final drop onto Tennessee Beach.

Our trail veers inland past Tennessee Valley Lagoon and soon begins a hill climb southward that makes this hike's past couple of climbs seem wimpy by comparison. Toward the top, there are clusters of wind-stunted conifers and a handful of bunkers built around World War II.

The panorama around here is so amazing, you may wish the world would temporarily turn into one of those sci-fi movies where time stands still, leaving you stranded in an envious and treasured spot. It all unfolds before your eyes—the vast blue sea, Rodeo Beach and its lagoon, Golden Gate Bridge, Mount Tamalpais, and Tennessee Valley.

The remainder of the journey is spent dawdling down the Coastal Trail, past Battery Townsley (scurry up nearby Tennessee Point to see more secluded beaches).

Hike 49

Back Ranch Meadows and Ridge Trails
in China Camp State Park

LENGTH: 6.4 miles round-trip as described; 4.6 miles round-trip if side trip to Bay Hills Trail is bypassed.

DIFFICULTY: moderate to strenuous.

TOTAL ELEVATION GAIN: 1,000 feet.

WATER: none; bring your own.

SEASON: all—slick spots on trails after a heavy winter rain.

MAP: China Camp State Park brochure or USGS topo San Quentin.

INFORMATION: China Camp State Park, (415) 456-0766.

DIRECTIONS TO TRAILHEAD: First drive to San Rafael, which is north of San Francisco on Highway 101. Take the North San Pedro Road exit, drive 3.3 miles, then park on the right side of the road near the trail signs.

The hustle and bustle of city life is mere miles away, but when you're deep in the quiet woods this view-filled hike offers, urbanization is fast forgotten. San Pablo Bay, San Francisco Bay's southerly neighbor, looks its absolute best from vantage points along China Camp State Park's most remote reaches, which is what this backcountry journey covers.

Nearby China Camp was once a thriving shrimp-fishing village run by the Chinese in the Gold Rush days. Interpretive exhibits now tell of their toils and way of life, and several ramshackle buildings still standing are now over a hundred years old.

The first 0.2 mile is spent traipsing in grassy Back Ranch Meadows, featuring sovereign valley oaks. A pair of 20-foot-tall buckeye trees and a massive California bay laurel shrub adorn the first signed trail junction at a quarter of a mile. A scattered grove of blue oak trees dots the slope on the left between another trail junction (bear left) a bit farther.

The Shoreline Trail, a well-trodden footpath, ascends gently in a hardwood forest of live oak, laurel, black oak, madrone, and toyon. At 0.7 mile, you come to a badly eroded clearing, where a steep climb

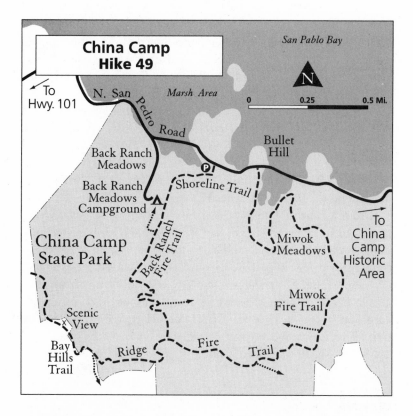

China Camp
Hike 49

San Pablo Bay

To Hwy. 101

N. San Pedro Road

Marsh Area

N

0   0.25   0.5 Mi.

Back Ranch Meadows

Bullet Hill

P

Back Ranch Meadows Campground

Shoreline Trail

China Camp State Park

Back Ranch Fire Trail

Miwok Meadows

To China Camp Historic Area

Scenic View

Miwok Fire Trail

Bay Hills Trail

Ridge   Fire   Trail

to the left promptly issues onto the Back Ranch Fire Trail above and beyond the campground (which was on the right). Manzanita shrubs now appear intermittently in sunny sections of this old dirt road, joining the aforementioned list of trees and shrubs that comprise the interior forest.

After making a right and then a left turn, the trail climbs 0.3 mile farther beneath the filtered shade of handsome live oak and madrone specimens. At the signed junction with the Ridge Fire Trail beneath a trio of large eucalyptus trees, venture right to access a top-of-the-world panorama. In less than a mile you reach an old Nike missile site, with views of Mount Tamalpais to the west, San Pablo Bay to the east, and Mount Diablo and Angel Island (Hike 50) to the southeast. By scanning the vast woods and bays, it's easy to picture how the Miwok thrived for centuries on fish, acorns, and land animals before the Spanish explorers settled here in the 1800s.

After retracing your steps back to the junction with the Back Ranch Trail, continue straight on the signed Ridge Fire Trail to complete the loop. You soon reach a clearing featuring a spectacular view of the merging point of San Pablo and San Francisco Bays, including the Richmond, Golden Gate, and Bay Bridges.

A steep climb immediately follows to another clearing where a 200-yard-long spur trail darts to the right to reveal a sprawling view of the previously mentioned bays and bridges. From this chaparral flat, a voyeur can gaze down on the steep and lushly vegetated canyon into the tiny community of Glenwood. Chamise shrubs grow to 8 feet here, and toyon reaches 18 feet high.

From a bench 0.2 mile farther on the Ridge Fire Trail, you're treated to an eastward vista of San Pablo Bay and its shore-hugging marshlands, which stretch and curve for miles. After a brief but extremely steep descent past eucalyptus, another bench displays a more revealing scene of marshlands and bay framed by two madrones.

Once on the signed Miwok Fire Trail, continue the descent while admiring northward views of San Pablo Bay, ignoring all other trails. To celebrate the journey, consider a picnic near the small pond at Miwok Meadows before walking the short distance to your car.

Hike 50

Angel Island—Perimeter Trail and Mount Livermore

LENGTH: 7 miles round-trip to Mount Livermore as described; 5 miles round-trip by skipping Mount Livermore and staying on Perimeter Trail.

DIFFICULTY: moderate.

TOTAL ELEVATION GAIN: 800 feet.

WATER: available from fountains along Perimeter Trail; or bring your own.

SEASON: all—most likely to get best bay views in the fall.

MAP: Angel Island State Park brochure or USGS topo San Francisco North.

INFORMATION: Angel Island State Park, (415) 435-1915 or (415) 456-1286.

DIRECTIONS TO TRAILHEAD: Take the ferry to Ayala Cove at

Angel Island from Tiburon, (415) 435-2131. From Highway
101 north of the Golden Gate Bridge, drive north to Marin,
then head east on Tiburon Boulevard (also Highway 131).
After 4 miles, park at one of the pay lots, then walk the short
distance to the Tiburon Ferry. Ferry boats also leave from
San Francisco and Vallejo to Angel Island: Call 1 (800)-BAY-
CRUISE.

The ultimate way to know San Francisco Bay up close is to gaze on
it from all directions while on Angel Island. On a clear day, even a
snapshot of the bay from this enchanted island tends to look like a
beautiful postcard.

The Bay Area's biggest island is also so historically rich (with constant examples along the hike), you may ask yourself if maybe you've
been here in a previous life. Perhaps during a 2,000-year span as a

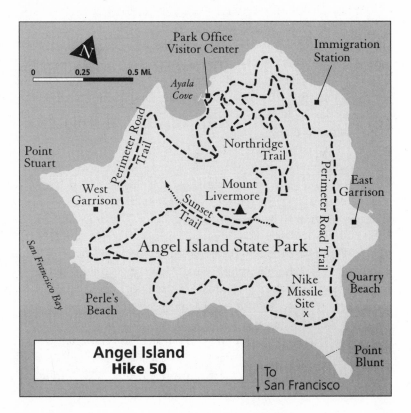

Miwok Indian, reaching the island with boats made of tule reeds to hunt, fish, or gather buckeyes and acorns. Or perhaps in 1775 as one of Juan Manuel de Ayala's Spanish sailors who anchored in Ayala Cove to record the first known maps of the bay. Or maybe even the early 1900s when major military installations and operations were developed. In 1905, North Garrison was converted to a controversial Immigration Station, where immigrants (97 percent from Asia) were processed, sometimes in inhumane fashion.

Shorebirds such as pelicans and blue herons swoop over the multiple-cove island for brief visits. Robins, scrub jays, sparrows, hummingbirds, flickers, owls, and hawks hang out indefinitely or live on the island. Many hikers wonder how some land animals such as deer and raccoons wound up on the island while others commonly found in Marin County woodlands such as squirrels, skunks, opossums, foxes, and coyotes are notably absent.

The signed Northridge Trail takes off to the left and ascends steeply as a footpath, with wooden boards improving the footing and easing the climb. Sturdy and youthful coast live oaks native to the island and windswept Monterey pines (native to Point Lobos—see Hike 70—and planted here by the military) join native giant toyon shrubs along this 200-foot climb. Sailboats gliding across San Francisco Bay highlight the view to the north with the San Rafael Bridge in the distance.

Mostly paved Perimeter Road Trail (turn left) stays flat most of the way and soon leads to lushly landscaped North Garrison, where cedars and eucalyptus trees hover above the neighborhood-like setting of large military structures. A bit farther, note the three-story-high hospital minus the window glass, built for 70 beds in 1911. Here U.S. military men with lingering tropical diseases were cared for and treated. From here the Bay Bridge is visible over some decrepit military barracks. A nearby grove of old Monterey cypresses partially shield the architecturally fancy quarters that once housed the officers.

A spur trail here leads down to wind-protected Quarry Beach, a half-mile strip of sand suitable for sand castle building and picnicking. A bit farther on the Perimeter Trail sits East Garrison, which consists of tall, sturdy structures used as barracks, mess halls, and a hospital. At one time, East Garrison trained some 30,000 military men per year for overseas duty.

The south face of Angel Island was once covered by immense stands of eucalyptus planted by the military. The bad news is that it'll take a long time for the island's native trees and shrubs (coast live oak, madrone, toyon, chamise, manzanita, and coyote brush) to return to lush status. The good news is the breathtakingly wide-open views of Alcatraz Island, with San Francisco looking like the Wizard's Emerald City behind it.

Sunset Trail takes off near a vantage point overlooking Perle's Beach (more on that later) and climbs relentlessly for about 500 feet to the summit of 781-foot-high Mount Livermore. The dirt footpath cuts through coastal scrub and chaparral, where the western fence lizard scurries. Dramatic scenes of all the world-class landmarks previously appreciated are captured here in an awesome 360-degree vista. Flat, dome-shaped Mount Livermore now has picnic tables, replacing the antiaircraft guns and Nike missile installation that were once fixtures here. Spiritually attuned campers can obtain permits to stay overnight on the island, often with the intent of admiring the glowing Golden Gate Bridge and the City By The Bay at night. Full-moon nights are extra special.

Perle's Beach is the perfect capper after hang time on Mount Livermore (retrace your steps). Loaded with spectacular views of Alcatraz Island, Golden Gate Bridge, and San Francisco's skyscrapers, the wind is often gusty and the waters choppy here.

Perimeter Trail now winds north, soon entering a shady grove of mature oaks, pines, cypresses, and eucalyptus. You're then treated to a choice of a view above or access to the classic military buildings comprising West Garrison. Still standing are the brick hospital, the chapel, barracks, and stables.

Hike 51

Golden Gate Promenade and Crissy Field to Fort Point

LENGTH: 6.6 miles round-trip; 4 miles round-trip from Fort Mason to Crissy Field.
DIFFICULTY: easy.
TOTAL ELEVATION GAIN: 100 feet.
WATER: from faucets; bring some also.

SEASON: all—more likely to get more comfortable weather in the fall.

MAP: USGS topo San Francisco North, or free Golden Gate National Recreation Area map.

INFORMATION: G.G.N.R.A., (415) 556-8371.

DIRECTIONS TO TRAILHEAD: Get on Highway 101, and get to the southern end of the Golden Gate Bridge. Take the Marina Boulevard exit and head east for 3 miles or so, then park at Fort Mason or Marina Green.

If you're going to San Francisco, be sure to wear some flowers in your hair (so the song goes), and take this hike. This leisurely walk departs from the typical wilderness journeys described throughout this book. Instead, this time you can take a tiny hiatus from remoteness and seclusion and capture a view-filled slice of San Francisco City. Plan on gusty afternoon winds and experiencing more than the beautiful San Francisco Bay Area scenery.

Witness people in motion, sailboats cruising, Frisbees flying, and volleyballs being spiked. The wide array of architecture is at its finest. This includes San Francisco's skyscrapers, Fort Point's massive pre–Civil War military fortifications, the Golden Gate Bridge, and the old-style designs of adjacent Marina Drive's apartments.

After passing a big kite-flying field called Marina Green on the left and the yacht harbor on the right, pick and choose your way to the old dirt road that leads to the end of a pier strip. The unique wave pipe organ here creates whalelike tones, especially when the winds kick up.

Back on the paved pathway, you soon reach grassy Crissy Field just beyond a small beach strip. This area marked the introduction of airplanes employed in the coastal defenses during the 1920s. The entire Golden Gate Promenade vicinity is a brisk, happening place —artsy and recreational. On a given morning when the path is dotted with runners and walkers, expect to hear drummers pounding, horn players tooting, and artists sand-sculpting. People also fish, skate, and ride mountain bikes here.

You'll soon reach the historic Fort Point facilities, where the U.S. Army was responsible for the underwater mines in and around the

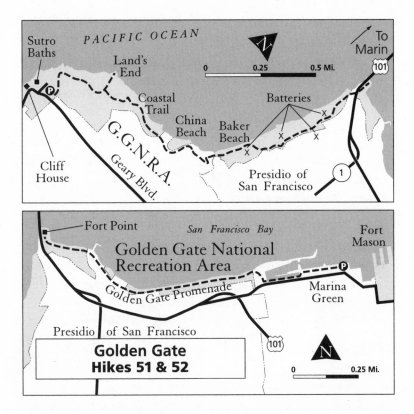

Golden Gate through World War II. You can spend some hang time at the nearby old pier or the small and rocky beach.

After a brief climb through a botanical garden setting, Battery East appears, where five huge guns once guarded the bay entrance in the 1870s. After passing under a tunnel, you get to look down on Fort Point proper, nestled beneath the Golden Gate Bridge. This fort of red brick was designed to mount 126 huge muzzle-loading cannons, but never had to fire a shot.

A few more hops, skips, and jumps put you on solid ground underneath the bridge. Feel free to hang from the sturdy bars just to say you once dangled from the Golden Gate Bridge. This is also the destination of Hike 52. By arranging a car shuttle or municipal transportation at the west end of Geary Boulevard, one can continue on the Coastal Trail for another 4 miles or so past Baker Beach and Land's End.

Hike 52

Land's End and Baker Beach to the Golden Gate Bridge

LENGTH: 8 miles round-trip as described; 4 miles round-trip to China Beach.

DIFFICULTY: easy.

TOTAL ELEVATION GAIN: 200 feet.

WATER: none—bring your own.

SEASON: all—very few people on a rainy weekday in winter; most likely to have clear weather in autumn.

MAP: USGS topo San Francisco North or free Golden Gate National Recreation Area map. See p. 147.

INFORMATION: G.G.N.R.A., (415) 556-8371.

DIRECTIONS TO TRAILHEAD: From San Francisco, get on Geary Boulevard and head west until it dead-ends at Cliff House next to the Pacific Ocean. From Highway 1 near Pacifica, get on Skyline Boulevard (Highway 35), then follow it west and north around Lake Merced, where it becomes the Great Highway. Park on a side street called Merrie Way that doubles as a big paved parking lot.

For splendid lookouts of vast beaches, crashing breakers, the South Bay, Golden Gate Bridge, and beyond, this hike is pure paradise. This excursion along coastal bluffs at the west end of San Francisco unveils outrageous views as fast as a jukebox plays the hits. The clearer the day, the better this hike will turn out.

As an added bonus, some Bay Area history unfolds on the way. At the outset, wander over to nearby Cliff House and ponder the large collection of historic exhibits and photographs. After watching from the Cliff House balcony the sea lions and seals basking on Seal Rocks, head for the Sutro Bath ruins. The cement foundations from several saltwater baths are all that remain from a fire in 1966.

The first half of this trip passes in and out of cypress groves, framing inspirational views of the Pacific Ocean, Golden Gate Bridge, and other prominent landmarks and place-names. This trail section follows the route of an abandoned turn-of-the-century train that

Baker Beach and Golden Gate Bridge.

used to take people to Cliff House. The remaining trail sections on this journey cover beaches and even sidewalks, as well as beach strips and a military roadway past several military installations such as Battery Crosby and Battery Dynamite.

A half mile or so into the journey you reach Land's End, which is so special it should be seen up close. This can be done by taking the spur trail past several standing but dead cypresses. From the chunky earth outcrop, one can get away from the other hikers while taking in photogenic sights of bridge and bay. This is another good spot for spying the Farallon Islands, Point Reyes shoreline, and Mount Tamalpais. The spur trail continues beyond Land's End and fades as it reaches a small and secluded beach strewn with large boulders. The big waves crashing against the rocks here sound like thunder.

Back on Coastal Trail, you soon come to a stretch two-thirds of a mile long that spans the seaside sidewalks of El Camino Del Mar and then Seacliff Avenue, along a pleasant and formally landscaped beachfront neighborhood. China Beach, much smaller than nearby Baker Beach, appears halfway along this fancy section. This family beach, nestled into the steep shoreline, was used by the Chinese fishermen as a campsite during Gold Rush times.

A little farther on, drop down onto pretty and popular Baker Beach (a long strip of clean sand featuring great views of Golden Gate Bridge). At the north end of the beach Battery Chamberlain points a 95,000-pound cannon toward the ocean from a hidden bunker. Park rangers demonstrate the procedure on weekends.

After a climb to Battery Boutelle, a cluster of old cement military structures with lots of stairways, Golden Gate Bridge looms large, with accompanying views of a secluded beach alongside Fort Point Rock. The Coastal Trail soon crosses beneath the grand bridge (feel free to safely swing from the bridge bars), reveals a view of Fort Point, then descends through a pretty botanical garden setting. At this point, you've connected with Hike 51. If a car shuttle or municipal transportation is planned, you can continue 3 miles or so along the Golden Gate Promenade to Marina Green.

San Mateo County/
Santa Cruz Mountains Area

Hike 53

Summit Loop Trail in San Bruno Mountain State and County Park

LENGTH: 4.4 miles round-trip.

DIFFICULTY: strenuous.

TOTAL ELEVATION GAIN: 1,200 feet.

WATER: available from faucets near restrooms and picnic area; pack plenty of your own.

SEASON: all—wildflowers in the spring; most likely to get the best views in the fall.

MAP: USGS topo San Francisco South or San Bruno Mountain State and County Park brochure.

INFORMATION: San Bruno Mountain State and County Park, (415) 587-7511 or (650) 992-6770.

DIRECTIONS TO TRAILHEAD: From Highway 101 north of South San Francisco, use the Cow Palace exit. Continue to Guadalupe Canyon Parkway, turn left and follow it 2.2 miles to the park entrance and paved parking lot on the right.

This is the Bay Area's ultimate peninsula excursion. Pack a windbreaker, for the winds are water cooled by the ocean to the west, San Francisco Bay to the north, and the East Bay to the east.

To gaze on all this water is to capture the essence of this hike. The price is a quadriceps-rejuvenating climb to the ridge, where a panorama awaits. From atop San Bruno Mountain's east-west ridgeline, the northernmost extension of the Santa Cruz Mountains, an avid wanderer can spend hours staring at the bays, ocean, San Francisco, and other major place-names. Take along binoculars for studying the red-tailed hawks that patrol the ridge, a camera for the sweeping scenery, and go on a clear day.

The entire park is home to the endangered and protected San Bruno elfin butterfly and the rare Montara manzanita.

Over the first part of the Eucalyptus Loop Trail, you get to check the progress of native plant restoration. Almost right away, views of the East Bay appear—just a tease for more outrageous scenes farther up. Heavy-duty climbing coincides with this inaugural view. The

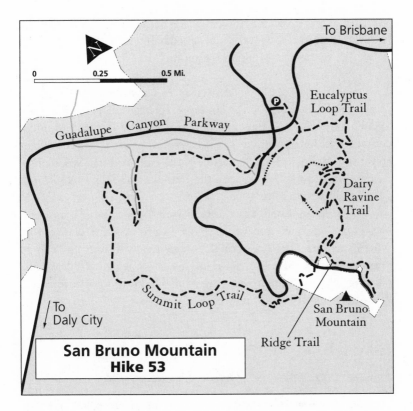

well-made footpath zips through coastal scrub consisting of coyote brush, occasional coffeeberry, and blue-blossom ceanothus. When catching your breath, admire the terrific combination of the Bay Bridge and Emerald City–like skyscrapers of San Francisco to the north. Just as the spectacular views of the Pacific Ocean and Mount Tamalpais arise, a trail junction appears at 0.7 mile. Bear left onto the signed Dairy Ravine Trail, where 2-foot-tall lizard's-tail shrubs and bracken ferns show up immediately. Meanwhile, the climb persists and the views improve.

At 1.2 miles Dairy Ravine Trail finishes, merging with Summit Loop Trail. Note the view-filled return route on the right, then continue climbing to the left. After investing in less than half a mile of continued ascent, your goal is reached at San Bruno Mountain's 1,314-foot-high summit.

All the previously mentioned place-names are included in the summit's panorama, as well as Mount Diablo some 28 miles as the hawk flies to the east. Montara Mountain (Hike 56) graces your gaze 9 miles to the south.

Up to the 1800s, Native American Indians roamed this mountain, periodically burning the land to encourage the growth of food and basketry plants. The irregular topography of this mountain combines with its several microclimates to support a variety of plant communities, including chaparral, grasslands, and oak woodlands. These communities, along with the coastal scrub atop this summit, are all visible from here.

The Summit Loop Trail (return route) continues to show off sweeping scenery, contouring the ridge in a northwesterly direction, which keeps the ocean in virtually constant view. If time and energy permit, consider strolling some of the short trails that leave the parking lot and traipse over grassy hillocks to the north to reveal splendid vistas of San Francisco.

Hike 54

Sweeney Ridge to the Portola Discovery Site

LENGTH: 4.4 miles round-trip from Skyline College; 5.0 miles round-trip via Shelldance Nursery.

DIFFICULTY: easy to moderate.

TOTAL ELEVATION GAIN: 600 feet via Skyline College; 1,000 feet via Shelldance Nursery.

WATER: none—bring your own.

SEASON: all—wildflowers in spring; best chance of clear weather in the fall.

MAP: USGS topo San Francisco South.

INFORMATION: Golden Gate National Recreation Area, (415) 556-8371 or (415) 556-0560.

DIRECTIONS TO TRAILHEAD: From Highway 1 in Pacifica south of San Francisco, turn east onto Sharp Park Road, travel 1.4 miles, then turn right onto College Drive. From Interstate 280 in San Bruno south of San Francisco, take the Westborough exit, drive west, then turn left onto Skyline

Boulevard (Highway 35), then soon turn onto College Drive. This road encircles the Skyline College. Simply park in lot 2 and get on the trailhead from the southeast section of the lot. If you hike in from Shelldance Nursery, find it on the east side of Highway 1 in Pacifica. The sign for the nursery is half a mile south of Sharp Park Road.

To fully appreciate the splendor of San Francisco Bay, and to notch perhaps the best 360-degree view in the Bay Area, do what Captain Portola did to discover the bay—climb Sweeney Ridge. Merely obtain a fog-free weather report, then climb past grasslands and brush highlighted by one great lookout after another all the way to the official Portola Discovery Site.

Two things are apt to cross your mind—how easy it is to snag such a special panorama of bay and sea, and how different and pris-

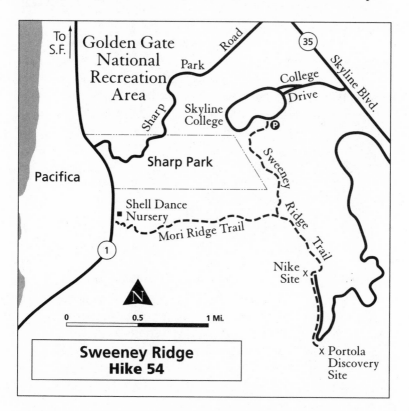

tine the views were in the autumn of 1769 when Gaspar de Portola stood gazing in awe atop Sweeney Ridge.

During a brief climbing burst away from Skyline College, coyote brush dominates the hillside, decorated by the spring-flowering goldfield, cow parsnip, paintbrush, lupine, California poppy, and yellow wild mustard. The Sweeney Ridge Trail levels for a bit at 0.2 mile, yielding your first grand views of the Pacific Ocean beyond Pacifica and a forest of eucalyptus. The lookouts of Daly City and the San Francisco Bay unfold soon after.

After a fleeting drop down and then up a gulch next to a eucalyptus and cypress grove, the trail, an old dirt road, soon switches to asphalt at 1.4 miles next to the Nike missile site. This is a flat spot consisting of a cluster of old and dilapidated cement buildings used during cold war times as a missile-launching and helicopter-landing site.

A mile's worth of virtually level strolling brings you to the Portola Discovery Site. It's hard to figure that a bay as important as the San Francisco Bay would be found on foot and not via sailing ships, as were most California coastal bays and coves. The bay's narrow opening and frequent fog shrouded it from passing ships for two centuries before Spain's Portola and his men sighted it from somewhere around where you now stand. They saw the bay and a bunch of mountains with no names and no shreds of civilization.

From your vantage point, the Farallon Islands look like a miniature mountain range rising from the sea. Power lines frame your view of the Point Reyes shoreline and Mount Tamalpais to the northwest. Long, light green, and naked San Bruno Mountain (Hike 53) shields the view of Angel Island to the north. Pointed Mount Diablo stands guard over the vast bay. Mount Hamilton east of San Jose shares the scene to the east with the San Mateo Bridge. Chaparral-clothed Montara Mountain (Hike 56) spreads across the south expanse.

During the return trip, you'll come back to the Mori Trail junction, which you passed on the way up. With some prior car shuttle planning, you can veer left here and take this trail down to Shelldance Nursery (directions to this trailhead were detailed earlier). For those preferring a better workout, they'll find it by doing the Mori Trail rather than starting from Skyline College. The Mori Trail is described with the assumption that a car shuttle was arranged.

This old dirt road furnishes an ongoing drop past open grasslands to the sea. The changing heights of the chaparral keep varying your views of the sweeping hills, Montara Mountain, Point Reyes seashore, and Mount Tamalpais. The blue-blossom ceanothus, coffeeberry, and coastal sage are even more abundant on the Mori Trail than the Sweeney Ridge Trail above. An occasional Monterey pine adds a nice touch to the landscape.

Hike 55

Hazelnut Trail in San Pedro Valley County Park

LENGTH: 4.8 miles round-trip.

DIFFICULTY: moderate.

TOTAL ELEVATION GAIN: 800 feet.

WATER: none; bring your own.

SEASON: all—very secluded in the winter; chaparral blooms in the spring.

MAP: USGA topo Montara Mountain or free San Pedro Valley County Park map.

INFORMATION: San Pedro Valley County Park, (415) 355-8289.

DIRECTIONS TO TRAILHEAD: From Pacifica south of San Francisco on Highway 1, turn east onto Linda Mar Boulevard and drive 2 miles to the parking lot at San Pedro Valley County Park.

If it weren't for this good trail through a major maze of thick bushes, nobody could ever be in this special place. Chaparral seldom gets as tall, wide, and dense as it does hovering over the Hazelnut Trail. It's a big bonus that the tough and heroic trail builders blazed this gem of a path for you and I to roam on. If you don't mind being overpowered by a pretty thicket, isolated beyond compare, then this hike's got your name written all over it. Besides, the bushes are a buffer from the at-times fierce winds that strafe the nearby beaches.

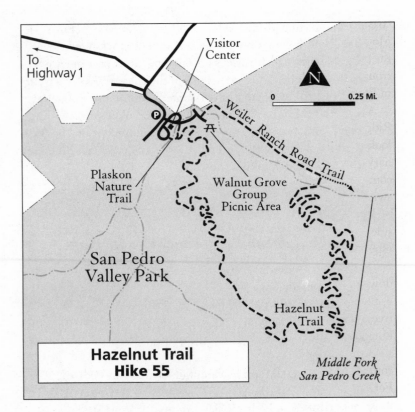

Hazelnut Trail
Hike 55

Plaskon Nature Trail

Walnut Grove Group Picnic Area

Visitor Center

To Highway 1

Weiler Ranch Road Trail

San Pedro Valley Park

Hazelnut Trail

Middle Fork San Pedro Creek

0   0.25 Mi.

The first quarter mile of this journey is enough to thrill native plant lovers seeking variety. This is due to an abrupt transition from riparian community along the Plaskon Nature Trail (pick up self-guided brochure at the Visitor Center) to coastal scrub. You'll find coast live oak, redwood, red dogwood, arroyo willow, red elderberry, gooseberry, thimbleberry, wood and sword ferns, and horsetail along San Pedro Creek. Soon after the climb commences on the Hazelnut Trail, you'll encounter blue-blossom ceanothus, cow parsnip, toyon, manzanita, poison oak, Pacific wax myrtle, coffeeberry, California huckleberry, coyote brush, and the rare giant golden chinquapin.

The chinquapin grows tall enough (up to 15 feet) to furnish welcome splashes of shade along with the intermittent eucalyptus trees that tower over this slender footpath. Initially the main lookouts are northward, featuring glimpses of Pacifica and the surrounding coastal foothills. The views switch southward at 0.6 mile of Montara Mountain's north flank and also a dense eucalyptus grove cloaking the canyon that empties into the South Fork of San Pedro Creek. A trout farm was operated there until a major storm washed it out in 1958.

On reaching the flat at 1.2 miles, you can study most of Sweeney Ridge to the northeast. Toward the trail's highest point be on the lookout for the Farallon Islands rising from the sea like the imaginary continent of Atlantis. Point Reyes shoreline and Sweeney Ridge comprise the main views once you begin descending the countless switchbacks.

The footpath in this section is so slender in spots and the canyonside is so clogged with chaparral, it's a good idea to check for ticks, especially if you're wearing shorts.

The things seen along this descent differ from the ascent. This downhill stretch has a shorter range of views, but it provides hawk's-eye focus down on the San Pedro Valley. The occasional madrone tree, absent on the climb, escorts you now. There's also more hazelnut, nettle, and coast silktassel.

At 3.5 miles, you get on the flat Weiler Ranch Road Trail, escorted along the San Pedro Valley by the arroyo-willow-lined Middle Fork of San Pedro Creek. If ever there was a trail for lovers, this one's it. The romantic scenes include some lush meadows (adorned in spring with California poppies, buttercups, and wild mustard), mature and shapely red alders that decorate the swirling creek, and people with smiles, often in pairs, admiring the eucalyptus groves and chaparral canyonsides you just came from. The Walnut Grove group picnic area rounds out the romantic scenes list, next to the Middle Fork of San Pedro Creek, which is one of the few remaining migratory steelhead spawning areas in San Mateo County.

Because this hike covers chaparral, streamsides, and meadows, the wildlife is abundant, including red-tailed hawks, quail, turkey vultures, scrub jays, and garter snakes. If you're super quiet and lucky, you may spot some of the sneakier wildlife, such as bobcats, gray foxes, and rabbits.

Nestled in the Santa Cruz Mountain range, the San Pedro Valley became an important mission outpost in the late 1700s. It offered fertile soil for growing wheat and fruits, and lots of cattle-grazing land.

A hawk's-eye view of Montara State Beach.

Hike 56

Montara Mountain via Old San Pedro Road Trail

LENGTH: 6 miles round-trip.
DIFFICULTY: strenuous.
TOTAL ELEVATION GAIN: 2,200 feet.
WATER: none, bring plenty of your own.
SEASON: year-round, best in mid spring.
MAP: USGS topo Montara Mountain.
INFORMATION: Half Moon Bay State Beaches, (650) 726-8820.
DIRECTIONS TO TRAILHEAD: Look for an unsigned gate on the east side of Highway 1 several yards north of Montara State Beach's access road, which is 10 miles north of Half Moon Bay. If this tiny lot is jammed, consider parking farther south at Gray Whale Cove parking area on the highway's east side or at the Montara State Beach parking lot.

Climb a wild and untamed mountain, biologically rich and geologically interesting, to a top-of-the-world view of the Pacific Ocean and the San Francisco Bay Area. You'll stroll past an impressive variety of wildflowers in a northern scrub community.

Montara Mountain belongs to the Santa Cruz Mountains, where they narrow to a 6-mile divider between the ocean and south San Francisco Bay. The summits here, at less than 2,000 feet elevation, are half the height of the neighboring summits to the south.

Since it's caught between and influenced by two large marine bodies, this mountain's maritime climate is characterized by exceptional dense fog and persistent salt-laden winds. Wet winter weather can be extreme enough to cause slide damage, forcing the closure of Highway 1. This happened during the near daily rains of January 1995, and the highway didn't reopen until nearly six months later. It's best to call ahead and check.

To start, stroll east on a path that parallels a grove of tall cypress trees. Turn sharply left onto unsigned Old San Pedro Road at 0.2 mile just in front of the ranger's residence. Fortunately, this dirt path is wide, because poison oak soon dominates trailside for a quarter mile.

At 0.5 mile walk past a shaded grove of scotch broom and pampas grass, examples of exotic plants that can be attractive but are out of control in many areas of the central coast, including here. Get set now for some heavy-duty climbing and improving views of the towns of Pacifica northward and Half Moon Bay behind you.

Go right at 1.4 miles onto a fire road called the Montara Mountain Trail. The steepest climbing occurs from 1.6 to 1.9 miles, accompanied luckily by spring-blooming California poppy and lupine.

Blue-blossom ceanothus (also called California lilac) dominates the trailside from 2.0 to 2.5 miles. These are the kings of the ceanothus genus, reaching heights of up to 20 feet.

Monumental rock outcrops, most composed of granite from the Salinian block, attract attention in the distance. Other prominent geologic formations along the flanks of Montara Mountain consist of shale, conglomerate, and sandstone.

Stray off the beaten path to climb a number of small peaks from 2.7 to 2.9 miles. If you're quiet enough, perhaps you'll spot some local wildlife, such as coyotes, bobcats, mountain lions, mule deer, chipmunks, wood rats, and gray foxes. The numerous bird species that

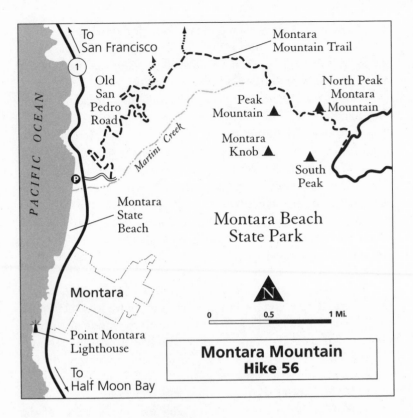

To
San Francisco

Montara
Mountain Trail

1

Old
San
Pedro
Road

PACIFIC OCEAN

Martini Creek

P

Peak
Mountain ▲

North Peak
Montara
Mountain ▲

Montara
Knob ▲

South
Peak ▲

Montara
State
Beach

**Montara Beach
State Park**

Montara

N

0   0.5   1 Mi.

Point Montara
Lighthouse

To
Half Moon Bay

**Montara Mountain
Hike 56**

dive, dart, and hover around these outcrops include peregrine falcon, California thrasher, red-tailed hawk, and American kestrel.

Back on the trail, you'll soon reach the microwave/weather station atop 1,898-foot-high North Peak Montara Mountain, the highest peak. As you check out the 360-degree view, admire Mount Diablo to the east, and Scarper's Peak and the Santa Cruz Mountains southeast. Half Moon Bay and its nearby beaches stretch below to the southwest, and Mount Tamalpais towers to the north above San Francisco's skyscrapers.

Montara Mountain has been a major barrier along this coastal section for thousands of years. Imagine Native Americans passing along the trail built over the mountain, connecting two isolated Ohlone villages. A large population of the long-lost native perennial flower Hickman's cinquefoil, a critically endangered species, was recently discovered on the southwestern flank of Montara Mountain.

Hike 57

The Tidepools, Beach, Bluffs, and Cypress Grove in Fitzgerald Marine Reserve

LENGTH: 5 miles round-trip to see it all; the trip can be substantially reduced by skipping parts of the beach and/or bluff trails.

DIFFICULTY: easy.

TOTAL ELEVATION GAIN: 200 feet.

WATER: available only from parking lot drinking fountain; bring your own.

SEASON: all—most likely to get better views in the autumn; blufftop flowers in the spring; fewer folks in the winter.

MAP: USGS topo Montara Mountain.

INFORMATION: Fitzgerald Marine Reserve, (650) 728-3584.

DIRECTIONS TO TRAILHEAD: From the tiny coastal community of Moss Beach on Highway 1 (a few miles north of Half Moon Bay and several miles south of San Francisco), turn west on California Street and drive 0.4 mile to the paved parking lot.

To San Mateo County residents, Fitzgerald Marine Reserve is a cherished shoreline for fabulous ocean views, tidepooling, and barefoot rock hopping on the beach. They return to their special strip of rugged coastline to philosophize along the coastal scrub bluffs or romanticize in wind-sculpted Cypress Grove.

For first-time visitors, it's a chance to be a kid, discovering a bountiful treasure of bullwhip kelp, sea stars, urchins, underrock crabs, and anemones. Show up at low tide, read the interpretive exhibits, wear good gripping shoes, and get set for an educational experience in the tidal reef and marine world.

For the hiker, it's the chance to do all of the above, leaving with memories galore and probably a few fine photos to boot. To explore Fitzgerald Marine Reserve is to sample what the locals have been appreciating for some time.

A cute little creek finishes into the ocean next to a couple of interpretive signs. Start here by darting left on the rocky beach if it's

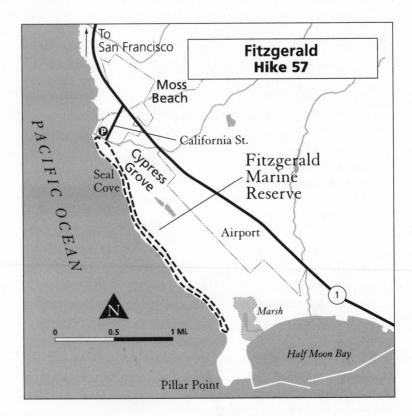

To San Francisco

Moss Beach

PACIFIC OCEAN

California St.

Cypress Grove

Seal Cove

Fitzgerald Marine Reserve

Airport

N

0   0.5   1 Mi.

Marsh

Half Moon Bay

Pillar Point

low tide. If the tide is still a tad too high but getting lower, climb and then head south on the bluffs, returning via the beach later.

It's a mini-thrill to do balancing acts on the dark, wave-washed rocks, negotiating your way toward Pillar Point, which guards the coastline to the south. The thick mats of brown seaweed floating in the calm and soupy sections of the surf are kelp forests that furnish refuge for lots of fish species. This colony of brownish plants provides the canopy for an extremely productive submarine forest. In this zone between the high- and low-tide marks, 49 species of plants and animals have been documented.

Fifteen thousand years ago this shoreline stretch was about 400 feet lower than now, reaching all the way to the Farallon Islands. Looking like the continent of Atlantis might have looked, these islands are visible directly west from here on a clear day.

While continuing south, it becomes apparent this reserve is also noted as a shorebird watcher's paradise (snag the bird checklist brochure at the parking lot station). Red-throated, Pacific, and common loons patrol the surf regularly along with brown pelicans, cormorants, western seagulls, and blue herons (watch for night herons at dusk). Also look for peregrine falcons, osprey, and friendly ravens.

Before reaching massive Pillar Point, exit stage left onto one of the spur trails that charge up the bluffs. From this coastal scrub bluff flat, the views are far-reaching. The rolling San Mateo foothills sprawl to the east with rocky beach and shiny sea adorning the west gazes. Coyote brush, coast, and lizard's-tail low-growing shrubs combine with yarrow and fennel herbs all along the flat. Several side paths lead directly to commanding vistas of the shoreline and ocean. Choose an inland side trail and gather great views of Montara Mountain (Hike 56) and Princeton Harbor. A number of dirt roads —take your pick—eventually lead briefly through a posh seacoast neighborhood (requires a short stint of pavement pounding).

The cypress grove, a rectangular forest of Monterey cypress trees planted long ago to buffer the fierce winds and control erosion, is this journey's final highlight. Your mission here is to find two deciduous small trees among this immense conifer jungle affectionately dubbed by the locals as "monkey tree" and "little monkey tree." You'll know them instantly because the temptation to climb in their many scaffold branches is irresistible.

There are a few ideal perches on the cypress grove's shoreside for viewing the surf and steep bluffs. Once an extensive mudflat, the mud along this shore was compressed into shale over geologic time. Later, marine sediments were uplifted by movements in the earth's crust. The exposed shale was then gradually eroded by waves, leaving the channels, crevices, and cracks that form the tidepools.

Hike 58

Soda Gulch Trail and Harkins Ridge in Purisima Creek Redwoods Open Space Preserve

LENGTH: 7.5 miles round-trip as described; 4.8 miles round-trip to Soda Gulch.
DIFFICULTY: moderate.

TOTAL ELEVATION GAIN: 1,200 feet.

WATER: available from Purisima Creek (purify); or bring your own.

SEASON: all—Purisima Creek is in its prime when swollen after heavy winter rains; flowering herbs in late spring.

MAP: Purisima Creek Redwoods Open Space Preserve brochure or USGS topo Woodside.

INFORMATION: Midpeninsula Regional Open Space District, (650) 691-1200.

DIRECTIONS TO TRAILHEAD: In Half Moon Bay, at the intersection of Highway 92, drive south on Highway 1. After 1.3 miles, turn east on Higgins-Purisima Road, then drive 4.5 miles to the trailhead next to Purisima Creek.

Thank Save the Redwoods League for donating $2 million to establish this preserve filled with stately redwoods. Few folks are aware that a tremendous redwood forest exists beneath Harkins Ridge along Purisima Creek. This journey takes you deep into this forest, then into natural herb gardens on the cloistered Soda Gulch Trail, and climaxes with hawk's-eye views of these redwoods from Harkins Ridge.

One tends to get in a relaxed and creative mood while walking among redwoods along a pretty creek. The 2.5 miles spent affectionately close to Purisima Creek settle the nerves and satisfy the soul. The word *purisima* means purity.

Purisima Creek Trail, a dirt road, stays comfortably level and shaded over the first mile. Alder and bigleaf maple trees share the banks of peaceful Purisima Creek with stalwart redwoods, as redwood sorrel and ferns blanket the needle-littered forest floor.

A large clearing at 1.1 miles is dotted with introduced thistles and poison hemlock, and native thimbleberry bushes and rushes. Purisima Creek Trail climbs a quarter mile farther on, after crossing a bridge canopied by a charming and drooping bigleaf maple. The Grabtown Trail junction pops up soon afterward (keep straight), followed by another bridge crossing guarding one of Soda Gulch's tributaries. Towering redwoods and giant maples help keep a creekside fern garden moist and shady here.

Following some gentle creek climbing, the trail reaches Soda

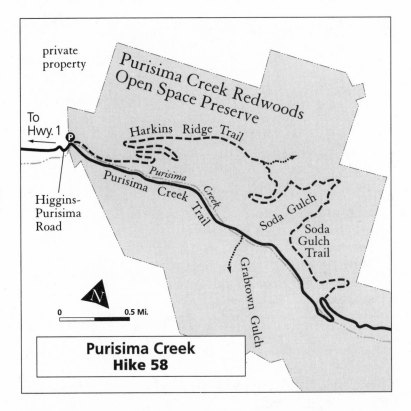

private property

To Hwy. 1

Purisima Creek Redwoods Open Space Preserve

Harkins Ridge Trail

Higgins-Purisima Road

Purisima Creek Trail

Purisima Creek

Soda Gulch

Soda Gulch Trail

Grabtown Gulch

N

0   0.5 Mi.

**Purisima Creek
Hike 58**

Gulch Trail (at 2.4 miles), onto which you turn. Purisima Creek becomes a pleasant memory as the slender footpath climbs moderately under scattered redwoods and herbs, including mugwort and mint.

After a mile on Soda Gulch Trail, you'll come to two huge redwoods joined at the base, and 0.2 mile farther your first view of the deep green Santa Cruz Mountains. It becomes obvious this well-made path required a lot of sweat to make, as it veers toward the ocean and then into dense chaparral.

While huffing and puffing your way to the top of a knoll, you'll come upon stunning views of the Santa Cruz Mountains sweeping into Half Moon Bay. Cow parsnip, California poppy, and yerba santa (bluish flowers in May) adorn the upper portion of Soda Gulch Trail. It soon leads to Harkins Ridge Trail at 4.8 miles (go left).

This dirt road escorts you past huge blue-blossom ceanothus specimens mingling with madrones. It's best to venture off the trail at times to gaze on the very redwood groves you roamed in earlier. The absorbing views of redwood groves and rolling Santa Cruz Mountains vanish after 1.4 miles. The trail bends toward Purisima Creek at 6.2 miles and descends more steeply through Douglas fir and tan oak to the trailhead.

Hike 59

Heritage Grove and Towne Trails
in Pescadero Creek County Park

LENGTH: 6.8 miles round-trip as described; 3 miles round-trip to Hiker's Hut on the ridgetop.

DIFFICULTY: moderate.

TOTAL ELEVATION GAIN: 1,300 feet.

WATER: refill at Hiker's Hut; also available at Towne Creek.

SEASON: all—ideal in winter; can be hot during summer.

MAP: Pescadero Creek County Park map or USGS topo La Honda.

INFORMATION: Pescadero Creek County Park, (650) 879-0238 or (650) 363-4020.

DIRECTIONS TO TRAILHEAD: From the peninsula on Interstate 280, take Highway 84 up the hill, and beyond Skyline Boulevard to La Honda. Turn left on La Honda/Pescadero Road and drive 1.1 miles, then turn left onto Alpine Road. Park in the small lot 1.2 miles farther. From Highway 1, south of Half Moon Bay, drive 8.5 miles on Highway 84, then turn right on La Honda/Pescadero Road.

Perhaps the best way to find out what the Santa Cruz Mountains are all about is to take this journey. It's a delightful climb through an ancient redwood forest to a ridgetop delivering extensive views of the conifer-clothed Santa Cruz Mountains sprawling onward to the sea. And as if that weren't enough, one also gets to ramble in these Santa Cruz Mountains to the confluence of Towne Creek, Pescadero Creek, and Jones Gulch.

At the onset, a redwood bridge crosses Alpine Creek and promptly enters an ancient redwood forest. Look at enough of the

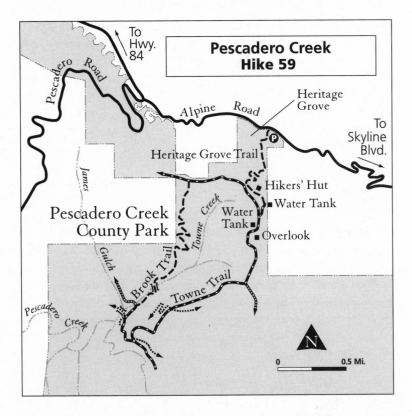

Pescadero Creek
Hike 59

To Hwy. 84

Pescadero Road

Alpine Road

Heritage Grove

To Skyline Blvd.

Heritage Grove Trail

James

Pescadero Creek County Park

Towne Creek

Water Tank

Hikers' Hut

Water Tank

Overlook

Gulch

Brook Trail

Towne Trail

Pescadero Creek

N

0   0.5 Mi.

huge trunks and you're bound to note yellow paint marks on a few. Loggers did this in 1973 to indicate which trees were coming down in a proposed logging operation. Concerned citizens united with the San Mateo County Board of Supervisors to protect this redwood legacy, creating a county park a year later.

Alpine Creek rapidly fades from sight and sound during a brief climb to Heritage Redwood Grove. A side trail skirts some majestic virgin redwoods. This worthy trail reveals a cluster of some of the biggest redwoods in the world.

Back on the densely shaded Heritage Grove Trail, massive Douglas firs replace redwoods as the climb continues underneath scattered tan oak stands and next to sword fern and redwood sorrel to the ridge field. After this aerobic workout consisting of 1.3 miles and a 600-foot climb, take the 0.2-mile spur trail up to Hiker's Hut. It's a well-designed A-frame lodge with benches and tables, nestled under a cluster of massive coast live oak and one giant Douglas fir. This picnic spot furnishes lots of chances to focus on the rugged Santa Cruz Mountains, which stretch to the Pacific Ocean.

Complete the Hiker's Hut loop, which includes the enticing 1,316-foot-high lookout knoll, then briefly descend past the water tank (after turning left onto a fire road called the Towne Trail). A spur trail soon departs the main trail and reveals a great vista of the dark and bumpy Santa Cruz Mountains.

Back on the Towne Trail, you promptly pass next to a scenic and statuesque coast live oak grove. Then the trail plunges dramatically past yellow bush lupine and orange bush monkeyflower.

You soon break into a dark Douglas fir forest, mixed with coast live oak. The trail stays level to a fork (go right), then begins a steady drop while heading west by southwest in dense fir shade that epitomizes much of the Santa Cruz Mountains.

You'll make four consecutive right turns (the idea is to get on the fire road called the Brook Trail, your return climb back to the ridge). Plan on a picnic at any of the beautiful spots down along the confluence of the above-mentioned streams, where California buckeye groves catch the eye.

Hike 60

Mill Ox, Jackson Flats, and Six Bridge Trails in Butano State Park

LENGTH: 5.3 miles round-trip.
DIFFICULTY: moderate.
TOTAL ELEVATION GAIN: 700 feet.
WATER: available from parking lot fountains and Little Butano Creek.
SEASON: all—occasional wet parts and washouts in winter; occasionally hot in the summer.
MAP: Butano State Park map or USGS topo Franklin Point.
INFORMATION: Butano State Park, (650) 879-2040 or (415) 330-6300.
DIRECTIONS TO TRAILHEAD: Coming from Interstate 280 near San Mateo, take Highway 92 west to Half Moon Bay. Turn

south on Highway 1 and drive 16 miles to Pescadero Beach, then turn east on Pescadero Road. Drive 2 miles and turn right onto Cloverdale Road, parking near the park kiosk 2.3 miles farther.

Variety is the spice of hikes, and the journey along these four fine trails keeps things interesting. You get to ramble through shady redwood forests and sunny grasslands and chaparral, with some oak woodland and riparian creekside strolling thrown in as a bonus. Fine vistas of the dark and rolling Santa Cruz Mountains and a bunch of bridge crossings add to the list of goodies.

Nobody can figure it out, but Butano State Park remains a well-kept secret. Hikers tend to encounter comparatively few people here, and many prefer to keep it that way. Other amblers may think the park is too small for their roaming pleasures. Yes, the park is

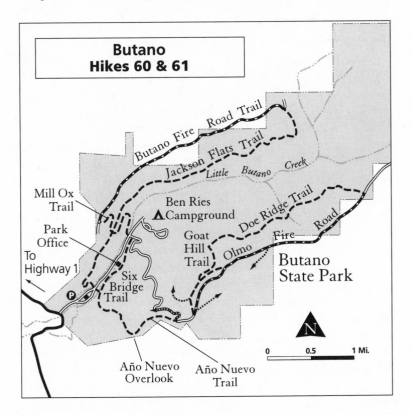

small in size, but highly concentrated in hikeability. The Jackson Flats Trail, a slender footpath, begins in a coastal scrub clearing of coyote brush, but quickly ducks under shady Douglas fir and then coast live oak as it climbs moderately. In their quest to reach the sunlight, these evergreen oaks are artistically pruned by time and nature, creating interesting multiple-trunked branch patterns. The clematis vine (soft white flowers in spring) drapes over salal and tan oak, adorning the trailside along with orange bush monkeyflower.

Listen for the soothing hum of Little Butano Creek while checking out some stands of ancient redwoods. A grove of them stand guard over a four-way signed trail junction at 0.7 mile, where you bear left and immediately commence ascent on the Mill Ox Trail. After ducking under a huge, fallen Douglas fir, the trail becomes a little overgrown in spots (check for ticks or wear long pants) with currant, bracken fern, mugwort, and vinca, then snakes west into a grove of Douglas firs that feature ghostlike naked limbs except for on top. This skeleton understory persists until reaching Butano Fire Trail (an unpaved service road) where you bear right.

This wide trail is dotted with sun and filtered shade, furnishing good glances into the Butano Canyon beyond ceanothus, salal, coffeeberry, elderberry, coast live oak, tan oak, and orange bush monkeyflower. Thank the stands of towering Douglas fir for the bulk of the shade, along with occasional redwood.

On reaching a handful of knobcone pines along an exposed trail section, take a brief break from the climb and look back for a vista of the Pacific Ocean beyond the Santa Cruz Mountains.

Toward the finish of this 1.8-mile-long trail, look for an old abandoned wooden shack nestled underneath a cluster of gargantuan redwoods. Loggers undoubtedly sought shelter there in the early 1900s, and thankfully didn't turn these masterpieces of nature into stumps. There are some large redwood stumps scattered in the park to remind us of the logging ventures that went on several decades ago. A hundred yards farther, look for a grove of chinquapin bushes, some higher than 20 feet and thriving in the all-day sun.

After getting to a clearing at 2.6 miles, featuring the best views yet of the sea and mountains, bear right back onto Jackson Flats Trail. It descends along a rocky section and through chaparral country, where the knobcone pine and manzanita outnumber the fir and oak; then, without warning, it switches abruptly into a dense forest of redwood and Douglas fir canopying California huckleberry and tan oak.

Half a mile past the junction with the Canyon Trail, the canyon wall drains into an alluvial flat, offering the best conditions for the biggest redwoods yet. Sword fern and low-growing redwood sorrel in some places here are virtually the only plants existing on this redwood forest floor.

Take a left onto the Mill Ox Trail at 4.5 miles, for a quiet and at times steep stroll down to Little Butano Creek. Cross the creek bridge, turn right on the paved road, then a quick left on a road leading to a gate. Turn right onto the footpath a few steps farther and begin a short climb onto a portion of the Six Bridges Trail.

The first bridge crossing features a tall and attractively lean bigleaf maple tree. Elderberry and red alder decorate Little Butano Creek at the next bridge. Arguably the hugest fir in the park (with a grotesquely broken-off main trunk) precedes the third bridge. The last bridge before reaching the parking lot features dogwood and red alder trees.

Hike 61
Doe Ridge and Año Nuevo Trails in Butano State Park

> **LENGTH:** 6.2 miles round-trip as described; 1.6 miles round-trip to view of Año Nuevo Island.
>
> **DIFFICULTY:** strenuous during Año Nuevo Trail climb; the rest is easy.
>
> **TOTAL ELEVATION GAIN:** 1,300 feet.
>
> **WATER:** none; bring your own.
>
> **SEASON:** all—slippery spots on Año Nuevo Trail during and after long rains.
>
> **MAP:** Butano State Park brochure or USGS topo Franklin Point. See p. 171.
>
> **INFORMATION:** Butano State Park, (650) 879-2040.
>
> **DIRECTIONS TO TRAILHEAD:** From Half Moon Bay on Highway 1, drive south for 15 miles, then turn east onto Pescadero

Road. After 2 miles, turn right onto Cloverdale Road, drive 2.3 miles, then park near the park kiosk.

Wander in these wild, yet whisper-quiet old-growth redwood forests to achieve refreshing peace, amazing solitude, and a total wilderness experience. There's peace because the redwood groves are mostly protected from wind, and the closest stream is usually out of hearing range. Solitude is virtually certain, since few souls are willing to invest in the 1,000 feet of hamstring-flexing climbing required right off the bat on the gorgeous Año Nuevo Trail. An ambitious wilderness adventure is guaranteed for all because there are distant ocean views on this journey, plus encounters with lush fern gardens, grand redwood groves, rare but striking flowers, fluffy mushrooms, and live oak woodlands.

While the majority of hikers are exploring the nearby and more popular Big Basin Redwoods State Park and Año Nuevo State Reserve, you can sometimes get equally beautiful and definitely less-visited Butano State Park almost to yourself.

A good way to start the hike is to study the exhibits and garden next to the kiosk, then begin the arduous climb on Año Nuevo Trail. The entire trail is like an imaginary fairy tale, with profuse fern gardens thriving beneath Douglas fir, covered with coexisting fungus and alga called staghorn lichen. Tree shade and persistent moisture from the nearby Pacific Ocean nourish this green jungle. The well-built footpath finally crests at 0.8 mile, where a bench features splendid views on clear days of Año Nuevo Island on the sea. The uncommon Douglas iris blooms here beneath a canopy of madrone and Douglas fir.

Go right at 1.1 mile onto signed Olmo Fire Trail. A bit farther hang a left, then a right shortly afterward on Goat Hill Trail. This level path is as tranquil and lush as the other trails on this hike, extending a half mile, where you take a right onto Doe Ridge Trail.

This serene trail stretches for 1.4 miles, all of it in an important old-growth redwood forest. There are countless stumps, sure signs of previously fallen giants. Note how many of the stumps are topped by actual California huckleberry bushes. These stately redwood groves survived two large lightning fires long ago, which explains the multitude of charred trunks. Colonies of bats often live in the hollow trunks. Twin redwood offshoots sharing one 10-foot-wide trunk catch your attention at 2.9 miles. If it's early spring, look closely for the purple calypso orchid in bloom on the needle-littered forest floor.

Olmo Fire Road stays level over a 1.8-mile stretch in a coast live oak woodland dotted with a few redwoods and Douglas fir. Chickadees, wrens, and warblers fill this open forest with song. Occasional views of the Pacific Ocean are earned here by departing the trail briefly when you see a chance and parting a few branches.

You reach a crest at 5.0 miles, walk downhill for 0.1 mile, then bear left back onto the Año Nuevo Trail. Returning on this enchanting trail, this time in rapidly descending fashion, is well worth it. You reacquaint with patches of mint, mugwort, ferns, thimbleberry, and cow parsnip to the parking lot.

For another great trip in Butano State Park, amid oak woodlands, dense chaparral, a pretty creek, and more redwoods, check Hike 60.

Hike 62

Franklin Point and Cascade Beach
in Año Nuevo State Reserve

LENGTH: 7.8 miles round-trip to Table Rock; 3.0 miles round-trip to Franklin Point.
DIFFICULTY: easy.
TOTAL ELEVATION GAIN: 200 feet.
WATER: available from Gazos Creek (purify); bring your own.
SEASON: all—most likely to get best views in the fall; blufftop and meadow flowers in the spring; virtual seclusion and best for whale watching in the winter.
MAP: Año Nuevo State Reserve brochure or USGS topo Año Nuevo.
INFORMATION: Año Nuevo State Reserve, (650) 879-2025.

DIRECTIONS TO TRAILHEAD: From the junction with Highway 92 in Half Moon Bay (south of San Francisco), it's a 24-mile drive south on Highway 1. From Santa Cruz, it's a 25-mile drive north on Highway 1. Park at Gazos Creek access parking area on the west side.

Escape the crowds and explore one of the most interesting and scenic stretches of California shoreline with this hiking endeavor. Along the way, Gazos, Whitehouse, and Cascade Creeks flow into the Pacific Ocean, which means lots of nearby marshes and riparian habitat supporting a wide variety of birds.

Sometimes it's aimless beach strolling, other times it's tidepooling or blufftop rambling—the whole hike offers constant photo opportunities of a curving and rugged coastline. It's hard to figure how this portion of Año Nuevo State Reserve can be so remote when just a couple miles south hordes of tourists are bound for Point Año Nuevo (Hike 63).

Whatever the case, Año Nuevo State Reserve, known for the elephant seals that look like monstrous slugs, is loaded with natural beauty and immense wildlife. It's possible to see brown pelicans swooping, California gray whales surfacing, harbor seals wallowing, and sea lions barking if you do this hike in winter or early spring.

At any time except during major high tides, walking south along uncluttered Gazos Beach to start the journey is doable, and preferred by most. Traipsing along the grassy dunes for variety's sake is always an option. A sandy spur trail adorned with nonnative ice plant and native lizard's-tail leads to a cluster of jagged rock outcrops called Franklin Point at 1.4 miles. There's lots of room for tidepooling for sea anemone and for rock hopping.

From atop the highest sand bluff, a soul can garner an inspirational panorama here. To the east, the sand dunes roll to a eucalyptus grove, which is backed by the deep-forested Santa Cruz Mountain range. Gazos Beach and Pigeon Point Lighthouse, a state historical landmark converted into a youth hostel, make for good photos to the north and northwest. Nearby Rumrunner's Cove and

Sea lions like to bask on Gazos Beach.

the distant Table Rock and Año Nuevo Island pull interest to the south. Somewhere just south of Pigeon Point, in the 1850s, two new clipper ships crashed into the rocks and were lost forever.

Sea stacks galore are the primary highlight of nearby Rumrunner's Cove. It got its name because people used to sneak booze via this isolated cove. Another outstanding feature of this cove is the wide range of colors in the rock, from orange and gray to black, white, and brown. Low-tide rock hopping and tidepooling are fun activities here, as well as playing hide-and-seek in the nearby dunes.

After departing Rumrunner's Cove, a slender path exits the dunes and then cuts through coastal scrub consisting of Pacific wax myrtle, coyote brush, lizard's-tail, buckwheat, and bush lupine. Soon the coastal scrub fades into grasslands, eventually leading to the mouth of Whitehouse Creek. The Qurosote, a group of Ohlone Indians, lived here for over 5,000 years, occupying a main village along this creek. They quarried chert and flint near here to make spear and arrow points and knives.

After crossing here next to a tiny pocket beach, you continue briefly on the bluff-hugging slender footpath. Splendid views of the gently curving Cascade Beach are virtually constant now. Access to this sandy beach, dotted with small and dark rock outcrops, comes later. The trail snakes around an eroded gulch, then heads through grasslands that, before 1971, used to be neatly plowed rows of brussels sprouts. For decades now, these former agricultural lands have been allowed to revert to their previous wild state. The various herbs and spring wildflowers are gradually yielding to ground-clinging native perennials. Douglas fir and Monterey cypress saplings are encroaching from near Highway 1, and eventually will complete the natural succession.

Turn right at the junction with the Cascade Trail for access to dark brown and flat Table Rock at the south end of clean, sandy Cascade Beach.

Hike 63

Point Año Nuevo and Cove Beach
in Año Nuevo State Reserve

LENGTH: 4 miles round-trip by starting on New Years Creek Trail.

DIFFICULTY: easy.

TOTAL ELEVATION GAIN: 100 feet.

WATER: none, bring your own.

SEASON: all—large crowds marvel at the huge northern elephant seals that come in the winter, when the reserve can be visited only on one of the regularly scheduled guided walks; most likely to get best scenic views in the fall.

MAP: Año Nuevo State Reserve brochure or USGS topo Año Nuevo.

INFORMATION: Año Nuevo State Reserve, (650) 879-2025.

DIRECTIONS TO TRAILHEAD: From the junction with Highway 92 in Half Moon Bay, it's a 28-mile drive south on

Highway 1 to Año Nuevo State Reserve entrance. From Santa Cruz, it's a 21-mile drive north on Highway 1.

Throngs of tourists gather at Año Nuevo State Reserve in the winter to witness a phenomenon—the curious breeding season of the northern elephant seals. It gets going in December, when the males, typically weighing a couple of tons, clash violently for harems. By late January, hundreds of pups, weighing up to 75 pounds apiece, are born. The northern elephant seals, resembling giant slugs, are best photographed with a telephoto lens.

For those preferring a dynamite hike with seclusion, variety, and natural beauty, go anytime after the elephant seals and gobs of people have left. April through November is prime time for this. Cove Beach then becomes a romantic getaway spot, especially on week-

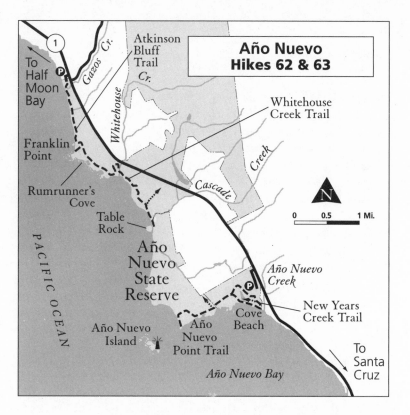

Riding the wild surf near Point Año Nuevo and Cove Beach.

days. Surfers ride the wild surf, while sea otters dive for food, harbor seals wallow on the rocks, and sea lions bark loudly and incessantly. As an added bonus, the myriad of habitats at Año Nuevo State Reserve creates a sanctuary for birds (ask for bird checklist brochure).

To start, get on New Years Creek Trail behind the Visitor Center, a renovated white barn once used along with other nearby relics as a dairy operation that thrived for 80 years until World War II. The sandy footpath passes through coyote brush and cypresses (planted long ago as windbreaks) and the deluxe Dickerman Steele house built in 1878. Veer left at the signed trail junction, then descend the wooden steps to an old cement bridge that crosses high above Año Nuevo (Spanish for New Years) Creek.

New Years Creek Trail then descends to Cove Beach at the mouth of the creek. The steep, brushy bluffs rise above the flat and gray sandy beach, as you now head north. It's a leisurely and daydreamy half-mile stroll with straight-ahead views of Año Nuevo Island and wave-worn Año Nuevo Point. Called Punta del Año Nuevo when sighted in early 1603 by Spanish maritime explorer

Viscaino, this low, rocky, windswept point has one of California's oldest place-names.

After studying the caves tucked into the rocky cliffsides on the beach's north end, find and climb the steps that eventually lead to Año Nuevo Point Trail. A sedge-lined pond that attracts waterfowl is the first highlight on the trail, which heads west. Año Nuevo Point Trail then climbs briefly to a coastal scrub flat blanketed almost entirely by coyote brush. The Pacific Ocean and the abandoned lighthouse perched atop Año Nuevo Island are constantly in view ahead, as are the heavily forested Santa Cruz Mountains to the east.

From an interpretive exhibit and trail junction at 1.2 miles (go straight), assorted Pacific wax myrtle, bush lupine, and lizard's-tail, all native shrubs, join the coastal scrub mosaic. A couple of spur trails dart south, leading to commanding vistas of Año Nuevo Bay and Cove Beach. The trail soon becomes gracefully rolling, beachgrass-lined sand dunes, which culminate at a narrow beach at ocean's edge.

On the return loop, consider for variety's sake taking the left fork —it reveals photogenic views of the aforementioned pond situated above the ocean. The path also passes by attractive coffeeberry shrubs. Another Año Nuevo State Reserve hike (Hike 62) features fantastic photo opportunities along Gazos and Cascade Beaches to ideal tidepooling spots such as Franklin Point.

Hike 64

Waddell Creek, Berry Creek Falls, and Skyline To The Sea Trail in Big Basin Redwoods State Park

> **LENGTH:** 16.4 miles round-trip as described; 3.6 miles round-trip to Twin Redwoods Trail Camp; 6.2 miles round-trip to Camp Herbert Trail Camp.
> **DIFFICULTY:** strenuous up McCrary Ridge, otherwise moderate.
> **TOTAL ELEVATION GAIN:** 1,700 feet.
> **WATER:** bring lots of your own.
> **SEASON:** all—the creeks become a beautiful torrent and the falls are mightier during late winter and early spring.

MAP: Big Basin Redwoods State Park brochure or USGS topos Big Basin, Davenport, Año Nuevo, and Franklin Point (topos don't have the trails on them).

INFORMATION: Big Basin Redwoods State Park, (408) 338-8860 or (408) 429-2851.

DIRECTIONS TO TRAILHEAD: From Santa Cruz, it's 18 miles north on Highway 1; from Half Moon Bay, it's 26 miles south on Highway 1. Park on the west side, next to the trailhead signed for Waddell Beach.

This variety-packed journey takes you past a marshland that's paradise for birds, then through a mixed evergreen forest featuring bay laurel groves and meadowlands. Those beautiful highlights are enough for some, but this journey has so much more.

Redwoods and lots of lush creekside enter the scene, followed by a circulation-enhancing climb through chaparral with views of the Santa Cruz mountainsides and ocean. Eventually, graceful yet powerful Berry Creek Falls climaxes the journey.

For the ultimate Skyline To The Sea journey, consider combining the first 4 miles of Hike 65 with the last half of this trip (backpackers must make advance reservations). Some folks who opt for all downhill park at park headquarters, then hike down to Waddell Beach to an arranged car shuttle.

If it's a nice midweek day, especially in fall, winter, or spring when less crowded, Waddell Beach is a nice place to start the hike or to unwind at journey's end. Skyline To The Sea Trail begins on the east side of Highway 1 at Rancho del Oso ("Ranch of the Bears") outpost, promptly reaching a huge marshland. Use binoculars from various vantage points to check for up to 150 species of birds that breed, nest, and rest here. One of the few relatively undisturbed bodies of freshwater left along the coast, this marshland is a year-round home to herons and ducks.

After passing through Horse Trail Camp, bear left at 0.3 mile and climb gently through a mixed evergreen forest mainly of coast live oak and knobcone pine. As the trail levels at 0.7 mile, gain a nice view behind of the marsh, ocean, and Waddell Beach. The hike continues past Douglas fir, redwood, and alder to Alder Camp, then crosses Waddell Creek at 1.4 miles. Named after a man who re-

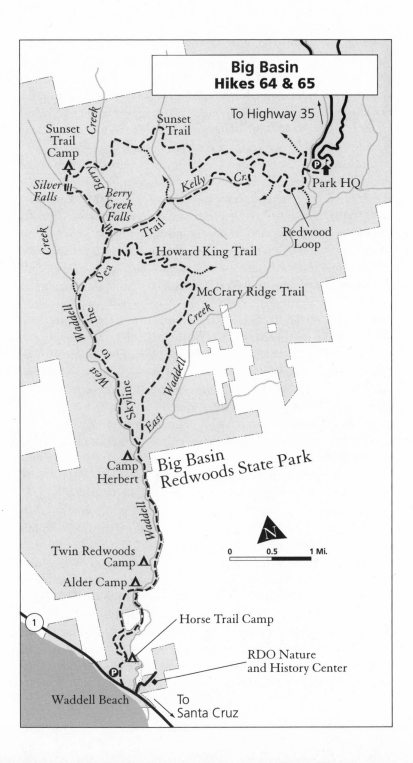

**Big Basin
Hikes 64 & 65**

To Highway 35

Sunset
Trail

Sunset
Trail
Camp

Creek

Kelly Cr.

P

Park HQ

Silver
Falls

Berry

Berry
Creek
Falls

Trail

Redwood
Loop

Creek

Sea

Howard King Trail

the

McCrary Ridge Trail

Waddell

to

Creek

West

Waddell

Skyline

East

Camp
Herbert

Big Basin
Redwoods State Park

N

0   0.5   1 Mi.

Waddell

Twin Redwoods
Camp

Alder Camp

Horse Trail Camp

RDO Nature
and History Center

1

P

Waddell Beach

To
Santa Cruz

portedly was mauled to death by a grizzly bear in the 1800s when these ferocious bears roamed Big Basin Redwoods, Waddell Creek lingers close to Skyline To The Sea Trail for 1.5 miles. Extra tall native riparian trees flourish in the sunlight and extra moisture, including bigleaf maple, alder, buckeye, Douglas fir, redwood, and California bay laurel. The understory lining the creek banks consists mainly of thimbleberry, redwood sorrel, fern, and horsetail.

Another backpack camp called Camp Herbert shows up at 3.2 miles, followed by a bridge crossing of East Waddell Creek, then a right turn onto signed McCrary Ridge Trail. This 3-mile-long footpath climbs in a mixed evergreen forest, then switches to chaparral mainly of manzanita and knobcone pine. Sprawling views of the Santa Cruz Mountains and glimpses of the ocean occur occasionally.

The trail and the brunt of the climbing climaxes at 6 miles with a right turn onto a fire road. Watch intently for a trail sign sometimes concealed by shrubs 0.2 mile farther, where you bear left onto Howard King Trail. This 2.5-mile-long trail drops gently in a shaded mixed evergreen forest of madrone, laurel, and Douglas fir.

On reaching West Waddell Creek, go right onto Skyline To The Sea Trail, then turn left 0.3 mile farther onto Berry Creek Falls Trail. After a few hops, skips, and jumps of ecstasy, you reach fabulous Berry Creek Falls, which plunges some 65 vertical feet into a tiny, frothy, but clear pool. From a well-built bench set on a wooden observation deck, hikers can feel the cool mist of the falls while gazing down on the entire scene, bordered by ferns. Nearby, constant cascades stream into perfect miniature pools. You've come this far; why not traipse another 0.6 mile to observe Silver Falls (Hike 65)?

After backtracking to Skyline To The Sea Trail, an old dirt ranch road, the final 6 miles of the journey is spent going gently downhill in soft shade along meandering Waddell Creek the whole way.

Plan to return several minutes before the bus comes (if you're taking it back to park headquarters) or prior to leaving in your car, so precious time can be spent barefoot on the sands of Waddell Beach. The Ohlone Indians fished from this beach, between trips up the same canyon you wandered in, where they hunted game. Check out nearby Waddell Bluffs, which have been in a constant state of erosion since the waves began washing the shore. These bluffs comprise a steep stone backdrop to the sky-blue ocean.

Hike 65

Berry Creek Falls, Silver Falls, and Sunset Trail in Big Basin Redwoods State Park

LENGTH: 11.5 miles round-trip as described; 0.6 mile round-trip on the Redwood Trail.

DIFFICULTY: strenuous.

TOTAL ELEVATION GAIN: 1,900 feet.

WATER: available from Kelly Creek and Berry Creek (purify); bring lots of your own.

SEASON: all—the roaring creeks in late winter inspire, when the falls and cascades are at peak power stage.

MAP: Big Basin Redwoods State Park brochure or USGS topos Big Basin and Franklin Point (topos don't have trails on them). See p. 183.

INFORMATION: Big Basin Redwoods State Park, (408) 338-8860 or (408) 429-2851.

DIRECTIONS TO TRAILHEAD: Get to the interchange of Highways 236 and 9 (6 miles west of Highway 35). Drive west on twisty Highway 236 for 8.4 steep miles to Big Basin Redwoods State Park headquarters. Or, from the town of Boulder Creek (on Highway 9, 13 miles northwest of Santa Cruz), drive 9 miles on Highway 236.

Stand under giant redwoods, then traipse deep into an old redwood forest that traces gorgeous creeks to renowned Berry Creek Falls. Then, explore dramatic Silver Falls and colorful cascades before getting on the Sunset Trail, which leads you through some chaparral in the park's remotest region before reuniting with towering redwoods. Big redwoods, clear and wild creeks, memorable waterfalls, splendid views—this journey is crammed with highlights throughout. Rest assured, there are some dues to be paid and a tradeoff to consider. There are several climbs of about 300–400 feet, most of it coming later. The trails are in such good shape and the hike is so popular, you'll likely share it with lots of people. However, relative solitude can be attained at midweek in winter, which is probably the best time to go anyway, because there's more water action.

This hike covers an enchanting portion of Skyline To The Sea Trail. To do the entire Skyline To The Sea adventure, combine the initial 4 miles of this hike with the last 7 miles of Hike 64. Backpackers need to reserve trailside camping in advance.

To start, do the 0.6-mile Redwood Trail loop through the park's largest grove of redwoods. This flat stroll can also be saved for last, as long as you seize the opportunity to take this self-guided nature walk (grab nearby trail brochure for a quarter). These grand redwoods are mighty. Father-of-the-Forest has probably lived more than 2,000 years, and Mother-of-the-Forest, at 329 feet, is the park's tallest tree. Chimney Tree has made it through many lightning fires.

To reach Skyline To The Sea Trail, head west from behind the fee kiosk, then follow the signs for it. Go left at the large signpost soon after crossing a wooden bridge.

Tall redwoods accompany a moderate descent to the crossing of Kelly Creek at 2.1 miles from the parking lot. A mile farther along this serene creek, reach a series of tiny pools near Kelly Creek's confluence with West Waddell Creek.

California huckleberry shrubs thrive along the banks of these two creeks. Before they were hunted to extinction, grizzly bears once gobbled these blue berries here. The Indians who roamed these lands long ago were aware of this, and they also knew grizzlies preferred the protection of these large redwood groves. Therefore, Native American Indians sensibly settled just outside the basin areas.

A wooden bench, ideal for admiring fabulous Berry Creek Falls roaring in the distance, is situated at trailside 4.1 miles onto Skyline To The Sea Trail. The trail then plunges another tenth of a mile to where Berry Creek flows into West Waddell Creek. A left turn here descends to Waddell Beach (Hike 64). Our hike proceeds right here for a 0.1-mile ascent to Berry Creek Falls, which plummets some 65 feet into a crystal-clear, sand-bottomed pool. Berry Creek Falls Trail also climbs to a vista from the top of the waterfall.

A half mile of light climbing puts you in touch with Silver Falls, which topple some 60 feet into a tiny, oblong clear body of water dammed by a large, fallen redwood trunk. A bit farther, the trail climbs to an inspirational view of Silver Falls, followed by scenes of strikingly splendid Golden Falls Cascade. Consisting of a quarter mile's worth of orange and brown pools and frothy white cascades,

Toppled redwood trunk and Silver Falls.

Golden Falls Cascade is flanked by rugged, rust-colored walls studded with tiny ferns and mosses.

You soon come to a signed trail junction at 5.2 miles, where a left turn leads 100 yards to Sunset Trail Camp, the park's most remote backpack camp. A right turn puts you on Sunset Trail, which suddenly breaks out of the redwoods and briefly through chaparral of chamise, manzanita, knobcone pine, and ceanothus. Serious climbing ensues, including the crossing of two canyonsides to a trail marker at 7.9 miles (bear left).

You gradually return to redwoods (they get bigger as you go). The final mile goes past three signed trail junctions (take a left and two rights), then alongside peaceful Opal Creek, where giant and stately redwoods take center stage.

Hike 66

Loch Lomond

LENGTH: 5.2 miles round-trip as described; 2.4 miles round-trip to Huckleberry Cove.

DIFFICULTY: moderate.

TOTAL ELEVATION GAIN: 700 feet.

WATER: available from Loch Lomond (purify), Newell Creek (purify), and faucets at boat launch.

SEASON: all—usually ideal temperatures in spring and fall; more seclusion in the winter.

MAP: Loch Lomond Recreation Area map or USGS topo Felton.

INFORMATION: Loch Lomond County Park, (408) 335-7424.

DIRECTIONS TO TRAILHEAD: From San Jose, take Highway 17 toward Santa Cruz, then go west on Mount Hermon Road for a couple of miles. Make a left on Graham Hill Road then another left on Zayante Road. After 5 miles, turn left on Lompico Road, drive 1.7 miles then turn left onto West Drive. After a half mile of winding and climbing, turn right on Sequoia and promptly reach the park. The trailhead begins near the launch ramp. From Felton, Ben Lomond, Big Basin Redwoods, and Highway 35, reach Ben Lomond

on Highway 9 then turn east on Glen Arbor Road. After 0.6
mile, go east on Quail Hollow Road. After 2 miles, turn left
on East Zayante Road, travel 0.7 mile, and then turn left on
Lompico Road. After 1.7 miles, go left on West Drive for 0.5
mile, then right on Sequoia to the park.

To the local folk, the natural riches of Lake Lomond are well known
and much visited. A stranger to the shores of this prized lake is apt to
find adventure roaming the conifer-ringed lake, leaving with good
vibes and good memories. It's easy to remember the primitive cry and
graceful flight of the great blue heron swooping low over the lake.
It's likely a newcomer will also fondly remember the enchanting
little island, the shoreline redwoods, and the hawk's-eye view of the
lake. The trip at first traverses the shoreline of the lake, where the
bullfrogs croak, the chipmunks and squirrels scurry, and the pond

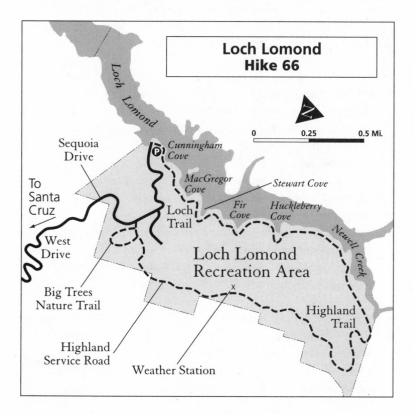

turtles submerge. Later, the trail climbs away from the lake and deep into the woods, where the mountain lions are (rarely) spotted sprinting away, and where the coyotes howl at night. The usually dry ridge grants views of the lake. From up here, alligator lizards and western fence lizards dart helter-skelter in the sun, while turkey vultures hover above for leftovers, and the red-tailed hawk dives for prey.

The Zayante group of the Ohlone Indians lived peacefully in Loch Lomond country, surviving on fish, acorns, and small game. The Ohlones lived the easy life, taking saunas, playing games, and singing songs.

At the start, Loch Trail heads for Cunningham Cove, featuring a dirt beach, a fishing ramp, and a huge, hollowed stump at the water's edge. Madrone, tan oak, and red alder adorn the shoreline here.

Redwoods shade a small beach at MacGregor Cove, where a small island with trees is situated nearby. The steep banks of neighboring Stewart Cove are laced with tanbark oak shrubs and trees, and California huckleberry shrubs. The Loch Trail crosses a narrow gulch clogged with toppled redwood logs, then winds around the rest of Stewart Cove in a redwood forest.

Fir Cove is partially discernible through a mixed redwood/hardwood forest and from the signed trail junction with the MacLaren Trail at 0.8 mile (keep left). The slender footpath continues its in-and-out/up-and-down shaded route past Huckleberry Cove, where hazelnut shrubs and live oak trees join the plant community. At this point, most of the people have been left behind, fishing.

Deer Flat, at the signed junction with the Highland Trail (go right), is tucked under an attractive mix of redwoods, coast live oak, and a handsome, multiple-trunked madrone tree.

The first 0.8 mile of the Highland Trail climbs 400 feet beneath the comfortable shade of tall redwoods, Douglas fir, tan oak, and madrone. As the trail levels, a mix of knobcone pines, chamise, manzanita, and the invasive (yellow-flowered) scotch broom appear in the more exposed sites.

A weather station is perched in a clearing at 3.1 miles, where good views can be had of Loch Lomond below. After a handful of short but steep ups and downs, Highland Trail meets the paved entrance road next to the Big Trees Nature Trail (well worth the 15 minutes to stroll through this grove).

Hike 67

San Lorenzo River and Eagle Creek Trails
in Henry Cowell Redwoods State Park

LENGTH: 6.3 miles round-trip as described; 4.2 miles round-trip excluding Eagle Creek Trail; 3.4 miles round-trip excluding Redwood Loop as well.

DIFFICULTY: easy.

TOTAL ELEVATION GAIN: 300 feet.

WATER: available from fountains near parking area; San Lorenzo River (purify) and Eagle Creek (purify).

SEASON: all—look for silver salmon spawning up the San Lorenzo River in winter; the river and creek are swifter and fuller in early spring.

MAP: Henry Cowell Redwoods State Park map or USGS topo Felton.

INFORMATION: Henry Cowell Redwoods State Park, (408) 335-4598.

DIRECTIONS TO TRAILHEAD: From Santa Cruz, take Highway 9 north for 6 miles, then turn right into Henry Cowell Redwoods State Park. From Felton on Highway 9, drive south for 0.7 mile to the park entrance. The trailhead is behind park headquarters near the meadow.

It's the true nature of a river—soft and smooth in the early autumn, swollen and intense in the late winter. The San Lorenzo River, full of silver salmon and steelhead in the winter, possesses these distinct dual characteristics. Much smaller Eagle Creek is still no slouch in early spring.

Why all the fuss about all this water? Because it's the centerpiece of this viewless walk. Strolls through a meadow and a grove of huge redwoods are bonuses that make this cool and serene journey well rounded and pleasant for the child in you and for kids in general.

The Meadow Trail splits a field of soft grasses, heading directly for the San Lorenzo River. Through timely prescribed burns, efforts are being made to gradually return this meadow of mostly introduced species into an even softer and more alluring green field of na-

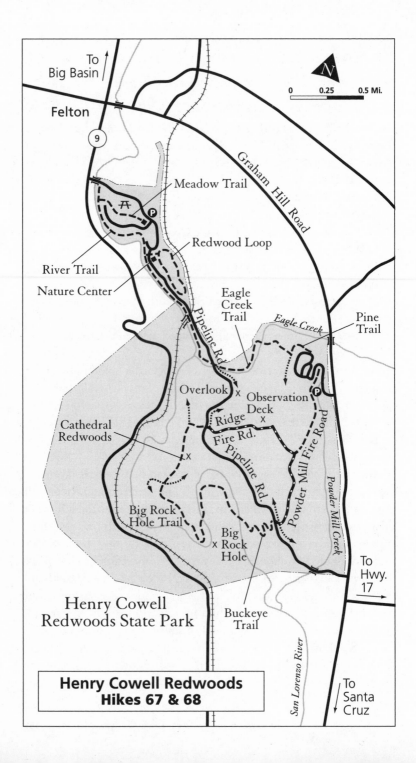

To
Big Basin

Felton

9

Meadow Trail

River Trail

Nature Center

Redwood Loop

Graham Hill Road

0   0.25   0.5 Mi.

N

Eagle
Creek
Trail

Pipeline Rd.

Eagle Creek

Pine
Trail

Overlook   x

Observation
Deck
x

Cathedral
Redwoods

Ridge
Fire Rd.

Pipeline Rd.

x

Powder Mill Fire Road

Powder Mill Creek

Big Rock
Hole Trail

Big
Rock
Hole   x

To
Hwy.
17

Buckeye
Trail

San Lorenzo River

To
Santa
Cruz

Henry Cowell
Redwoods State Park

**Henry Cowell Redwoods
Hikes 67 & 68**

tive grasses, sedges, and wildflowers. The shrubs and trees that decorate this meadow are native—willows, bay laurel, tanbark oak, coast live oak, and box elder.

Shade and serenity greet you on the River Trail, which hugs the banks of the San Lorenzo River. At 0.7 mile into the journey, River Trail breezes past the backside of the Nature Center. Go in front of this wooden building for a 0.8-mile promenade through a grove of gargantuan redwoods. A helpful interpretive guide of wheelchair-accessible Redwood Loop is available from the Nature Center. One can never get enough of grand groves like this sheltered forest of ancient redwood giants.

Back on the River Trail, one of the many joys of taking this flat and dusty path is to note how frequently the San Lorenzo River—rarely out of sight—alternates between calm swimming pools with gently flowing currents and whitewater mini-rapids. A room-sized fishing tank sits above the river at its confluence with Eagle Creek (bear left here), underneath an old railroad bridge.

Mellow Eagle Creek generally flows faster than the San Lorenzo River, and is situated in a steeper canyon. Eagle Creek Trail, a wide footpath, hugs the meandering banks most of the way. It shows off a near constant barrage of miniature cascades spilling into tiny pools, often draped with fallen redwood and tanbark oak logs.

The sometimes filtered but mostly deep shade of this trail keeps things cool, and the subliminal lure of Eagle Creek is pleasantly distracting, easing the climb through second-growth redwoods.

Just before its union with the Pine Trail, the path suddenly climbs into an open woodland/chaparral community. Ponderosa pine, coast live oak, and California bay laurel rise above ceanothus, manzanita, coffeeberry, and chamise. From here to the campground 0.3 mile farther, the gentle climb through this sunny plant community continues. The campground itself is mostly shaded by coast live oak, with madrones, Douglas firs, pines, and bay laurel mixed in.

Hike 68

Cathedral Redwoods and Big Rock Hole Trail in Henry Cowell Redwoods State Park

LENGTH: 5 miles round-trip as described; 2.2 miles round-trip to the Overlook for ocean views.

DIFFICULTY: moderate.

TOTAL ELEVATION GAIN: 1,200 feet.

WATER: available from campground faucets, Observation Deck, and San Lorenzo River (purify).

SEASON: April through November—call ahead after heavy rains to determine if the river (no bridges) is crossable.

MAP: Henry Cowell Redwoods State Park map or USGS topo Felton. See p. 192.

INFORMATION: Henry Cowell Redwoods State Park, (408) 335-4598.

DIRECTIONS TO TRAILHEAD: From Santa Cruz at the junctions of Highways 1 and 17, take Graham Hill Road north 5 miles to the Cowell campground and park entrance. From San Jose, take Highway 17 south, turn right after several miles on Mount Hermon Road, drive 3 miles and then turn left on Graham Hill Road at Felton. It's just over 2 miles to the campground. Find the Pine Trailhead between campsites 47 and 49.

This trip features several benefits a hiker looks for—seclusion, big redwoods, ocean vistas, and trail variety. It even includes a classic swimming hole, a deep spot of the San Lorenzo River, where earlier in the year silver salmon and steelhead spawned.

As an added bonus, the beginning and end of the journey is spent in an elfin forest—chaparral where the coyote sneaks, the bobcat prowls, and raccoon tracks appear on the trail.

If ever there was a custom hike to explore the distinct plant communities, varying topography, and other nuances of the Santa Cruz Mountains, this one's it.

Henry Cowell Redwoods State Park features diversity, including the flowering native buckeye tree.

The Pine Trail departs Powder Mill Creek, passes through open woodlands consisting mainly of mature coast live oak, then darts right in chaparral at the junction with Powder Mill Trail (the return trail). Knobcone pines stand above poison oak, manzanita, coffeeberry, chamise, and ceanothus here.

After a brief climb, you reach Ridge Road Trail (go left) and the Observation Deck, which includes a water tank, picnic tables, and a drinking fountain. The promised ocean views come later—the view here is down into Scott's Valley. A botanical mystery exists around this vista point. These ponderosa pines, which normally have prickly cones, have cones gentle to the touch like ponderosa pine's closest cousin, the Jeffrey pine. Both are yellow pines, but the closest stand of Jeffreys are in the Sierra, in much higher elevations. How did these ponderosas get crossed, or did they? Who knows?

After a brief descent, Ridge Road Trail intersects with paved (but closed to motorized vehicles) Pipeline Road. Turn left here and after a brief stroll, you'll come to Overlook, which encompasses far-reaching views of the San Lorenzo River gorge, sprawling Santa Cruz Mountains, and Monterey Bay, all in one gaze.

After doubling back to and going left on the Ridge Road Trail, you soon come to and go left on the Big Rock Hole Trail. After 0.2 mile of mostly level walking, you come to an intersection with Rincon Road Trail at 2 miles into the journey. Known as Cathedral Redwoods, the peaceful grove of huge second-growth redwoods here are home to great horned owls, which look down on the squirrels and banana slugs in the duff. A larger grove of redwoods are part of Hike 67.

Big Rock Hole Trail now plunges 400 feet in half a mile to the gracefully meandering San Lorenzo River, flowing over granitic rock. Bear left here onto the Buckeye Trail and promptly reach Big Rock Hole. Shaded by redwood, red alder, and tan oak trees, this deep, clear swimming hole invites a dip to stay cooler for the climb that follows. While stretched out on this large granite boulder, be on the lookout for kingfishers and herons swooping over the river gorge. Chances are, the Ohlone Indian children jumped off this rock long ago.

After swirling clockwise along the river, Buckeye Trail crosses it again, then climbs via switchbacks in a forest of second-growth redwoods, tan oak, and Douglas fir, then crosses Pipeline Road. You're now on Powder Mill Fire Road (go left at its fork), where you traipse in nearly level mixed woodland and chaparral back to the campground.

Monterey/Big Sur Area

Hike 69

China Beach, Bird Island, and Whaler's Cove in Point Lobos State Reserve

LENGTH: 4.5 miles round-trip as described; 1 mile round-trip to Pelican Point.

DIFFICULTY: easy.

TOTAL ELEVATION GAIN: 200 feet.

WATER: available from parking lot and Cannery Point faucets.

SEASON: all—fewer people in winter; more flowers in spring and summer; more clear days for great views in fall.

MAP: Point Lobos State Reserve map or USGS topo Soberanes Point.

INFORMATION: Point Lobos State Reserve, (408) 624-4909.

DIRECTIONS TO TRAILHEAD: From Carmel, it's a 4-mile drive south on Highway 1 to the Point Lobos State Reserve entrance station. Follow the main park road until it dead-ends at a large, paved parking lot.

It took nature millions of years to create an amazing interaction between land and sea that typifies Point Lobos. It'll take you about three hours to see the result—irregular coves, pristine beaches, brazen headlands, and rolling meadows. Throw in some far-reaching views and some extremely rare natural stands of native conifers and this becomes an all-encompassing, awe-inspiring journey.

The numerous destinations for this adventure require some careful and frequent map studying—the idea is to get greedy and not miss a single highlight.

First item on the hiking agenda is China Beach, covered with shimmering white sand compared to dark and pebbly Hidden Beach nearby (see Hike 70). The clear and calm aquamarine water contained within China Cove is as pretty as it gets. Its two-way sea tunnel is another attraction. From various lookouts above, the profusion of brown kelp can resemble several-legged sea monsters.

A good loop trail escorts you to a point for garnering great views

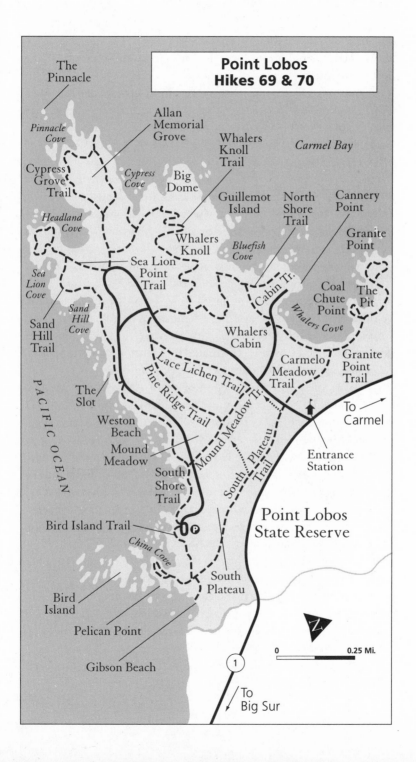

The Pinnacle

Pinnacle Cove

Carmel Bay

Allan Memorial Grove

Whalers Knoll Trail

Cypress Grove Trail

Cypress Cove

Big Dome

Guillemot Island

North Shore Trail

Cannery Point

Headland Cove

Granite Point

Bluefish Cove

Whalers Knoll

Sea Lion Point Trail

Cabin Tr.

Coal Chute Point

The Pit

Sea Lion Cove

Sand Hill Cove

Whalers Cove

Sand Hill Trail

Whalers Cabin

Granite Point Trail

PACIFIC OCEAN

The Slot

Lace Lichen Trail

Carmelo Meadow Trail

To Carmel

Pine Ridge Trail

Mound Meadow Tr.

Entrance Station

Weston Beach

Mound Meadow

South Plateau Trail

South Shore Trail

Bird Island Trail

Point Lobos State Reserve

China Cove

Bird Island

South Plateau

Pelican Point

0   0.25 Mi.

Gibson Beach

1

To Big Sur

Point Lobos
Hikes 69 & 70

out on Bird Island. This steep rock knob is often occupied by so many black cormorant sea birds, it almost looks like a distant alpine mountain dotted with dwarf conifers.

A network of wooden steps, similar to those that lead to China Beach, also descend to nearby Gibson Beach. Although larger and with lots more white sand to frolic on, Gibson Beach is less private because a posh neighborhood overlooks it from the east. A stroll on the level, needle-littered South Plateau Trail is spent in the comfortable shade of native Monterey pines, with a few coast live oaks in this open forest, along with coffeeberry, blue-blossom ceanothus, poison oak, and orange bush monkeyflower. Much of the poison oak here shows its amazing adaptability to shade by climbing like a vine up many of the pines. After crossing the park road near the entrance station, our trail switches to the Carmelo Meadow Trail, which shows off a variety of pretty grasses, rushes, sedges, and herbs. After crossing this pretty meadow, our journey comes to an ocean view of calm and kelp-covered Whaler's Cove (bear right onto Granite Point Trail).

The waves gently kiss the narrow brown strip of lengthy beach here, and this large cove is punctuated by a cluster of imposing rock outcrops just beyond Cannery Point. Although most of the landscape along the north coast section of Point Lobos is composed of coarse-grained Santa Lucia granite that solidified underground 110 million years ago, Whaler's Cove is composed of the Carmelo Formation. This 60-million-year-old sedimentary rock is more easily eroded, hence its water-rounded rocks. The brief loop trail around Coal Chute Point is graced by ancient, wind-sculpted, and naturally growing Monterey pines and Monterey cypresses. This is one of the few spots in the park where the two mesh. Figure that there are only three areas where Monterey pines grow naturally, and only two remaining places on earth where the Monterey cypress still grows naturally, then it's easy to see why this is a rare spot.

A variety of low-growing native succulents in the dudleya genus, such as bluff lettuce, adorn the steep, north-facing banks above a neighboring cove called the Pit. The beach tapers downward to meet the gentle waves—its lower portion consists of brown sand while the upper section is coated with dark pebbles.

From various vistas along the Granite Point Loop Trail, a hiker

A typical rocky surf zone at Point Lobos State Reserve.

can look in all directions beyond coastal scrub and granite boulders. Carmel River State Beach and the fancy homes above it can be surveyed on a clear day as well as the two previously mentioned coves and points. On doubling back, continue west on the Granite Point Trail past a grassy section of Carmelo Meadow laced with coyote brush on the left, and more chances to admire Whaler's Cove on the right. Registered scuba divers explore a portion of the park's marine habitats here, which is one of the richest in the state. Whaler's Cove was the site of a whaling station in the 1800s, and an abalone cannery was once operated along this large cove as well.

Shaded by huge, gnarled Monterey cypress trees, Whaler's Cabin consists of two wooden structures (one is now operated as a museum) with whale bones and two huge whaler's pots once used to melt down whale blubber into oil situated nearby.

Laced with views of Whaler's Cove and Granite Point, Whaler's Cabin Trail splits dense chaparral of poison oak, coyote brush, and orange bush monkeyflower. The views vanish the instant you stroll into another grove of native Monterey pines. Take the spur trail right signed North Shore Trail to take in closeup scenes of Cannery Point and Bluefish Cove.

On returning, stay on the North Shore Trail as it heads west awhile, and step over a network of large pine roots that lace the trail. You peer through the pine trunks to study the stark and steep rock cliffs that semisurround beachless Bluefish Cove.

The Whaler's Knoll Trail darts left and climbs gently and briefly past large patches of fragrant wood mint. The climbing is done when you bear left at another signed trail junction (going straight takes you atop Whaler's Knoll—see Hike 70).

Lace Lichen and Mound Meadow Trails feature quiet strolling in an open, level Monterey pine forest with pleasing glimpses of the meadow, and lead to the South Shore Trail. By turning left, you can check out a scenic section of the Point Lobos rocky shoreline (also the first part of Hike 70) for a couple hundred yards before returning to your car.

Hike 70

Sea Lion Rocks and Cypress Grove Trail
in Point Lobos State Reserve

LENGTH: 4.3 miles round-trip.

DIFFICULTY: easy.

TOTAL ELEVATION GAIN: 300 feet.

WATER: available from parking lot faucets.

SEASON: all—fewer people in the winter; most likely to get clear views in the autumn; most wildflowers in spring and early summer.

MAP: Point Lobos State Reserve map or USGS topo Soberanes Point. See p. 201.

INFORMATION: Point Lobos State Reserve, (408) 624-4909.

DIRECTIONS TO TRAILHEAD: From Carmel near Monterey, it's a 4-mile drive south on Highway 1 to the Point Lobos State Reserve entrance station. Follow the paved main park road until it dead-ends at a large, paved parking lot.

Everyone who takes this rocky seaside stroll will be touched by something special. It may be the noisy sea lions barking and basking on Sea Lion Rocks, or the southern sea otters sleeping peacefully and resembling dark logs in the floating brown seaweed.

Or it could be the contorted and gnarled Monterey cypresses that amazingly survive the salty air and feisty winds encompassing the outermost granite cliffs on the continent's edge. It's a reflective yet energizing excursion showing off a series of irregularly shaped sea stacks and rocky coves. Even in a deep fog, each step is precious and every view is breathtaking. Note how each beach and cove contrasts strikingly, and each view seems to rival or surpass the previous one.

After getting a kick out of the world's tamest squirrels at the parking area, get on the South Shore Trail and promptly saunter down the stone steps that lead to Hidden Beach. This tiny, rock-encased pocket beach is as small as they come. Coated with refreshingly uncommon gravel rather than sand, this enticing beach stays clean, dark, and wave washed.

The next stopover involves a free scramble atop a conglomerate rock face that allows you to feel you're out on the ocean looking in to an unnamed pocket beach. These conglomerate rocks are sedimentary and over 60 million years old. The rounded pebbles and cobbles were cemented together by pressure and naturally occurring chemicals.

Neighboring Weston Beach is lined with colorful pebbles and scattered with small driftwood. A maze of nearby flat and smooth rock faces are ideal for sun and wave worshiping.

The Slot is a narrow channel that proves how strong waves can be. They persistently push through this rock-surrounded slot onto another attractive pocket beach laced with pebbles.

Sand Hill Cove features several awe-inspiring scenarios. Partially bordered by a 100-foot-tall, steep sedimentary rock cliff face (ideal for watching the floating brown kelp), this cove also includes a pebbly beach. Choose your favorite perch along the bluffs to gaze at the waves that crash in three directions. There's as much foamy whitewater as gray-blue water here.

You're bound to see the quiet harbor seals resembling fat cigars, basking on rocks, or treading water close to shore. They don't move about on rocks as well as the larger and darker sea lions, which are often heard barking out on Sea Lion Rocks. It's easy to imagine the continent of Atlantis and Sea Lion Rocks being one and the same because of the fantastic, irregular rock formations.

A little side trip via Sea Lion Point Trail over to Headlands Cove offers an exciting opportunity to get close to some major whitewater wave action. Hear the waves explode loudly against a cluster of nearby rock outcrops. Serene Headlands Cove Beach contrasts with the wave action, and qualifies as the perfect sandy beach—smooth, clean, dark, and soft.

The Cypress Grove Trail briefly passes through coastal scrub consisting of orange bush monkeyflower, golden yarrow, California sage, coyote brush, and poison oak. There are a couple of prime spots for peering at the Pinnacle past wind-stunted, nature-sculpted Monterey cypresses.

The orange, velvety, stringy things clinging to its branches are actually green algae. The color change comes naturally from carotene, the same pigment in carrots. These algae, like the green lace lichens that drape over the dead and shaded understory limbs, are harmless to these rare cypresses.

After completing the much visited Cypress Grove loop, veer left en route to Whaler's Knoll. Pass briefly through coastal scrub, bear right onto the signed Whaler's Knoll Trail, then negotiate a 200-foot climb through an open Monterey pine forest.

Before the trail veers inland, be sure to check out a dense pyramidal mass covered with Monterey pines called Big Dome. Toward the top of this mostly flat knoll, abundant lace lichens droop from the pines. There's a huge granddaddy Monterey pine at the unsigned trail junction (bear right) gradually stripped by time of its needles on its lower half. This monument is easily twice as wide as the neighboring conifers.

After a brief descent, bear right again at another unsigned trail junction, pass beneath another huge Monterey pine specimen, cross the paved road, then get on the signed Pine Ridge Trail after briefly strolling the signed Lace Lichen Trail.

The aptly named Pine Ridge Trail, mellow and seldom visited, highlights an open forest of Monterey pine in various stages of growth from sapling size to mature height. It's a level stroll to the rhythm of chirping white-crowned sparrows and the softly purring sea, amid chaparral shrubs such as ceanothus, coffeeberry, and orange bush monkeyflower. It differs drastically from the South Shore Trail you started on, but variety is the spice of a good loop hike.

Hike 71

Soberanes Canyon and Rocky Ridge
in Garrapata State Park

LENGTH: 5.9 miles round-trip as described; 4.5 miles round-trip skipping the Peak Trail; 3 miles round-trip skipping Rocky Ridge Trail.

DIFFICULTY: moderate; strenuous climbing Rocky Ridge.

TOTAL ELEVATION GAIN: 1,800 feet.

WATER: along Soberanes Creek; bring lots of your own.

SEASON: all—flowers and ticks galore in summer; clearest days for views in the fall.

MAP: USGS topos Point Sur and Soberanes Point or small Garrapata State Park map.

INFORMATION: Garrapata State Park or Pfeiffer Big Sur State Park, (408) 667-2315.

DIRECTIONS TO TRAILHEAD: From Carmel heading south on Highway 1, it's a 9-mile drive to Gate 13 (20 miles going north from Pfeiffer Big Sur State Park), where you can park in the small dirt lot on the east side of the road if the small dirt lot on the west side is full.

Here's a case where underdevelopment is a blessing. It tends to save precious land for the roamers of the world—you and me. At Garrapata State Park, there are no bathrooms, or special signs, or large paved parking lots, or guided tours, or drinking fountains. Just lots of room for wandering in the Big Sur area's best redwood grove, and climbing past profuse wildflowers dotting steep hillsides to view after view of the rugged and rocky shoreline.

A fire road leaves a Monterey cypress stand, then abruptly veers north to the junction of Soberanes Canyon and Rocky Ridge Trails. It makes good hiking sense to do this loop counterclockwise, beginning with the Soberanes Canyon Trail. This way you snag a little more shade during a portion of the climb, then get rewarded with constant views of the Carmel coastline face first down the Rocky Ridge Trail.

The Soberanes Canyon Trail depicts a curiously weird scene at the onset. Impenetrable cactus mesh in the coastal scrub. Some cacti actually thrive in tandem with creekside willows. This drastically uncommon botanical setting can take place because the soil stays well drained enough for the cactus on the slope of Soberanes Creek, while the surrounding willows have enough lateral roots to dapple further into the moist streambed.

The first third of this trail passes along steep and sprawling coastal scrub hillsides, cloaked in late spring and early summer with flowering orange bush monkeyflower and golden yarrow (no relation to the more common white yarrow, which also grows in the scrub).

An ideal site for a picnic awaits at 0.5 mile right where a 5-yard sandy path transfixes you to a quiet creekside scenario nestled under a couple of towering multiple-trunked redwoods. Their large surface roots can be sat on, as well as any of several flat boulders. True, most of the other redwood hikes described in this book boast redwoods even taller than these, but the journey through this redwood grove rates as the most mystical and magical of them all. Delicately wandering Soberanes Creek drifts into one miniature pool after another, beckoning a wayfaring daydreamer to dip a pair of bare feet into its cool, clear waters.

Ground-hugging redwood sorrel is so lush in some spots, it resembles a thick carpet of clover. Ferns, thimbleberry, and ninebark shrubs comprise the rest of the understory, while a few stands of California bay laurel trees and an occasional bigleaf maple snugly hug the taller redwoods. There are a number of delightful wooden bridges to cross and unsigned trail loop junctions to choose from (they all trace the creek and return to the main trail).

At 1.5 miles, you reach an interesting trail junction where the edge of the redwood community meets the wide-open coastal scrub. By going right onto the North Fork Trail, you can further explore Soberanes Canyon for another half mile or so.

The moderate climbing of the Soberanes Canyon Trail is now

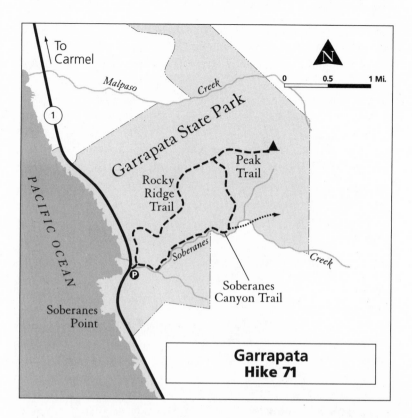

To
Carmel

Malpaso *Creek*

Garrapata State Park

1

PACIFIC OCEAN

Peak
Trail

Rocky
Ridge
Trail

Soberanes

Creek

P

Soberanes
Canyon Trail

Soberanes
Point

**Garrapata
Hike 71**

replaced with a steep and exposed climb on the Rocky Ridge Trail past a variety of low-growing, summer-flowering shrubs, including bush monkeyflower, lupine, buckwheat, California sagebrush, and the nonnative yellow-flowering wild mustard.

After just a few minutes of panting, one can pause and admire the Pacific Ocean. In the same view, rugged and undulating Soberanes Canyon can be traced to the sea.

After a hefty 1-mile hike, consisting of a 1,000-foot climb, you reach a signed trail junction at one of Rocky Ridge's many gaps. The views here are scintillating and far reaching, but slightly more so atop a knob after a 0.7-mile climb east on the Peak Trail. Grasses and more great views escort you on this 300-foot ascent, which includes two brief downhill stints.

The knob at the end of Peak Trail allows generous vistas to the east of the Santa Lucia Mountains. Views of the ocean, Soberanes

Canyon, and Malpaso Creek watershed can be appreciated along the way from various small rock outcrops.

The easy but occasionally steep stroll down the Rocky Ridge Trail is even more delightful if one follows the sun sinking over the ocean at twilight time. The hills are alive along this scenic stretch, and they do resemble the hills that Julie Andrews frolicked on in the *Sound of Music*.

From a wooden bench almost halfway down, you can bask in the sun and study the rocky shoreline and more coastal sage hillside sprawling below.

Hike 72

Big Sur River, Molera Beach, and Ridge Trail in Andrew Molera State Park

> **LENGTH:** 8 miles round-trip as described; 2.4 miles round-trip through Creamery Meadow to Molera Beach.
> **DIFFICULTY:** moderate to strenuous.
> **TOTAL ELEVATION GAIN:** 1,000 feet.
> **WATER:** from Big Sur River; fill up from the parking lot faucets.
> **SEASON:** all—check ahead during the winter to see if the bridge over Big Sur River can be crossed; great views more likely in the autumn.
> **MAP:** Andrew Molera State Park map or USGS topos Big Sur and Point Sur.
> **INFORMATION:** Andrew Molera State Park, (408) 624-7195.
> **DIRECTIONS TO TRAILHEAD:** From Carmel, drive south 21 miles on Highway 1 to the Andrew Molera State Park entrance. It's a 0.1-mile drive on paved road to the huge dirt-and-gravel parking lot. Cross the Big Sur River on foot via wood planks to pick up the trail proper.

A swirling river that climaxes into the sea at a beach is the ultimate bird sanctuary. Such is the case on this eventful journey tracing the south shoreline of clear Big Sur River to cormorant-covered Molera Point and Molera Beach, patrolled by western seagulls. The yard-tall

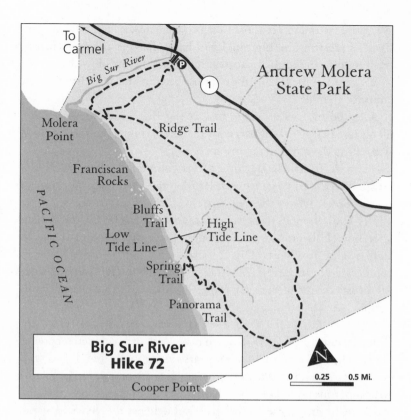

To Carmel

Big Sur River

Andrew Molera State Park

1

Molera Point

Ridge Trail

Franciscan Rocks

Bluffs Trail

High Tide Line

Low Tide Line

Spring Trail

Panorama Trail

PACIFIC OCEAN

**Big Sur River
Hike 72**

N

0   0.25   0.5 Mi.

Cooper Point

great blue heron swoops over the Big Sur River as the belted kingfisher frolics in the willow and red alder thickets hugging the river shore. Later in the journey, you may spy a red-tailed hawk hunting prey in a coast live oak grove adorning the Ridge Trail.

Even if all the birds suddenly decided to hide, this excursion is loaded with neat scenes. You get to walk between the river's edge and a meadow, an ideal strip for spotting wildlife. After some bare-foot traipsing on pretty Molera Beach, there's more flat strolling atop the bluffs overlooking the coastline. Then the far-reaching views unfold during the Panorama Trail climb, continuing along the mostly flat Ridge Trail.

The hike begins on a tiny, sandy beach, surrounded by willows along the Big Sur River. Veer right onto the Beach Trail at the trail junction (the trail on the left will be the return trail) and immediately enter Creamery Meadow. The wide and sandy trail escorts you past sycamore trees and occasional cottonwoods towering above willow thickets pressing the Big Sur River bank. Patches of coyote brush, bush lupine, and annual oatgrass highlight the meadow. Lush and lovely green in the spring, the oatgrass becomes tall and dry through summer and fall.

Get the nice view to the east as the Big Sur River meanders alongside a large gravel bar, with the steep, rolling, and grassy hills decorating the scene in the distance.

A maze of driftwood forts greets you at 1.2 miles, where the waves break loudly against slender Molera Beach. Kids like to play on the beach where the Big Sur River empties into the sea. The Bluffs Trail provides the best perches for focusing on the immediate shoreline. This mostly flat and sandy path stays close to the steep bluff's edge for most of its 2 miles. The yellow-flowered bush lupines highlight spring. Yard-tall perennial bunchgrasses and coyote brush comprise the year-round backbone on this coastal scrub field.

Once on the Bluff's Trail, there's but one access to Molera Beach. Take the curvy Spring Trail down to a scenic and secluded section of the beach, which virtually disappears during high tide. From atop the bluffs, several grand views can be had of Franciscan Rocks and the numerous pocket beaches. Soon after crossing a second gully, the workout begins as the Panorama Trail delivers the views its name implies while ascending steeply in sections, 1,000 feet of climbing overall in just over a mile.

The sweaty effort is rewarded, as the best is saved for last on the Ridge Trail. It further proves that Andrew Molera State Park is the panorama capitol of the Monterey/Big Sur area.

Some of the grand lookouts are next to or through ancient coast live oaks that take center stage on the first section of the Ridge Trail. The views of the floating brown kelp in the calm, soupy spots just beyond the beach are unsurpassed. A trio of Monterey cypress tree statues are serenely silhouetted at twilight time atop chunky and rectangular Molera Point.

Further north, Point Sur Light Station (well worth visiting) can be admired, anchored atop a massive block of volcanic rock. Before it was built in 1889, this rugged area was the site of several disastrous shipwrecks. The low-growing coastal scrub of coyote brush, coast sage, and orange bush monkeyflower dotting the Ridge Trail never impedes the far-reaching vistas.

Finally, the Ridge Trail displays Creamery Meadow and the Big Sur River outline to Molera Point. This old fire road then descends moderately, eventually connecting with a south loop trail bordering the meadow (bear right here to head back to the car).

Hike 73

Oak Grove Trail to Pfeiffer Falls and Valley View

LENGTH: 5.2 miles round-trip as described; 2.2 miles skipping the Oak Grove Trail and starting at the lodge.

DIFFICULTY: easy to moderate.

TOTAL ELEVATION GAIN: 600 feet.

WATER: available from Pfeiffer Redwood Creek; fill up from parking lot faucets.

SEASON: all—slick trail sections in winter; the falls and Pfeiffer Redwood Creek are more spectacular in early spring.

MAP: Pfeiffer Big Sur State Park map or USGS topos Pfeiffer Point and Big Sur.

INFORMATION: Pfeiffer Big Sur State Park, (408) 385-5434.

DIRECTIONS TO TRAILHEAD: Drive south on Highway 1; from Carmel it's about 26 miles, from Big Sur about 2 miles to the Pfeiffer Big Sur State Park entrance. Follow the paved park road along the north side of the Big Sur River, then park in the large paved lot near the softball field. The trail begins as a gated and paved fire road, which soon merges with the signed Oak Grove Trail.

Coast live oak groves like the ones along the Oak Grove Trail are a masterpiece in progress, attaining more grace as time passes slowly. You get to wander into them, on the way to a close encounter with Pfeiffer Falls, where a hiker can feel its eternal shower as it tumbles into an intimate pool.

These spots, including the territory along the aptly named Valley View Trail, were first settled on long ago by the Esselen Indians. They roamed the woodlands and coastal plains from Point Sur to Lopez Point, hunting the animals and gathering from the plants of land and sea. Spanish soldiers occupied this rugged country in the late 1700s, causing the Esselen tribe to move into the missions. Along came European diseases such as cholera and smallpox, wiping out nearly everybody so fast that little else is known about all these people. Big Sur country was left uninhabited for decades, but it was the Spaniards who called the area El Pais Grande del Sur, which means "the big country of the south." Later the nickname Big Sur took hold.

The first attraction a hiker sees on the journey is the Homestead Cabin, which consists of one square wooden room. It features steps that lead to a wooden porch, some old caged windows, and an old wood stove inside.

The Oak Grove Trail proceeds briefly into a statuesque coast live oak open forest, then commences an open climb in chaparral country made up of coyote brush, coffeeberry, black sage, poison oak, and orange bush monkeyflower. After 300 feet worth of climbing, the trail peaks in an ancient coast live oak grove, where the burly and gnarled trunks look even more imposing than the apple tree trunks from the *Wizard of Oz*.

After the meeting point with the unsigned Mount Manuel Trail (good access into the Ventana Wilderness—permit required), your trail continues straight, and begins a series of ups and downs (canyon hopping). A few California sycamore and California bay laurel trees appear in the gulches with coast live oak, while chaparral dominates the exposed portions of this steep hillside. Prior to reaching the much visited Pfeiffer Falls Trail, the less hiked Oak Grove Trail passes into a final monumental coast live oak grove.

The Pfeiffer Falls Trail climbs gently under the shade of an ancient redwood forest, crossing several wooden bridges over slender and gracefully winding Pfeiffer Redwood Creek.

Two flights of stairs lead to a wooden observation deck with benches overlooking 60-foot-long Pfeiffer Falls. Two steady streams of whitewater plunge vertically over a jagged rock face into a living-

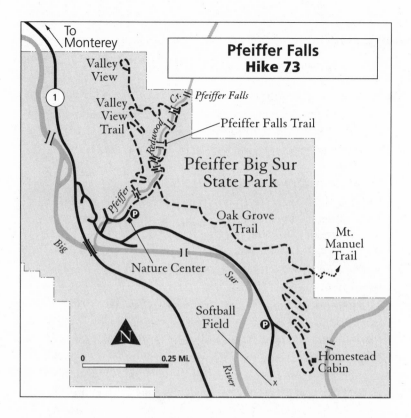

room-sized, clear and shallow pool. Most of the year you can be like a kid and wade into this invitingly cool pool to actually touch the falls. The Valley View Trail, via switchbacks, climbs through a tan oak and California bay laurel forest, then levels in a coast live oak grove. It soon comes to a signed trail junction, where you bear right to acquire the best views yet. After a 0.3-climb, a bench on a flat spot makes a good perch for hawk's-eye views into the Big Sur Valley and nearby Andrew Molera Park (see Hike 72).

Back at the trail junction, the remainder of the Valley View Trail descends moderately in open shade. If a car shuttle is arranged at the Pfeiffer Falls Trailhead, bear right at the next junction. Otherwise, turn left, then make a quick right to retrace your steps on the Oak Grove Trail.

Hike 74

Partington Creek and Tanbark Trail in Julia Pfeiffer Burns State Park

LENGTH: 8 miles round-trip as described; 2 miles round-trip for Partington Point and Partington Creek section.

DIFFICULTY: moderate; last section of Tanbark Trail is strenuous.

TOTAL ELEVATION GAIN: 2,000 feet.

WATER: available from Partington Creek; bring your own.

SEASON: all—Partington Creek is even more wild and gorgeous in the winter; winter is also ideal for watching gray whales migrating southward.

MAP: Julia Pfeiffer Burns State Park map or USGS topo Partington Ridge.

INFORMATION: Julia Pfeiffer Burns State Park, (408) 385-5434, or (408) 667-2315.

DIRECTIONS TO TRAILHEAD: From Big Sur (22 miles south of Carmel), drive south on Highway 1 for 11 miles, then park in the small dirt lot on either side of the highway (it's 1.8 miles north of the Julia Pfeiffer Burns State Park entrance).

For the ambitious adventurer seeking scenery and seclusion, this excursion through a creekside redwood forest, then up into the park's chaparral interior, is a match made in paradise. But for those who want a lot of beautiful Big Sur coast photos for just a little bit of family-style hiking, this trip can easily be abbreviated.

From the onset, watching for sea otters playing in the sea from Partington Point, to the inspirational vista point near the journey's end, the highlights keep coming all the way. Wild Partington Creek is a close companion during the first third of the hike, then eventually a climb in high chaparral country unfolds countless lookouts over the rugged and rocky Big Sur shoreline and out to the infinite sea.

To begin, zip down the dirt road past the iron gate and soon pass through the rocky cliff via a 30-yard-long tunnel. Kelp-laden Partington Cove was once used by ships to haul tanbark (from nearby tanbark oaks) from what is now the remains of an old dock.

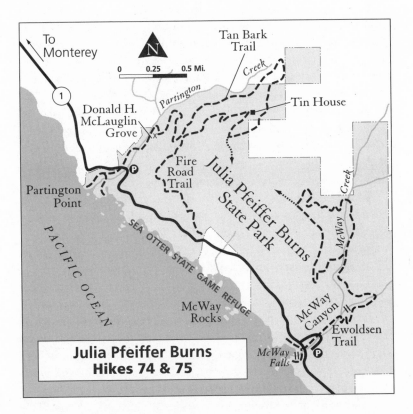

The Sea Otter State Game Refuge sprawls from Partington Point southward for a couple of miles. Experienced and registered divers probe these 1,680 acres for their splendid diversity—from the caves, canyons, and tunnels to the spectacular array of colorful marine animals and plants.

After doubling back to the car, the Tanbark Trail (starts as two trails—the north trail is in better shape and more shaded) soon crosses a wooden bridge between a small grove of large California sycamore trees. It stays flat and redwood-shaded for the next 0.2 mile past a series of pools, cascades, and rapids. A large, flat boulder perched over Partington Creek next to an ambling cascade makes for an ideal picnic spot in the shade. The rapids and cascades continue as the trail climbs moderately above these clear waters.

At 1.2 miles into the journey, you reach Donald H. McLaughlin Grove, a pretty water seepage area trickling from a gulch, featuring ferns and redwood sorrel shaded by tall redwoods. The trail departs Partington Creek here. There's also a 0.1-mile-long spur trail here that culminates in a needle-littered flat spot alongside a swirling section of the creek and beneath a huge redwood with a gnarled and buttressed trunk that grips a huge boulder.

The Tanbark Trail now climbs away from the creek in a shaded forest of redwood, madrone, tanbark oak, and California bay laurel. In spots, you can peer west through the limbs and get sneak previews of the sea. These views get better the higher one goes, eventually climbing past coast scrub, chaparral, and finally grasslands.

The trail snakes steeply toward the sea, eventually climaxing at 2,000 feet in elevation at the flat-topped Tin House, a good resting place featuring stunning coastal views. This upland area serves as home to raccoons, gray squirrels, gray foxes, and possums, as well as less frequently seen cougars, bobcats, wild pigs, and coyotes.

The Fire Road Trail begins as steep and grassy hillsides overlooking coastal scrub and mixed chaparral rising from the gray-blue ocean. You soon drop into the scrub and chaparral consisting of black sage, coyote brush, blue-blossom ceanothus, poison oak, coast sage, and white-flowered yarrow. The further down you go, the more the views improve of the dark and jagged shoreline and kelp-covered coves. The final quarter of a mile drops steeply, with the last 200 hundred yards plunging into a shady redwood canyon. The aptly named Vista Point stands just across Highway 1. If a car shuttle is arranged here at this paved parking lot, all that's left to do is check out the views a final time. Otherwise, you'll have to hoof it 0.7 mile up Highway 1.

Hike 75

McWay Falls and McWay Canyon
in Julia Pfeiffer Burns State Park

LENGTH: 5 miles round-trip as described; 4 miles round-trip skipping McWay Falls; 3 miles round-trip to loop junction.
DIFFICULTY: moderate; a steep climb in chaparral.
TOTAL ELEVATION GAIN: 1,400 feet.

WATER: available from McWay Creek and parking lot faucets.

SEASON: all—winter best for whale watching; late spring best for chaparral flowers.

MAP: Julia Pfeiffer Burns State Park map or USGS topo Partington Ridge. See p. 217.

INFORMATION: Julia Pfeiffer Burns State Park, (408) 385-5434, or (408) 667-2315.

DIRECTIONS TO TRAILHEAD: From Big Sur, drive south on Highway 1 for 13 miles (35 miles from Carmel) to the park entrance.

Waterfalls are always special, but when they tumble 80 feet onto a sandy beach as McWay Falls does, they become extra special and even rare. This and the spectacular surrounding shoreline scenery is one of this hike's many highlights. Far reaching coastal views of the legendary Big Sur country from atop chaparral clad hilltops is another feature. As an added bonus, there's the redwood journey up rugged McWay Canyon.

The mostly flat route to McWay Falls leads past spring-flowering dogwoods and blue-blossom ceanothus, then under Highway 1 via a tunnel. Superb vistas of the jagged shoreline rocks that epitomize the Big Sur coastline unfold outside the tunnel from the face of a steep bluff rising some 100 feet above the sea. Peer down into McWay Cove and admire slender McWay Falls. Note the luxuriant masses of reddish-brown kelp subtly floating in the cove. Sea palms, a smaller green kind of kelp, mount the granite rocks and absorb the crash of repeated waves that surge over them. Some environmental campsites are situated under a grove of Monterey cypress trees.

When you're done checking out these two small bluff trails, double back and then get on the signed Ewoldsen Trail that departs near the paved parking lot's restrooms. It climbs gently through a pleasantly shaded redwood forest. Clear and soothing McWay Creek, which flows year-round, escorts you past some steep and astonishing rocky landscapes. It's surprising how many communities of fern and redwood sorrel tend to thrive wherever there's sufficient soil situated between the rock faces in steep and rugged McWay Canyon.

To check out an unnamed 20-foot-high waterfall, take the 0.2-

mile-long Canyon Spur Trail. Soon the confluence of McWay Creek and its unnamed tributary form a "Y" beneath a vast rock outcrop. This slim waterfall drops straight down into the tributary, where a picnic bench is nestled in the redwood shade.

Back on the Ewoldsen Trail, some serious climbing ensues, briefly away from the tributary, and thankfully under the shade of redwood and tanbark oak. Once it crosses a wooden bridge at 1.8 mile into the journey, the Ewoldsen Trail climbs steadily north, past sunny chaparral sections of ceanothus and live oak shrub forms, alternating with forest sections dominated by California bay laurel. There are some inspiring scenes of the sea forefronted by the McWay watershed.

The slender footpath levels as it reunites with McWay Creek through a small grove of mostly lightning-charred tall redwood trees. At 2.3 miles, you come to another footbridge, gorgeously shaded by four uniquely shaped and large tan oaks and a cluster of tall redwoods. Bear right here at this signed loop junction, and commence climbing past more redwoods.

The next half mile covers hauntingly lonesome country that typifies Big Sur territory to a final crossing of McWay Creek. The steepest part of the journey now begins along with top-flight views of McWay Rocks and Partington Point below. Even better news is that you get to see these shoreline scenes with musical accompaniment from chirping Big Sur chaparral birds such as bushtits, swallows, sparrows, flycatchers, and scrub jays. Orange bush monkeyflower, wild mustard, and smaller Indian paintbrush decorate trailside, flanked by taller coyote brush, coffeeberry, chamise, and poison oak.

Eventually the trail veers southward and drops quickly back into a forest of tan oak, California bay laurel, madrone, and redwood. It then swings eastward, climbs a short stint, and then reunites with the aforementioned footbridge.

Appendix 1

Park Information Addresses

Phone numbers are listed in the Information sections in hike chapters. Addresses and phone numbers are subject to change.

Andrew Molera State Park, Big Sur Station 1, Big Sur, CA 93920

Año Nuevo State Reserve, New Year's Creek Road, Pescadero, CA 94060

Armstrong Redwoods State Reserve, 17,000 Armstrong Redwoods Road, Guerneville, CA 95446

Austin Creek State Recreation Area, 17,000 Armstrong Redwoods Road, Guerneville, CA 95446

Big Basin Redwoods State Park, 21,600 Big Basin Way, Boulder Creek, CA 95006

Butano State Park, P.O. Box 3, Pescadero, CA 94060

China Camp State Park, East San Pedro Road, San Rafael, CA 94901

Del Norte Coast Redwoods State Park, P.O. Drawer J, Crescent City, CA 95531

Del Norte County Park, 840 Ninth Street, Crescent City, CA 95531

Fitzgerald Marine Reserve, P.O. Box 451, Moss Beach, CA 94038

Golden Gate National Recreation Area, Marin Headlands, Building 1056, Fort Cronkite, Sausalito, CA 94965

Gualala Point Regional Park, P.O. Box 95, Gualala, CA 95445

Henry Cowell Redwoods State Park, 101 North Big Trees Road, Felton, CA 95018

Jedediah Smith Redwoods State Park, 1375 Elk Valley Road, Crescent City, CA 95531

Jughandle State Reserve, P.O. Box 440, Mendocino, CA 95460

King Range National Conservation Area, BLM, P.O. Box 1112, Arcata, CA 95521

Loch Lomond County Park, 100 Loch Lomond Way, Felton, CA 95018

MacKerricher State Park, P.O. Box 440, Mendocino, CA 95460

Manchester State Beach Park, P.O. Box 440, Mendocino, CA 95460

Marin Water District, 220 Nellen, Corte Madera, CA 94925

Midpeninsula Regional Open Space District, 330 Distel Circle, Los Altos, CA 94022

Mount Tamalpais State Park, 801 Panoramic Highway, Mill Valley, CA 94941

Muir Woods, Muir Woods National Monument, Mill Valley, CA 94941

Patrick's Point State Park, 41,250 Patrick's Point Drive, Trinidad, CA 95570

Pfeiffer Big Sur State Park, Big Sur, CA 93920

Point Lobos State Preserve, Route 1, P.O. Box 62, Carmel, CA 93923

Point Reyes National Seashore, Point Reyes, CA 94956

Prairie Creek Redwoods State Park, 600-A West Clark Street, Eureka, CA 95502

Redwood National Park, 1111 Second Street, Crescent City, CA 95531

Russian Gulch State Park, P.O. Box 440, Mendocino, CA 95460

Salt Point State Park, 25,050 Coast Highway 1, Jenner, CA 95450

Samuel P. Taylor State Park, P.O. Box 251, Lagunitas, CA 94938

San Bruno Mountain County Park, 600 Oddstad Blvd., Pacifica, CA 94044

San Pedro County Park, 600 Oddstad Blvd., Pacifica, CA 94044

Sinkyone Wilderness State Park, P.O. Box 245, Whitethorn, CA 95489

Sonoma Coast State Beaches, P.O. Box 123, Duncan Mills, CA 95430

Tomales Bay State Park, Star Route, Inverness, CA 94937

Van Damme State Park, P.O. Box 440, Mendocino, CA 95460

Appendix 2

Club and Activist Group Addresses

California Coastal Commission, 45 Fremont St., Suite 2000, San Francisco, CA 94105-2219, (415) 904-5200

California Native Plant Society, 1722 J St., Suite 17, Sacramento, CA 95814, (707) 664-8031

Campaign To Save California Wetlands, P.O. Box 20,651, Oakland, CA 94620, (510) 654-7847

National Audubon Society, 2530 San Pablo Avenue, Suite G, Berkeley, CA 94702, (510) 843-2222

Point Reyes National Seashore, Point Reyes, CA 94956, (415) 663-1200

Save The Redwoods League, 114 Sansome Street, Room 605, San Francisco, CA 94104

Sierra Club, 923 12th Street, Suite 200, Sacramento, CA 95814, (916) 557-1100

U.S. Fish and Wildlife Service, 2800 Cottage Way, Room E-1803 Sacramento, CA 95825-1846, (916) 979-2110

Appendix 3

Author's Ultimate North Coast Backpack Trips

Call for permits, maps, etc.

1 Klamath River and Hidden Beach to Damnation Beach—see Hikes 4 and 5

2 Ossagon Rocks, Gold Bluffs Beach, and Skunk Cabbage Creek—see Hikes 6 and 10

3 Prairie Creek, Miner's Ridge, Fern Canyon, Gold Bluffs Beach, James Irvine Trail loop trip—see Hikes 7 and 8

4 Dolason Prairie, Tall Trees Grove, and Redwood Creek—see Hikes 11 and 12

5 Mattole River, Punta Gorda to Shelter Cove—see Hike 14

6 Hidden Valley, Chemise Mountain, Whale Gulch, and Needle Rock—see Hikes 16 and 18

7 Bear Harbor to Usal Camp—see Hikes 19 and 20

8 Austin Creek, Gilliam Creek, and East Ridge Trail—see Hikes 28 and 29

9 Drake's Estero, Limantour Beach, and Coast Trail to Arch Rock—see Hikes 34, 36, and 37

10 Bear Valley Trail, Arch Rock, Wildcat Beach, and Pelican Lake—see Hikes 38 and 40

11 Muir Beach to Rodeo Beach—see Hike 48

12 Perimeter Trail, Sunset Trail, and other trails to Mount Livermore on Angel Island—see Hike 50
13 Año Nuevo Trail, Doe Ridge Trail, Canyon Trail, and Jackson Flats Trail loop trip—see Hikes 60 and 61
14 Kelly Creek, Berry Creek Falls, and Skyline To The Sea Trail—see Hikes 64 and 65
15 Pfeiffer Falls, Oak Grove Trail, and Ventana Wilderness—see Hike 73

Appendix 4

Author's Suggested Hikes to See Birds

Most of these hikes encompass ocean and fresh water.

HIKE 1   Point St. George, Pelican Bay, and Lake Earl
HIKE 5   Klamath River to Hidden Beach and False Klamath Rock
HIKE 14 Lost Coast—Mattole River to Shelter Cove
HIKE 19 Lost Coast—Bear Harbor to Wheeler Camp
HIKE 21 Lake Cleone and Laguna Point
HIKE 25 Lake Davis and Alder Creek
HIKE 26 Gualala River and Gualala Point
HIKE 31 Bodega Dunes and South Salmon Creek Beach
HIKE 34 Drake's Estero and Sunset Beach
HIKE 36 Limantour Beach via Muddy Hollow and Estero Trails
HIKE 40 Pelican Lake and Wildcat Beach
HIKE 52 Land's End and Baker Beach to Golden Gate Bridge
HIKE 57 Fitzgerald Marine Reserve
HIKE 62 Franklin Point and Cascade Beach
HIKE 63 Point Año Nuevo and Cove Beach
HIKE 64 Waddell Creek and Berry Creek Falls
HIKE 69 China Beach, Bird Island, and Whaler's Cove
HIKE 72 Big Sur River and Molera Beach

Appendix 5

Author's Suggested Hikes for Seeing Flowers

Go in the spring and summer.

HIKE 3	Little Bald Hills Trail
HIKE 5	Klamath River to Hidden Beach
HIKE 6	Fern Canyon to Ossagon Rocks
HIKE 11	Redwood Creek to Tall Trees Grove
HIKE 12	Dolason Prairie Bald Hills
HIKE 14	Mattole River to Shelter Cove
HIKE 20	Usal Camp to Little Jackass Creek
HIKE 22	Ecological Staircase
HIKE 25	Lake Davis and Alder Creek
HIKE 26	Gualala River and Gualala Point
HIKE 27	Pygmy Forest and Stump Beach Trail
HIKE 28	Austin Creek and Gilliam Creek Trails
HIKE 30	Goat Rock, Blind Beach, and Peaked Hill
HIKE 31	Bodega Head
HIKE 32	Tomales Point
HIKE 37	Coast Trail in Point Reyes National Seashore
HIKE 39	Bolinas Ridge and Shafter Trails
HIKE 40	Pelican Lake and Wildcat Beach
HIKE 42	Bon Tempe and Alpine Lakes
HIKE 45	Stinson Beach, Dipsea, and Matt Davis Trails
HIKE 48	Muir Beach, Tennessee Beach, and Rodeo Beach
HIKE 53	Summit Loop Trail/San Bruno Mountain
HIKE 54	Sweeney Ridge
HIKE 58	Soda Gulch Trail and Harkins Ridge
HIKE 62	Franklin Point and Cascade Beach
HIKE 69	China Beach, Bird Island, and Whaler's Cove
HIKE 70	Sea Lion Rocks, Cypress Grove Trail
HIKE 71	Soberanes Canyon and Rocky Ridge

Appendix 6

Author's Special-Pick Hikes with Grand Views

Do these hikes on a day with blue skies or high clouds. Autumn is the best time. Note—you may not have to do the whole hike to snag the view.

Appendix 7

Author's Suggested Ancient Redwoods Walks

Appendix 8

Hikes Dogs Can Go On (at least part of the way)

Appendix 9

Hikes That Allow Mountain Bikes
(at least on some of the trails)

Appendix 10

Hikes for Horseback Riding

HIKE 1   Pelican Bay
HIKE 25   Lake Davis
HIKE 28   Austin Creek
HIKE 32   Tomales Point
HIKE 34   Drake's Estero
HIKE 35   Inverness Ridge
HIKE 36   Estero Trail
HIKE 37   Coast Trail
HIKE 38   Arch Rock
HIKE 39   Bolinas Ridge
HIKE 49   China Camp State Park
HIKE 58   Purisima Creek
HIKE 73   Oak Grove Trail
HIKE 75   McWay Canyon

Appendix 11

Wheelchair-Accessible Hikes (part of the way)

HIKE 9   Lost Man Creek
HIKE 13   Patrick's Point
HIKE 21   Lake Cleone
HIKE 23   Russian Gulch Creek
HIKE 24   Van Damme State Park
HIKE 26   Gualala Point Regional Park
HIKE 27   Gerstle Cove
HIKE 34   Drake's Estero
HIKE 35   Inverness Ridge
HIKE 36   Muddy Hollow
HIKE 38   Arch Rock
HIKE 47   Redwood Creek
HIKE 67   Henry Cowell Redwoods State Park
HIKE 70   Point Lobos State Preserve

INDEX

ABOUT THE AUTHOR

Marc J. Soares, born in 1955, is a landscape consultant in the Redding area and coauthor of *One Hundred Hikes in Northern California*. He writes gardening columns for newspapers and teaches gardening and landscape classes for Shasta College Community Education.